GUINNESS WORLD RECORDS 2011

GUINNESS WORLD RECORDS

GAMER'S EDITION

British Library Cataloguing-in-Publication Data: a catalogue record for this book is available from the British Library.

ISBNs:
US 13:
978-0-7440-1261-3
US 10: 0-744012-61-9
UK 13:
978-1-4053-6546-8

Check the official **GWR Gamer's Edition** website – **www.guinnessworld records.com/gamers** – regularly for record-breaking gaming news as it happens, plus exclusive interviews and competitions.

© 2011 Guinness World Records Ltd, a Jim Pattison Group company

GAMER'S EDITION 2011

EDITOR-IN-CHIEF
Craig Glenday

MANAGING EDITORS
Matt Boulton, Ben Way

GAMING EDITOR
Gaz Deaves

EDITORIAL TEAM
Rob Cave, Matthew White

INDEX
Chris Bernstein

PRODUCTION MANAGER
Jane Boatfield

PRODUCTION ASSISTANT
Erica Holmes-Attivor

DIRECTOR OF PROCUREMENT
Patricia Magill

VP OF PUBLISHING
Frank Chambers

PICTURE EDITOR
Michael Whitty

DEPUTY PICTURE EDITOR
Laura Nieberg

PICTURE RESEARCHER
Fran Morales

ORIGINAL PHOTOGRAPHY
Paul Michael Hughes,
Shinsuke Kamioka,
Ryan Schude

CONCEPT CREATION & LAYOUT
Itonic Design Ltd,
Brighton, UK

COLOUR ORIGINATION
FMG, London, UK

GAMER'S CONSULTANTS
Best Of & Action-Adventure Games:
Chris Schilling

Shooting Games:
Michael French

Sports Games & Racing Games:
David Crookes

Party Games:
Ellie Gibson

Fighting Games:
Simon Parkin

Puzzle Games:
Mark Walton

Role-Playing Games:
Wesley Yin-Poole

Strategy & Simulation Games & Instant Gaming:
Martyn Carroll

GUINNESS WORLD RECORDS

ABBREVIATIONS & MEASUREMENTS: Guinness World Records Limited uses both metric and imperial measurements. The sole exceptions are for some scientific data where metric measurements only are universally accepted, and for some sports data. Where a specific date is given, the exchange rate is calculated according to the currency values that were in operation at the time. Where only a year date is given, the exchange rate is calculated from December of that year. "One billion" is taken to mean one thousand million.

GENERAL WARNING: Attempting to break records or set new records can be dangerous. Appropriate advice should be taken first and all record attempts are undertaken at the participant's risk. In no circumstances will Guinness World Records Limited have any liability for death or injury suffered in any record attempt. Guinness World Records Limited has complete discretion over whether or not to include any particular records in the book. Being a Guinness World Record holder does not guarantee you a place in the book.

GUINNESS WORLD RECORDS 2011

GUINNESS WORLD RECORDS

GAMER'S EDITION

ONTENTS

OU DON'T FANCY STARTING AT THE INTRODUCTION, THIS SHOULD HELP YOU FIND YOUR FAVOURITE RECORDS

KEY GAMES AND SERIES ARE HIGHLIGHTED AS "CRITICAL HITS!"

NUMBER RECORDS HIGHLIGHT AN INTERESTING VIDEOGAME FACT OR RECORD IN FIGURES.

ORIGINAL PHOTOGRAPHY AND THE BEST IMAGES FOR THE LATEST RECORD-BREAKING GAMES BRING EACH SPREAD TO LIFE IN DRAMATIC STYLE.

"TRIVIA TRAIL" AND "DID YOU KNOW" BOXES HIGHLIGHT A VARIETY OF FUN GAMING FACTS.

"TOP 10" TABLES FOR EVERY GENRE.

CLASSIC QUOTES QUIZ RUNS ALONG THE BOTTOM OF EACH PAGE – FIND THE ANSWERS ON P.214.

ACCURACY

As with all Guinness World Records books, every effort has been made to bring you the most accurate and up-to-date records. If, however, you believe that you know of a more impressive achievement or a higher score, please let us know.

NEW AND UPDATED RECORDS

Each year in *Gamer's Edition*, we strive to bring you either completely new or updated records, to keep the book as fresh and current as we possibly can. Where we've done this, you will see the following icons before the record title:

» NEW RECORD » UPDATED RECORD

Of course, we've included some classic old records as well, because sometimes oldies are goodies.

INTRODUCTION

» NEW RECORD
» UPDATED RECORD

THE GAMER'S BIBLE IS BACK! *GUINNESS WORLD RECORDS GAMER'S EDITION 2011* IS HERE WITH THE LATEST AND GREATEST GAMING RECORDS, GIVING YOU THE LOW-DOWN ON THE MOST POPULAR DOWNLOADS AND CHARTING THE MOST CRITICALLY ACCLAIMED GAMES IN THE WORLD!

»LARGEST GAME OF TETRIS

Holder: *The Gadget Show* **(Five, UK)**
The hosts of *The Gadget Show* are renowned for their unique take on all things technology-based, so when we got a call from them saying they wanted to break the record for the biggest-ever game of *Tetris* (Alexey Pajitnov, 1985), we were intrigued to know what they had planned. When our own Gaz Deaves headed to the National Exhibition Centre in Birmingham, UK, to adjudicate the attempt on 15 September 2010, he found they'd created a playing area made up of 200 Fireball PAR Can LEDs split into 20 rows of 10 that covered 105.79 m^2 (1,138 ft^2). The game was so vast that presenter Jason Bradbury had to go up in a crane to shout directions down to fellow team members Pollyanna Woodward, Ortis Deley, Suzi Perry (pictured, left to right) and Jon Bentley, who were on the ground operating the switches that controlled the familiar *Tetris* blocks.

Guinness World Records *Gamer's Edition* is now in its fourth edition and we reckon it just gets better every year. As ever, it's crammed full of record-breaking gaming facts and feats, fantastic features, incredible images and a great **new Top 50 survey**, which this year features the top videogame characters of all time as voted for by *Gamer's Edition* readers.

In addition to our regular line-up of records arranged by genre there are also some new additions to the mix, including our **Critical Hits!** (see box, opposite), informative **"Top 10" tables** and our **Classic Quotes Quiz** (see box, opposite), and as you can see, we also have a sharp new design put together for us by Itonic Design in Brighton, UK.

So, what have we been up to this year? Well we've been busier than ever out on the road adjudicating *Gamer's Edition* events all over the US, the UK and beyond (see box, left), and we've received record claims from countries across the globe, including Canada, Brazil,

RECORDS FROM AROUND THE WORLD

For *Gamer's Edition 2011* we travelled the globe to track down the videogame world's most talented players and most dedicated collectors. Wherever they were located, we visited record-claiming gamers so that we could see their skills in action and verify their claims. For the best of the best, our picture editor, Michael Whitty, took a camera crew along to capture exclusive photos of gamers in action, such as Annie Leung (USA, pictured), who set the record for the **highest score for a single track on** *Guitar Hero III* **(female)** in California, USA. You can find out more about Annie on p.82.

"HEY MONKEY, DO YOU KNOW WHAT AN ICE CREAM IS? WELL, BECAUSE YOU SEEM TO HAVE ONE STUCK ON YOUR HEAD."

NEW YEAR, NEW GAMES

The past 12 months have been packed with the launches of hundreds of hotly anticipated games and peripherals. We've been lucky enough to be there to check the coolest releases out in person, such as the new controller-free Kinect system for Xbox, which launched at E3 in Los Angeles, USA, in June 2010. We also called in at the UK launch of the blockbusting *Halo: Reach* (Microsoft, 2010), where we presented a couple of spartans with the certificate marking the **most popular videogame beta test**. Check out our *Halo* Critical Hit! spread on pp. 54–55 for full details of this and other records from the mega-selling *Halo* series.

CRITICAL HITS!

This year we've added an exciting new element to *Gamer's Edition* in the shape of "Critical Hit!" spreads. Speaking to gamers, we discovered that although you love the genre spreads, sometimes you'd like to see your favourite games featured in more depth. So, our Critical Hit! spreads focus on the very best videogame series and the latest record-breaking releases in great detail, including *Civilization*, *World of Warcraft*, *Halo*, *Fallout*, *The Legend of Zelda* and more. You'll find one or two Critical Hits! in each section.

Japan, the Netherlands, South Africa, Malaysia and even Inner Mongolia, which just goes to show how far the *Gamer's Edition* message is now reaching.

Not all of the claims that came in to us were successful, of course (it's not easy becoming a world record holder, you know), but you'll find those that made it through our strict claims procedure on the pages of this book. Remember – we are always looking out for new record claims, so if you have a special gaming skill or ability and want to see yourself in next year's *Gamer's Edition*, turn the page and find out how you can become the holder of a *Guinness World Records Gamer's Edition* certificate, and then head on to read about the very best in gaming achievement.

TRIVIA TRAIL

On our trip to the *Halo: Reach* launch (above) we came across a spartan with a surprise – he was equipped with a working jetpack! This supersoldier might not have spent as long in the air as his equivalents from the game, but he did get to fly around Nelson's Column in London, UK!

»MOST COMPETITION WINS ON STREET FIGHTER GAMES

Holder: Ryan Hart (UK)

It's been quite a year for *Street Fighter IV* (Capcom, 2009) champ Ryan Hart. Not only did he set the record for the **most consecutive wins against a human opponent** (see p.119 for details), he also claimed the record for the **most national and international tournaments won on *Street Fighter* games**, chalking up 30 titles over the course of his knockout 15-year career playing various incarnations of Capcom's classic combat game.

CLASSIC QUOTES QUIZ

We know that fans of videogames are always trying to out-do each other by showing off their knowledge of the minutest details of the most obscure videogames. So we thought we'd appeal to the inner nerd in all of you (and us, let's face it) by compiling a classic videogames quotes quiz. On the bottom of each page you'll see a quote from a classic videogame – test yourself and see how many of them you recognize. You'll find the answers on p. 214.

{ "AT LAST YOU ARE ASLEEP. FOR THREE NIGHTS EACH ATTEMPT TO REST HAS BROUGHT YOU STARTING FROM YOUR BED IN FRIGHT, WITH NO MEMORY OF WHAT HORRIFIED YOU SO, WITH A SICKENING SENSE OF DÉJÀ VU, YOU BEGIN TO DREAM...." }

WWW.GUINNESSWORLDRECORDS.COM/GAMERS **007**

HOW TO BE A RECORD BREAKER

RECORDS DON'T BREAK THEMSELVES – SHOW US WHAT YOU CAN DO!

TIRED OF BEING CALLED A N00B BY TROLLS ON TEH INTERNETS? WANT TO PROVE YOUR GAMING SKILLZ ONCE AND FOR ALL? THEN READ ON! HERE'S OUR STEP-BY-STEP GUIDE TO ACHIEVING RECORD BREAKING IMMORTALITY AND MAYBE EVEN GETTING YOUR NAME INTO THE *GUINNESS WORLD RECORDS GAMER'S EDITION*…

≫ LONGEST MARATHON PLAYING DANCE DANCE REVOLUTION

Holder: Chris McGivern (UK)

Getting his groove on, Chris McGivern danced for 13 hr 33 min 56 sec on the latest *Dance Dance Revolution* arcade machine *Dance Dance Revolution X2* at the Funland arcade, London, UK, on 23 October 2010. For the first five hours, Chris danced on the game's lowest difficulty setting, selecting a harder mode for the second five hours, and an even harder setting at the 10-hour mark. Such considerations didn't deter Chris, who danced like a crazy guy for the first 12 hours of the attempt without a single break!

{ "PSYMON SAYS, YES!!!" }

»LARGEST HANDHELD GAMES CONSOLE PARTY

Holder: National Media Museum

The National Media Museum in Bradford, UK, was the place to be on 27 July 2010 – especially if you had a handheld console. Urged on by local station Real Radio, a total of 659 gamers, each armed with a Nintendo DS, descended upon the museum for a gaming session. *Gamer's Edition*'s Gaz Deaves adjudicated, aided by the creator of the *Broken Sword* series, Charles Cecil.

1. SELECT YOUR CHALLENGE

Decide the game and record you're going to attempt. Remember that Guinness World Records need to be measurable, breakable and verifiable. We need a score or time that we can count that proves your achievement.

2. TELL US!

Go to our website at www. guinnessworldrecords. com/gamers and follow the links. You'll need to register on our website, and then you'll be able to tell us the game you're playing, what you're doing and how you'll measure it. When we receive your record idea,

we'll decide whether or not it fulfils our criteria – remember that not every new record idea will be approved by us.

3. GET THE GUIDELINES

If we like your record idea, we will send you the guidelines: a brief set of rules that explain the

game settings you'll need to use for the record and any glitches you're allowed to employ. For endurance records, the guidelines explain how and when you can take breaks. Most importantly, the guidelines tell you what evidence you need to record for your evidence. Here are the kinds of things we need:

- A letter from you explaining the who, what, where, when and why of your record attempt.
- A letter from an independent witness who saw you perform the attempt.
- Photos and/or videos of the attempt.

4. GET YOUR GAME ON

Go ahead and carry out your record attempt, making sure that you follow the guidelines. Good luck!

5. SHOW US YOUR SKILLS

When you've completed your challenge, we need to see the evidence, so put everything together in an envelope and mail it to us.

6. LEAVE THE REST TO US

When we get your evidence we'll review it and let you know the results. If you've been successful you'll get your very own Guinness World Records certificate recognizing your world-beating achievement. If you're very lucky your record might even be selected for next year's *Gamer's Edition*!

» **NEW RECORD**
» **UPDATED RECORD**

»MOST PERFECT GAMES ON Wii SPORTS: BOWLING

Holder: John Bates (USA)

A dedicated Wii enthusiast, 84-year-old John Bates of Onalaska, Wisconsin, USA, has been playing *Wii Sports* (Nintendo, 2006) since he bought a Wii back in 2009. He wrote to us in August 2010 to tell us about his 2,850 perfect games on the bowling challenge of the game. Thanks to his detailed score logs, we were able to approve his record swiftly.

GUINNESS WORLD RECORDS CHALLENGERS

Want to see how you measure up against various Guinness World Records online? Guinness World Records Challengers is a new video-based social-gaming community that enables you to do that and more besides – see how you stack up against real record-holders, or just your friends!

All you have to do is find a record challenge you like, film yourself making an attempt, then upload it to our website to see how you rank overall, or against other people in your country or age group. As you upload attempts and perform other actions on the site, you'll earn tokens that you can spend in the Token Store to customize your own Challengers homepage!

Best of all, if you're good enough to rank #1 overall in a challenge, you could be a new Guinness World Record holder, and maybe even appear in the next book!

Can't wait to get involved? To create your account and start taking on some records, head on over to www.guinnessworldrecords.com/challengers.

"WHEN I REALIZED THAT I HAD NO HOPE OF BEATING CLAVES, I RAN AWAY. WHAT ABOUT YOU? ARE YOU LIKE ME? DO YOU RUN AWAY FROM SITUATIONS WHERE YOU KNOW YOU CAN'T WIN, TOO?"

RECORDS.COM/GAMERS   **009**

GAMING AWARDS ROUND-UP

THE DARLINGS OF THE GAMES INDUSTRY ARE HONOURED ONCE AGAIN. AND THE WINNERS ARE…

Best Action/Adventure Game
Portal 2

GAME CRITICS AWARDS: BEST OF E3 2010

Award	Winner
Best of Show	Nintendo 3DS
Best Original Game	Dance Central
Best Console Game	Rage
Best Handheld Game	God of War: Ghost of Sparta
Best PC Game	Portal 2
Best Hardware	Nintendo 3DS
Best Action Game	Rage
Best Action/Adventure Game	Portal 2
Best Role Playing Game	Star Wars: The Old Republic
Best Fighting Game	Marvel vs. Capcom 3: Fate of Two Worlds
Best Racing Game	Need for Speed: Hot Pursuit
Best Sports Game	NBA Jam
Best Strategy Game	Civilization V
Best Social/Casual Game	Rock Band 3
Best Motion Simulation Game	Dance Central
Best Online Multiplayer	Assassin's Creed: Brotherhood
Special Commendation for Graphics	Rage

BAFTA VIDEO GAMES AWARDS 2010

Award	Winner
Academy Fellowship	Shigeru Miyamoto
Action	Uncharted 2: Among Thieves
Artistic Achievement	Flower
Best Game	Batman: Arkham Asylum
Family & Social	Wii Sports Resort
Gameplay	Batman: Arkham Asylum
Handheld	LittleBigPlanet (PSP)
Multiplayer	Left 4 Dead 2
Original Score	Uncharted 2: Among Thieves
Sports	FIFA 10
Story	Uncharted 2: Among Thieves
Strategy	Empire: Total War
Use of Audio	Uncharted 2: Among Thieves
Use of Online	FIFA 10
BAFTA Ones to Watch Award	Shrunk!
GAME Award of 2009	Call of Duty: Modern Warfare 2

Academy Fellowship
Shigeru Miyamoto

» **NEW RECORD**
» **UPDATED RECORD**

{ "HEY, AMMY, DOESN'T IT FEEL THAT WE'VE BEEN MEETING LOTSA BABES LATELY? WHEN WAS THE LAST TIME WE RAN INTO A GUY?" }

12: THE NUMBER OF AWARDS GIVEN TO *UNCHARTED 2: AMONG THIEVES*, INCLUDING TWO GAME OF THE YEAR AWARDS, MAKING IT THE MOST CELEBRATED GAME OF 2010.

GAME DEVELOPERS CHOICE AWARDS 2010

Award	Winner
Game of the Year/Best Game	Uncharted 2: Among Thieves
Best Debut Game	Runic Games (for Torchlight)
Best Handheld Game	Scribblenauts
Best Downloadable Game	Flower
Best New Social/Online Game	FarmVille
Excellence in Audio	Uncharted 2: Among Thieves
Excellence in Game Design	Batman: Arkham Asylum
Best Technology	Uncharted 2: Among Thieves
Excellence in Visual Arts	Uncharted 2: Among Thieves
Excellence in Writing	Uncharted 2: Among Thieves
Game Innovation Spotlights	Scribblenauts
Lifetime Achievement Award	John Carmack (Doom series)
The Pioneer Award	Gabe Newell
Ambassador Award	Jerry Holkins, Mike Krahulik and Robert Khoo

Ambassador Award Jerry Holkins, Mike Krahulik and Robert Khoo for Gabe & Tycho

GOLDEN JOYSTICK AWARDS 2010

Award	Winner
Ultimate Game of the Year	Mass Effect 2
Download Game of the Year	Plants vs. Zombies
Action-Adventure Game of the Year	Assassin's Creed II
Fighting Game of the Year	Street Fighter IV
Music Game of the Year	Guitar Hero 5
The One to Watch	Call of Duty: Black Ops
Online Game of the Year	League of Legends
Portable Game of the Year	Pokémon HeartGold/SoulSilver
Puzzle Game of the Year	World of Goo
Racing Game of the Year	Forza Motorsport
RPG Game of the Year	Mass Effect 2
Shooter of the Year	Call of Duty Modern Warfare 2
Soundtrack of the Year	Final Fantasy XIII
Sports Game of the Year	FIFA 10
Strategy Game of the Year	Plants vs. Zombies

Ultimate Game of the Year **Mass Effect 2.**

INDEPENDENT GAMES FESTIVAL AWARDS 2010

Award	Winner
Seumas McNally Grand Prize	Monaco (Pocketwatch Games)
Excellence in Visual Art	Limbo (PlayDead)
Excellence in Audio	Closure (Closure Team)
Excellence in Design	Monaco (Pocketwatch Games)
Nuovo Award	Tuning (Cactus)
Technical Excellence	Limbo (PlayDead)
Audience Award	Heroes of Newerth (S2 Games)
D2D Vision Award	Max & The Magic Marker (Press Play)
2010 IGF Student Showcase Winners	Continuity (Ragtime Games)

"WE LIVE IN GRIM TIMES INDEED, IF THE YOUNG ARE TOO WORLD-WEARY TO BELIEVE IN MAGIC. MOST CHILDREN YOUR AGE BELIEVE EAGERLY."

GAMES OF THE YEAR: TOP 3

IF YOU DIDN'T BUY THESE GAMES WHEN THEY CAME OUT, THEY WERE SURELY ON YOUR CHRISTMAS LIST...

A THRILLING 2010 HAS SEEN THE RELEASE OF A BUMPER CROP OF GAMES, AND WITH THREE SEQUELS TOPPING THIS YEAR'S CHART, IT GOES TO SHOW THAT GAMERS CAN'T GET ENOUGH OF A GOOD THING.

TRIVIA TRAIL

To celebrate the 25th anniversary of the *Super Mario* franchise in 2010, Nintendo published a special boxed set featuring the first three *Super Mario* games (and the *Lost Levels*) reformatted for the Wii, a CD soundtrack of the series' music and a DVD documentary all about the plump plumber.

SUPER MARIO GALAXY 2

(Nintendo, 2010)
After the critical and commercial success of 2007's *Super Mario Galaxy*, a second trip around the universe for Mario was definitely going to be on the cards. Thankfully, the team at Nintendo really excelled themselves with *Galaxy 2* giving us more power-ups, more inventive gameplay elements and, most importantly, more Yoshi!

The only down side was that *Super Mario Galaxy 2* was quite a bit more difficult than the first game, but the sheer variety of things to do, from floating around to drilling through planets, meant there was plenty of fun for everyone in Mario's latest cosmic adventure.

DID YOU KNOW?

Super Mario Galaxy 2 was originally planned to reuse *Super Mario Galaxy*'s soundtrack, but during production the game's designers realized that its new gameplay techniques would really benefit from a new symphonic score. Nintendo composer Koji Kondo (Japan) eventually recruited 60 musicians for the orchestra that performed the *Super Mario Galaxy 2* score – 10 musicians more than worked on the first game.

] "LISTEN, MY FATHER ONLY TAUGHT ME THE BASICS OF FIGHTING. THEN HE WENT AND GOT HIMSELF KILLED, LEAVING ME THE HEIR TO THE WHIP! THIS WHIP I CAN'T EVEN USE. HE WAS ALWAYS SO SELFISH." [

RED DEAD REDEMPTION

(Rockstar, 2010)
A sequel of sorts to *Red Dead Revolver*, Rockstar's western from 2004, *Red Dead Redemption* gave the franchise a much-needed makeover using the winning gameplay mechanics behind the *Grand Theft Auto* series. With an extensive campaign mode packed with side quests and plenty of multiplayer options, *Red Dead Redemption* kept us busy for most of the year. But the game's biggest strength was its landscape, so take some time to sit back and watch the buffalo roam the next time you play.

"EARLY IN THE PRE-PRODUCTION STAGE WE EXPERIMENTED WITH ALL KINDS OF DIFFERENT GAMEPLAY. WE FOCUSED ENTIRELY ON THAT, AND NOTHING ELSE."
/TREYARCH STUDIO HEAD MARK LAMIA ON PLANNING *CALL OF DUTY: BLACK OPS.*

TRIVIA TRAIL

Showing that zombies never lose their popularity, both *Red Dead Redemption* and *Call of Duty: Black Ops* have downloadable content that includes some undead enemies to shoot. No word yet on plans for *Left 4 Dead* downloadable content featuring soldiers or cowboys...

CALL OF DUTY: BLACK OPS

(Activision, 2010)
Moving on from their traditional role of developing *Call of Duty* titles set in World War II, developer Treyarch's latest addition to the series turned its attention to hidden conflicts set within the Cold War. With missions in hot spots such as Vietnam, Cuba and Laos, the varied gameplay ensured that there was far more to the game than the standard first-person shooter action.

GAMES OF THE YEAR: 4 TO 10

WHETHER YOU LIKE DRIVING, SHOOTING OR EXPLORING NEW WORLDS, 2010 HAD THE GAMES FOR YOU.

FIFA 11

(EA, 2010)

In a league of its own, EA's FIFA franchise continued to innovate in 2011, making other football simulation games look like they'd taken their eye off the ball. New features in this year's game included an updated passing system that rewarded accuracy and punished sloppy play, and the merger of the "pro" and "manager" modes into a single "career" mode that allows you to track your progression over 15 seasons. The latest game also proved particularly popular with goalkeepers – there were significant AI improvements to the computer-controlled netminders, and for the first time players were able to put themselves in goal, which at last created the opportunity for true 11-a-side multiplayer action.

HALO: REACH

(Microsoft, 2010)

Going back to their roots for one last adventure, Bungie, the developer who spawned the *Halo* franchise, took gamers to an event that was merely alluded to in the past – the epic fall of the human colony of Reach. You know it's a losing battle from the start and none of the extra power-ups, jetpacks and vehicles will help you turn the tide of the battle, but that is a significant part of the fun of *Reach*'s campaign mode.

With its games engine entirely overhauled since *Halo 3*, Bungie really pushed the Xbox 360 to its limit with *Reach*'s beefed-up artificial intelligence, which turned every firefight into a tactical challenge. The game's rich variety of multiplayer options also ensure years of replayability as well as putting a fitting cap on what is still the finest platform-exclusive shooter out there.

WORLD OF WARCRAFT: CATACLYSM

(Blizzard, 2010)

The third great expansion pack for the global phenomenon that is *World of Warcraft* brought two new races – goblins and lupine creatures known as the Worgen – 3,500 new quests, a host of new and updated locations to explore and an upper skill level limit that has been raised to 85. Those guys at Blizzard know exactly what *World of Warcraft* fans are after, and have all but guaranteed that the pre-eminent MMORPG will be with us for a long time yet.

"AS I MENTIONED, I AM BUT A SIMPLE BUN MASTER, WITH A DEAR WIFE WHO HAS TURNED MY LIFE INTO A MISERABLE CESSPOOL DEVOID OF HUMOUR AND EXCITEMENT. BLESS HER SOUL."

MASS EFFECT 2

(Bioware, 2010)

Bioware's sci-fi RPG sequel gave you the chance to revisit Commander Shepard and his (or her) friends from the original *Mass Effect* – quite literally. If you had a save from the completed first game you could import your character into *Mass Effect 2*. The consequences of your decisions in previous games then carried a greater weight in this game's world – characters you could save in the first game only appeared in *Mass Effect 2* via imported saves. So, if you fail to save the Korgan Wrex in the first game, he won't be alive in this game. With its multiple endings, not all of which Shepard survives, *Mass Effect 2* kept us coming back for more throughout 2010.

7

ENSLAVED: ODYSSEY TO THE WEST

(Namco Bandai, 2010)

Based on novelist Alex Garland's updating of the classic Chinese narrative *Journey to the West*, developer Ninja Theory gave their game a futuristic twist – setting it on a world ravaged by rampaging robots. But what really made *Enslaved* stand out from the crowd wasn't its setting but its gameplay, in which you are forced to act as a bodyguard to your companion and be ever alert to the dangers that threaten you both as you navigate the legions of hostile robots on your journey westwards.

8

9

FALLOUT: NEW VEGAS

(Bethesda, 2010)

Moving the action to the Mojave Wasteland, *Fallout: New Vegas* rejuvenated the post-apocalyptic RPG franchise with a completely new cast and setting, plus overhauled systems of combat, allegiance and reputation. Thankfully developers Obsidian didn't meddle with the core gamplay elements that made *Fallout 3* such fun to play – why mess with success?

STARCRAFT II: WINGS OF LIBERTY

(Blizzard, 2010)

Over a decade after the first *StarCraft* – the game that defined turn-based strategy for a generation – Blizzard released its much-anticipated sequel. Many fans were concerned that the new game wouldn't be as good as the original, but they needn't have worried as Blizzard don't release sub-standard games and *StarCraft II* is no exception. This is a game that will hook you in for many years to come, and you'll find that the time to the release of *StarCraft III* will just fly by.

10

"ATTENTION HUMANS. I AM CRYPTOSPORIDIUM OF THE PLANET FURON. THIS PLANET IS NOW A TERRITORY OF THE FURON EMPIRE. RESIST THIS."

WWW.GUINNESSWORLDRECORDS.COM/GAMERS **015**

YEAR IN REVIEW: OCT TO MAR

WHAT A YEAR IT'S BEEN! HERE ARE JUST A FEW OF OUR HIGHLIGHTS OF THE LAST 12 MONTHS.

TRIVIA TRAIL

In October 2009, former NFL player Jim Brown lost a court case against EA Sports over the use of his likeness in the *Madden NFL* series. Brown claimed that he featured in two of the game's historical line-ups, though presiding judge Florence-Marie Cooper claimed that "the *Madden NFL* videogames are expressive works".

OCTOBER 2009

- Sony launched the PSPgo (right), resulting in a 120% increase in PSP sales in Europe (300% in the US) during its first week of release.
- Will Wright's *Spore* (EA, 2008) became the latest videogame to get its own movie tie-in, as 20th Century Fox announced plans for an animated CGI film version from Blue Sky Studios, makers of the *Ice Age* series.
- *FIFA 2010* (EA, 2009) became the **fastest-selling sports game ever**, shifting 1.7 million copies across Europe in its launch week.
- *LostWinds 2: Winter of the Melodias* (Frontier Developments, 2009) was the 100th game to be released on Nintendo's WiiWare download service.
- With over 11 million copies sold, *Wii Play* (Nintendo, 2006) was revealed to be the **best-selling game not to be bundled with a console** – being bundled with a controller probably helped its sales figures though.

NOVEMBER 2009

- Activision's *Call of Duty: Modern Warfare 2* (2009, right) dominated the month, breaking several records on its debut. It achieved the highest first-day sales for a videogame in the UK, shifting 1.23 million copies. Worldwide, the game's day-one sales topped 5.5 million, generating a total of $401 million (£242 million).
- Well over 1 million votes were cast for the 27th Annual Golden Joystick Awards, with *Fallout 3* (Bethesda Softworks, 2008) winning the coveted accolade of Ultimate Game of the Year.
- Nintendo celebrated more sales milestones as *Wii Sports* (2006) passed the 50-million barrier and *New Super Mario Bros.* (2006) for the DS reached 20 million and counting.
- Nintendo launched the DSi XL handheld in Japan (under the DSi LL brand), shifting over 100,000 units in its first two days on sale. By comparison, Sony's PSPgo sold 28,275 units in its first week on sale.

DECEMBER 2009

- The PlayStation brand celebrated its 15th birthday this month – the original PlayStation console having been released in Japan on 3 December 1994. The first PS has gone on to sell in excess of 100 million units worldwide, making it one of the most successful consoles ever made.
- Sega's *Aliens vs. Predator* (2010, left) was refused classification ahead of its planned release in Australia, leading to a number of people speaking out against the Australian Classification Board, including game designer David Jaffe. Sega refused to make any cuts to the game, instead appealing the decision. The publisher won, and the game was awarded an MA15+ certificate.
- A report by *The Daily Telegraph* stated that more money was spent on videogames in the UK during 2009 than on film, including both cinema and DVD releases. Research company Chart-Track claimed £1.73 billion ($2.7 billion) was spent on games in the year ending September 2009, while approximately £1.2 billion ($1.89 billion) in revenue was earned at the box-office and from DVD and Blu-Ray releases over the same period.

"I USED TO FREAK OUT WHEN MY AMP CAUGHT ON FIRE, BUT NOW I KINDA DIG THE TONE."

18.36 MILLION: THE NUMBER OF GAMES FEATURING TIGER WOODS' NAME IN THE TITLE SOLD BY EA SPORTS SINCE THE FIRST RELEASE IN 1998.

JANUARY 2010

- EA Sports polled gamers to ask whether or not Tiger Woods' extra-marital affairs had affected their opinions of the publisher's golf games starring the player. Despite the company's public support of Woods, the questionnaire asked: "Has the controversy made you more or less likely to buy a Tiger Woods-related videogame in the future?" We must assume that gamers didn't mind Woods' indiscretions, as EA went ahead and published *Tiger Woods PGA Tour 11* later in the year.
- Capcom announced that *Gears of War* heroes Marcus Fenix and Dominic Santiago would be appearing in *Lost Planet 2* (Capcom, 2010) as exclusive characters for the Xbox 360 version.
- Movie website Rotten Tomatoes gave *Street Fighter: The Legend of Chun-Li* (USA, 2009) its Golden Tomato award for the worst-rated film of 2009. The videogame adaptation achieved a rating of just 4% from the site.
- After months of rumours, Steve Jobs announced the forthcoming release of Apple's iPad tablet computer at a press conference in San Francisco, California, USA, leading many games companies to join the rush to develop games in time for its launch.

TRIVIA TRAIL

In January 2010, peripheral creator Mad Catz admitted that it had actually paid money not to be involved with the hugely successful *Guitar Hero* series. CEO Darren Richardson told website Kotaku.com that his company was set to make an Xbox version of the original game, but paid $300,000 (£170,000) to escape the contract to avoid a legal dispute.

FEBRUARY 2010

- Non-profit videogame publisher OneBigGame released the music-themed puzzler *Chime* on Xbox Live Arcade. All proceeds from sales of the game went to the Save the Children and Starlight Children's Foundation charities.
- *Uncharted 2: Among Thieves* (Sony, 2009, right) swept the board at the Academy of Interactive Arts and Sciences Awards, winning 10 awards including Game of the Year. In the same week, it was revealed as the **fastest-selling first-party title for the PlayStation 3**, with over 3.5 million worldwide sales.
- The British Academy of Film and Television Arts (BAFTA) confirmed that Shigeru Miyamoto would be receiving the prestigious BAFTA Fellowship. Miyamoto was only the third recipient of the award from the games industry, following Nolan Bushnell in 2009 and Will Wright in 2007.

MARCH 2010

- Microsoft launched the retro-gaming service *Game Room* (left) for Xbox 360 and PC, allowing users to download and play hundreds of arcade classics on their console or computer. Microsoft has promised to make more than 1,000 arcade titles available to players over the next three years.
- Two key figures from developer Infinity Ward, responsible for the *Modern Warfare* games, were sacked by publisher Activision. The studio's president Jason West and CEO Vince Zampella were allegedly fired due to "breaches of contract and insubordination". The pair went on to form a new studio, named Respawn Entertainment.
- *Batman: Arkham Asylum* (Eidos, 2009) was the big winner at the BAFTA videogame awards, earning the coveted BAFTA masks for Best Game and Best Gameplay.
- The videogame industry showed the first signs that it was emerging from the global recession. Combined hardware, software and accessory sales hit $1.52 billion (£950 million), up 6% over March 2009's total.

GAME ROOM ™

» NEW RECORD
» UPDATED RECORD

"I'M NO HERO. NEVER WAS. I'M JUST AN OLD KILLER... HIRED TO DO SOME WET WORK."

WWW.GUINNESSWORLDRECORDS.COM/GAMERS **017**

ASIDE FROM ALL THE NEW RELEASES, SUMMER 2010 WAS AWASH WITH NEWS ON GAMES IN THE PIPELINE.

APRIL 2010

- On 8 April, FirstPlay – Europe's first console-based interactive videogame web series – launched for PlayStation 3. The show is updated weekly and produced by the team behind the UK's *Official PlayStation Magazine*.
- April saw the UK's hotly debated Digital Economy Bill passed in the House of Commons by a majority of 142. The act made the Pan-European Game Information (PEGI) classification system for games legally binding in the UK, though it won't be fully implemented until April 2011.
- *Call of Duty: Modern Warfare 2* (Activision, 2009) downloadable multiplayer map pack the Stimulus Package (left) broke Xbox Live download records in its first week of release, with over 2.5 million players purchasing the 1,200-Microsoft-Point (£10.20, $15) pack.
- Ubisoft's *Just Dance* hit a whopping 2 million sales, making it the top-selling rhythm-action game in 2010 (it has since gone on to sell 4.2 million copies by October 2010).

MAY 2010

- Apple's iPad sold its first million units after just 28 days on the market. By comparison, the iPhone took more than twice as long to reach the same figure, reaching the 1 miliion mark in 74 days.
- Nintendo announced that DS sales had outstripped those of the Game Boy series of handhelds, with close to 130 million sales up to the end of the financial year in March, when the DS XL launched in the USA.
- US President Barack Obama claimed that games consoles were distracting students from the importance of education. Admitting that he didn't know how to work "iPods and iPads, Xboxes and PlayStations", Obama stated that with these devices "information becomes a distraction, a diversion, a form of entertainment, rather than a tool of empowerment… the means of emancipation".
- ES revealed that digitally distributed first-person shooter *Battlefield 1943* had sold 1.5 million copies on Xbox Live Arcade and PlayStation Network.
- Sony confirmed that British developer Media Molecule was hard at work on a sequel to the popular and critically adored *LittleBigPlanet* (right), which is set for release in January 2011.

JUNE 2010

- *Super Mario Galaxy 2* was released in Europe to huge critical success, while in Japan the game sold 340,000 copies in its first week of release. This outstripped its predecessor's 2007 debut and was more than four times as many copies as its closest chart rival sold that week.
- At the trade show E3, a wide variety of developers and publishers announced plans for their latest games – even comics publishers and film studios were getting in on the act with Marvel Comics showing off their latest fighter *Marvel vs. Capcom 3* and Disney previewing *Tron: Evolution* to tie into the upcoming film *Tron Legacy* (USA, 2010).
- Microsoft's hands-free controller Kinect was unveiled at E3, and at the same time the publisher revealed the first-party line-up of games planned for its November release. Microsoft's *Kinectimals*, *Joy Ride* and *Kinect Sports* joined bundled title *Kinect Adventure* for the launch.
- Nintendo revealed that it would be remaking *The Legend of Zelda: Ocarina of Time* (1998) for its upcoming 3DS handheld. A demonstration of the remake (left) featured at Nintendo's E3 press briefing.

"I'VE BEEN USING A GUN LIKE THIS SINCE I WAS EIGHT YEARS OLD. I'M MORE COMFORTABLE WITH IT THAN I AM WITH A BRA."

JULY 2010

• Declaring he was unhappy with "the horrible concept of demos", UK game designer Peter Molyneux announced that his latest title *Fable III* (Microsoft, 2010) would be available for purchase in digital episodes as well as a traditional retail release, with the first chapter, which is around one hour long, made available as a free download.
• Review aggregator site Metacritic claimed that game quality was improving in 2010, despite declining sales. For the first half of the year, the average review scores were higher than for games released in the same period a year earlier. What's more, seven games released in the first six months of 2010 scored 90% or better on Metacritic.
• At the E3 Critics Awards, id Software's open-world FPS *Rage* (left) and Nintendo's 3DS console were the big winners, raising expectations ahead of their predicted 2011 release dates.

TRIVIA TRAIL

On 6 July 2010, NASA released free-to-play MMO game *Moonbase Alpha* on the digital download service Steam. The game, set in 2032, tasks players with maintaining a lunar base and repairing the installation after a meteor strike. Designed as an educational game, it is intended to encourage interest in space travel.

AUGUST 2010

• *Starcraft II: Wings of Liberty* topped the UK sales chart on its first week of release, becoming the first PC-exclusive title to reach number one in 2010.
• Warner Bros. officially announced plans to release *Batman: Arkham City* (right) in 2011, the sequel to the critically acclaimed *Batman: Arkham Asylum* (Eidos, 2009). The new game will feature Catwoman and has Two-Face competing with the Joker for control of Gotham City.
• Irrational Games showed off its latest planned addition to the *Bioshock* franchise, *Bioshock: Infinite*. Set on the floating city of Columbia in 1912, the game will be released in 2012. An early demonstration received glowing praise from the press, and it was acclaimed as one of the most anticipated titles to be previewed at European games festival Gamescom.

SEPTEMBER 2010

• Microsoft revealed that their Kinect hands-free controller would support three languages at its November launch: English, Mexican Spanish and Japanese. The device's voice recognition support for mainland European languages won't materialize until the device is released in those territories in Spring 2011.
• Developer Gearbox Software announced they were the new custodians of the long-awaited *Duke Nukem Forever*. The game, previously in production at 3D Realms, had been in development for 12 years. Publisher 2K hope to finally release the game in 2011.
• EA's controversial shooter *Medal of Honor* (2010, left) was effectively banned from sale at US military facilities after the Army and Air Force Exchange Services asked for the game to be removed. The request was made after it was revealed players could play as Taliban fighters against US military characters in the game's multiplayer mode.
• One of the games industry's most creative games designers, Keita Takahashi (Japan), left his position at publisher Namco Bandai. The *Katamari Damacy* (Namco, 2004) creator's latest plan is to pursue his long-time dream project, which is to create a children's playground.

HARDWARE

YOU CAN MAKE THE BEST GAME IN THE WORLD, BUT IT'S NOTHING WITHOUT THE KIT TO PLAY IT ON.

»FASTEST-SELLING PORTABLE GAMING SYSTEM

Holder: iPhone 4 **(Apple, 2010)**

Analyst estimates place the first-day sales of the iPhone 4, released on 24 June 2010, at 1.5 million units, making it the fastest-selling portable gaming device in history. For comparison, the PSP shifted 200,000 units on its launch date in 2005, and the DS took a week to move 500,000 consoles in November 2004. While not solely a gaming device, the iPhone now boasts over 30,000 available games, which is a larger library than any other portable system. Furthermore, with web browsing and E-reader capabilities in both the PSP and DS, the features of both devices are clearly close enough for them to be considered as competitors.

"NOTE TO SELF, NEED MORE HENCHMEN, GOOD ONES THIS TIME."

$5.445 BILLION:

THE REVENUE (EQUIVALENT TO £3.612 BILLION) GENERATED BY iPHONE SALES IN THE FIRST QUARTER OF 2010.

Retina Display full frame

polygon smoothing

WHAT ARE THEY?

It has been another great year for hardware junkies, with Microsoft and Sony catching up to the motion control bandwagon that Nintendo have been happily riding solo since 2006. Elsewhere, you'd be forgiven for thinking it was 1992 again with all the talk of 3D gaming (albeit this time it's the glasses kind of 3D rather than the rendering kind). The hardware section is dedicated to all the shiny pieces of gaming technology that live under our TVs, on our desks and, more than ever, in our pockets. Let the fanboy flamewars begin!

WHO SAYS SO?

Chris Schilling (UK) is an experienced videogames writer whose work has featured in *The Daily Telegraph*, *The Observer*, Eurogamer.net and *GamesTM*. Chris has been an avid fan of videogames since the age of five. He has more consoles than he can play and is always looking to add to his gaming armoury, making him just the man to give us the lowdown on what's happening in the hardware world.

CONTENTS

BEST OF XBOX 360

SLIMLINE CONSOLES AND A HANDS-FREE CONTROL SYSTEM MADE THIS A BIG YEAR FOR XBOX HARDWARE.

SYSTEM UPDATE

It was both an evolutionary and revolutionary 2010 for Microsoft, as it upgraded its console hardware and readied the release of a peripheral promising a brand new way to play games. Announced at its E3 conference – and made available immediately to North American gamers – the Xbox 360 S is a slimmer, smaller and much quieter console than any previous 360 model. At the same event, Microsoft revealed that its Project Natal motion-control camera was to be called Kinect and set a November 2010 release date for the device.

NOT CONTENT TO RELY SOLELY ON SEQUELS TO POPULAR GAME FRANCHISES, MICROSOFT SPENT 2010 SUPPORTING INNOVATION IN GAMING, BOTH THROUGH PROMOTIONS OF INDIE TITLES ON ITS XBOX LIVE ARCADE DOWNLOAD SERVICE AND THROUGH THE DEVELOPMENT OF ITS KINECT CONTROL SYSTEM.

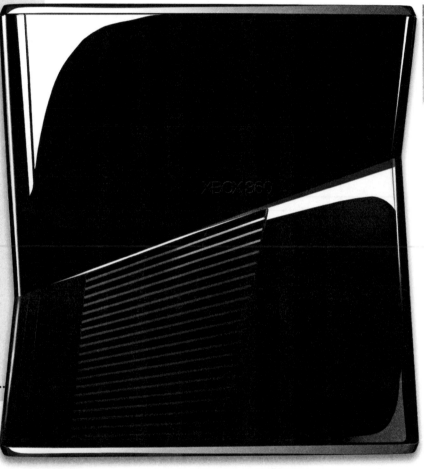

XBOX 360 S

(Microsoft, 2010)
Though a new version of the console had long been rumoured, US gamers were still surprised to learn that they would be able to get their hands on the new Xbox 360 S within four days of Microsoft's press conference at the E3 videogames expo. The console is now available as a 250 GB version retailing for £199.99 ($299) and one with a smaller 4 GB hard drive, priced at £149.99 ($199). The more expensive model features a glossy black finish while the 4 GB console has a matte casing. Both are described as "whisper-quiet" and are Wi-Fi compatible, unlike previous versions. To make way for this new console rollout, Microsoft discontinued their old Elite and Arcade units, bidding farewell forever to the beige boxes of old.

KINECT

(Microsoft, 2010)
Pitched as a "natural user interface", Microsoft's newest control device, which aims to break down the barrier between users and technology altogether, launched in November 2010. An unassuming box filled with cameras and other sensors, the Kinect tracks players by their movement, mapping it on to on-screen avatars in real time. Original games developed for the Kinect include *Kinect Sports* (Microsoft, 2010) and *Kinectimals* (Microsoft, 2010), with many more titles in the pipeline.

» **NEW RECORD**
» **UPDATED RECORD**

"TOUGH TALK FOR SOMEONE WHO STOOD ON THE SIDELINES WHILE HIS NOBODY FLUNKIES DID THE FIGHTING!"

"ACCESSIBILITY IS A KEY DESIGN PRINCIPLE IN LIMBO – A LOT OF DECISIONS RAN FROM THAT."
/MADS WIBROE, PRODUCER OF *LIMBO*.

SUMMER OF ARCADE

(Various, 2010)
Returning for its third year in 2010, Microsoft's Summer of Arcade promotion highlighted five top Xbox Live Arcade titles with discounts for gamers who bought four or five of them. The first to be published was Microsoft's own critically acclaimed 2D platform adventure *Limbo* (pictured), followed by arcade boat racer *Hydro Thunder Hurricane*, *Castlevania: Harmony of Despair*, multiplayer shooter *Monday Night Combat* and *Lara Croft and the Guardian of Light*.

HALO: REACH

(Microsoft, 2010)
Hyped as the last *Halo* game from Bungie, the series' original developer, *Halo: Reach* was released in September 2010 to massive critical acclaim. The game details the events leading up to 2001's *Halo: Combat Evolved*, with the player guiding a super-soldier known as Noble 6 through a series of battles against Covenant forces as they fight to defend the eponymous colony world. The game features a number of changes from previous games, including a suite of improved level-creation tools in the "New Forge World" mode, making it a worthy epitaph to Bungie's iconic first-person shooter franchise.

ALAN WAKE

(Microsoft, 2010)
After close to six years in development, Remedy Entertainment's psychological horror-thriller was finally released in 2010. The hero of the title is a struggling novelist who attempts to get over his writer's block by taking his wife on holiday to the seemingly idyllic town of Bright Falls. Once there, he discovers there are dark forces at work, which he has to battle using limited equipment at night while investigating the town's numerous mysteries during the day. Enemies are especially sensitive to light, so Alan uses torches and flares to strip them of their powers, reserving his limited firearms ammunition to finish them off.

As you might expect from a game that relies heavily on the distinction between night and day, *Alan Wake* features impressive shadow effects. Another key feature is the game's episodic TV-series-like structure, with recaps of previous events at the start of each new chapter. Now gamers just have to sit back and wait for the first trailers for the game's second season.

"GOOD AFTERNOON MISS CROFT. MY RESEARCH DEPARTMENT HAS RECENTLY TURNED ITS FOCUS TO THE STUDY OF ANCIENT ARTEFACTS, AND I'M LEAD TO BELIEVE THAT WITH THE RIGHT INCENTIVE, YOU'RE JUST THE WOMAN TO FIND THEM FOR ME."

BEST OF PLAYSTATION 3

SONY MOVED INTO NEW TERRITORIES IN 2010, EXPLORING 3D GAMING AND MOTION-CONTROL.

SYSTEM UPDATE

Sony had a strong year as the PS3 Slim continued to perform well, particularly in Japan and Europe. In April 2010, Sony released system software update 3.30, which allowed the system to utilize stereoscopic 3D for those with televisions capable of displaying three-dimensional images. PlayStation Network games such as *WipEout HD*, Super *Stardust HD* and *PAIN* were patched to include 3D support, while later in the year Sony released a special cut-down version of *Motorstorm: Pacific Rift* on its download service, which offered a selection of the game's tracks to be played in 3D. Meanwhile, in September 2010, Sony launched the PlayStation Move controller, its entry into the motion-control market.

WITH NO SIGN OF A NEW CONSOLE ON THE HORIZON, SONY LOOKED TO PROVIDE NEW IMMERSIVE EXPERIENCES FOR FANS OF THE PLAYSTATION 3, TAKING A LEAP INTO THE THIRD DIMENSION OF GAMING AND A DETERMINED MOVE INTO MOTION-CONTROL.

PLAYSTATION MOVE

(Sony, 2010)
Having been in development for several years, Sony's motion controller was finally launched in September 2010. The Move is a wand with a glowing orb at its tip, which allows the PlayStation Eye camera to track its movements accurately. As it can read the controller's depth as well as the direction in which it is facing, it offers precision 1:1 control.

Original games have been developed for the Move, while titles such as *Heavy Rain* and *EyePet* were released in new Move-compatible versions.

DID YOU KNOW?

Premium subscription service PlayStation Plus (or PS+) was announced at Sony's E3 2010 press briefing. The service offers a number of benefits over the free PlayStation Network, including exclusive demos, freebie games, discounts and the ability to have firmware updates and patches download automatically to your PlayStation console.

"THE PERFECT SET-UP [FOR MOVE] IS THE KIND OF ENVIRONMENT YOU WANT TO WATCH TELEVISION IN."
/SONY'S RICHARD MARKS EXPLAINS.

TRIVIA TRAIL

Though most gamers were happy to see *Yakuza 3* get a Western release, others were disappointed that elements were left out. The game's strip clubs and their associated missions were removed, and four mini games were also excised, including Shogi chess and Mahjong. Sega released a statement to say it had cut "portions we felt didn't resonate with Western culture".

HEAVY RAIN

(Sony, 2010)
David Cage's (France) narrative-driven adventure was a platform exclusive title quite unlike any other, as players controlled four different characters in a dark and moody thriller, shaping the game's story with their decisions and actions. The game, which used motion-captured actors for added realism, won critical acclaim and gained commercial success, selling over 1.5 million copies.

DEMON'S SOULS

(Sony/Namco Bandai, 2009)
A rare third-party exclusive, this celebrated Japanese action RPG won a substantial cult following overseas, and it finally arrived on UK shores in June 2010 courtesy of Namco Bandai. The kingdom of Boletaria is under the control of a demon named The Old One, and the game's hero is charged with retrieving the demon's souls to gain the power required to defeat him. It's a game renowned for its high difficulty level, but it's one of the most rewarding experiences on PS3.

YAKUZA 3

(Sega, 2009)
Hugely popular in its country of origin, Sega's series based on Japan's gangster life was a late arrival in the West. It tells the tale of Kazuma Kiryu, hero of the first two games in the series, who has retired from his role as head of the Tojo Clan to run an orphanage in the sleepy port town of Okinawa. He is eventually dragged back into his old lifestyle in an action RPG that blends storytelling with beat-'em-up style action. Its brutal street brawls allow players to grab almost any object to pummel their opponents, while undertaking dozens of side-quests to accumulate money, experience and new weaponry. It tells an expansive and surprisingly emotional story using professional actors and real Japanese brands for extra authenticity, and offers faithful, detailed recreations of the two featured districts.

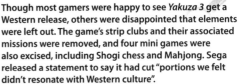

BEST OF Wii

NINTENDO SHOW THAT WHEN IT COMES TO MOTION-CONTROL, THEY STILL HAVE ALL THE MOVES.

HISTORY

Late 2009 saw Wii's first major price-cuts in Japan, from 25,000 yen to 20,000 yen (£170 to £136; $271 to $216), and Europe, from €249 to €199 (£224 to £179; $356 to $285). In December 2009, it set a new monthly record for home console sales in the US, with over 3 million units sold. In the same month, it surpassed the total sales of the original Nintendo Entertainment System, making it »**Nintendo's best-selling home console ever.**

By September 2010, the Wii had consolidated its position as the **most popular home console**, with over 74 million sales in total. Nintendo of America president Reggie Fils-Aime (USA) said the company wouldn't start thinking about a successor to the Wii until "[a] software developer comes forward with an idea that can't be executed on the current platform".

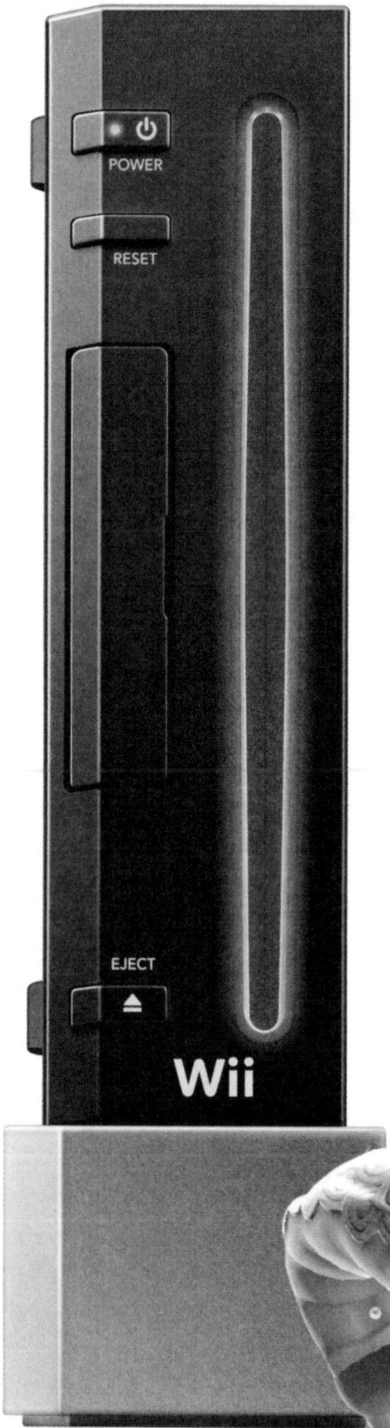

THE Wii CONTINUED ITS REMARKABLE SUCCESS IN 2010, WITH A NUMBER OF TOP-QUALITY EXCLUSIVES BOLSTERING ITS SOFTWARE LINE-UP AND CONTRIBUTING TO ITS SALES. BUT WITH RIVAL MOTION-CONTROL SYSTEMS MOVE AND KINECT COMING ONTO THE SCENE, WILL THE RECORD-BREAKING CONSOLE CONTINUE TO PROSPER?

SUPER MARIO GALAXY 2

(Nintendo, 2010)
Many critics thought Nintendo would struggle to better the original *Super Mario Galaxy* (2007), but were then surprised to discover that the games giant had managed to do just that. This critically lauded sequel strips back the story elements and introduces a new spaceship hub and level select that allows players to get into the action much quicker than before.

Featuring more galaxies than the first game, *Super Mario Galaxy 2* uses a number of clever perspective shifts and changes of gravity, and even introduces some puzzle elements to the platforming. Within each world is a well-hidden or hard-to-reach Comet Medal, which adds a new twist to the level, from speed runs through purple coin hunts to challenges from a mischievous chimp. Beat all the galaxies and you'll unlock a brand new feature that gives the game substantial replay value. With some of the best graphics and sound you'll find on the Wii, there's little wonder it's so highly rated.

POWER

RESET

EJECT

Wii

Wii

» NEW RECORD » UPDATED RECORD

"IT'S COMMON KNOWLEDGE THAT IRRADIATED CATS HAVE 18 HALF-LIVES."

METROID: OTHER M

(Nintendo, 2010)
In the latest *Metroid* title, series creator Yoshio Sakamoto (Japan) and *Ninja Gaiden* developer Team Ninja, delve into the past of heroine Samus Aran, detailing her history with the Galactic Federation Army. The game adopts a side-scrolling perspective, though a Wii Remote-friendly first-person view is also available.

TRIVIA TRAIL

On 20 November 2009, Nintendo released the Classic Controller Pro in Europe, a variation on the standard model with more traditional grips for each hand and different button placement. *Monster Hunter Tri* producer Kenzo Tsujimoto (Japan) revealed he was consulted on the device during its development, and the Pro was subsequently bundled with copies of the game.

> "THE WORLD IS MOVING MORE AND MORE DIGITAL— AND SO ARE WE." NINTENDO OF AMERICA'S REGGIE FILS-AIME.

SILENT HILL: SHATTERED MEMORIES

(Konami, 2009)
A reimagining of the original *Silent Hill* (Konami, 1999), *Shattered Memories* is an innovative take on the classic survival horror franchise. Framing the story is an interview with a therapist, through which the player is psychologically evaluated according to their responses. The game that follows is subtly adapted depending on the answers provided. There are adaptations to the control interface too, enabling players to use their Wii Remote as a mobile phone, on which they can check the map, take pictures and listen to messages.

MONSTER HUNTER TRI

(Capcom, 2009)
Nintendo struck a deal with Capcom to promote and distribute this epic action RPG in the West. As with previous *Monster Hunter* games, this one has a substantial solo campaign but can also be played co-operatively, split screen or online by up to four players at a time. The game was even sold with Nintendo's Wii Speak microphone peripheral, allowing players to communicate more easily.

BEST OF PC

DEVELOPERS WILL ALWAYS PRODUCE QUALITY GAMES FOR PCs WHILE THEY REMAIN THE STRONGHOLD OF MMOGs.

SYSTEM UPDATE

Digital distribution continued to be the dominant force in the PC market, with Valve's Steam platform reportedly accounting for 70% of all digital sales. With over 1,100 games available and regular special promotions, the service goes from strength to strength.

Though some consider the PC to be struggling at traditional retail, it continued to receive the best versions of many multiplayer titles. The release of *StarCraft II: Wings of Liberty* in July 2010 proved that the biggest PC titles can still top the sales chart, with 1 million copies sold in its first 24 hours.

NO OTHER PLATFORM OFFERS SUCH A WIDE RANGE OF EXPERIENCES AS THE PC. FROM INDIE CLASSICS TO MEGA-BUDGET BLOCKBUSTERS, IT'S GOT ALL BASES COVERED. AND YOU CAN EVEN USE IT TO WORK ON A SPREADSHEET IF YOU FEEL THE NEED.

STARCRAFT II: WINGS OF LIBERTY

(Blizzard, 2010)
Over a decade on from the release of the original *StarCraft* (Blizzard, 1998), its sequel was one of the most eagerly anticipated releases of 2010 and it didn't disappoint its millions of fans. *StarCraft II*'s epic campaign sees Jim Raynor attempting to overthrow the Dominion Emperor and then take on the Terrans' old foes, the Protoss and the Zerg. Its fast-paced gameplay requires quick thinking as you attempt to micromanage your army. The single-player game is only a small part of the fun, too – with challenge and skirmish modes bolstering the game's multiplayer options this is an essential PC title.

» **NEW RECORD**
» **UPDATED RECORD**

»MOST CUSTOMIZABLE GAMING MOUSE

Holder: Cyborg R.A.T. 7
With a total of 1,344 different physical configurations in addition to its customizable driver software, the Cyborg R.A.T. 7 is the most adaptable input device of its kind. The mouse is sold with extra body plates to change its form factor, and options to alter its weight and length. It also features variable sensitivity to make for more precise aiming – perfect for pro-gamers.

"GOOD GOD, IT SMELLS LIKE GRANDPA GOAT'S GARLIC FACTORY IN HERE!"

MINECRAFT

(Markus Persson, 2009)

The brainchild of one man, Swedish independent developer Markus Persson (aka "Notch"), *Minecraft* (below) is a sandbox adventure game that sees players plunged into a randomly generated world made from different kinds of block. The goal is simply to survive, which you do by building a safe haven and exploring the world to track down valuable resources. You can mine ores, cut down trees for timber or indulge in a bit of farming by harvesting your own crops. Venture further away from home and you may need to craft weapons and armour in order to protect yourself from enemies. Alternatively, you can focus on creating an ever more elaborate home for your character. Essentially, *Minecraft* is an entirely open-ended gameplay experience where no two players will adopt the same approach, and if you're finding this huge world a little lonely, you can even invite friends and take a collaborative approach to survival and world-building.

AMNESIA: THE DARK DESCENT

(Frictional Games, 2010)

Amnesia (above), from Swedish developer Frictional Games who are responsible for the *Penumbra* series, is a first-person adventure game that plays like a survival horror. You play as an amnesiac called Daniel who must explore a dark and dangerous castle while attempting to recover his own memories. The only instruction you have is an apparently self-written letter, telling you to find the castle's basement and kill a man you don't know. The lack of weaponry makes each enemy encounter all the more intense, and with Daniel unable to even look at these horrific creatures in case he descends into madness, *Amnesia* is a truly unnerving experience. It's not for the faint-hearted – but if you can handle the scares, it's one of the most atmospheric PC games around.

PLAIN SIGHT

(Beatnik Games Ltd, 2010)

Plain Sight is described as "a multiplayer arcade game about suicidal ninja robots". You are armed with a katana, which you use to slice your opponents into ribbons so that you can use their left-behind energy to grow more powerful. The object is then to attract the attention of other players before blowing yourself up, gaining points for each opponent you take out in the blast before upgrading your abilities and starting all over again. With five gameplay modes, this is one of the most innovative multiplayer experiences on PC.

TRIVIA TRAIL

While PC owners continue to wait for *Diablo III*, Seattle, USA-based developer Runic Games successfully filled the dungeon-crawling void for many in 2009 with *Torchlight*, which sold 750,000 copies in less than a year. The game was developed in under 11 months, remarkable for such a polished title, and a sequel has been announced for Spring 2011.

"HERE'S A LOCKPICK. IT MIGHT BE USEFUL IF YOU THE MASTER OF UNLOCKING – TAKE IT WITH YOU."

WWW.GUINNESSWORLDRECORDS.COM/GAMERS **029**

BEST OF DS

SYSTEM UPDATE

By the middle of 2010, Nintendo's family of DS handheld consoles had sold an estimated 135 million units, bringing it close to the PlayStation 2's massive user base of 140 million. The PS2's sales figures had previously seemed unbeatable. Indeed, by the time you read this, Nintendo's dual-screened portable may be the most successful games console of all time! Its sales have been helped significantly by the launch of the DSi XL (known as the DSi LL in Japan) and look set to take another leap with the launch of the 3DS.

THE PAST 12 MONTHS HAVE SEEN THE RELEASE OF AN UPSCALED NEW MODEL AND PLENTY OF COMPELLING GAMES FOR THE DS, BUT REALLY WE'VE ALL SPENT THE YEAR IN ANTICIPATION OF THE LATEST WORD IN HANDHELD GAMING – THE 3DS.

DID YOU KNOW?

Pokémon Black & White (Nintendo, 2010) introduced a new graphics engine and a more dynamic battle system to the *Pokémon* series, which enabled "Triple Battles" – a new mode that allows players to pit their pokémon into three-on-three contests. On top of this, there are 150 brand new pocket monsters to collect and many ways to import old favourites.

NINTENDO 3DS

(Nintendo, 2011)
Announced at E3 2010, the 3DS is Nintendo's plan to bring 3D gaming to your handheld without the need for special 3D glasses. The device works by producing an image that contains slightly different information for each eye, displayed under a thin layer of material called a parallax barrier. The barrier contains a series of holes that are positioned so that at a certain "sweet" viewing position the left eye can only see the parts of the image intended for the left eye and the right eye can only see the parts intended for the right eye and together these parts make a 3D whole. While the 3DS will be compatable with previous DS cartridges, 3DS games won't work on old DSi or DS Lites – time to start saving for what promises to be Nintendo's latest hit handheld.

"TEN YEARS, ATHENA! I HAVE FAITHFULLY SERVED THE GODS FOR TEN YEARS! WHEN WILL YOU LEAVE ME OF THESE NIGHTMARES?"

WARIOWARE: DO IT YOURSELF

(Nintendo, 2010)

WarioWare games are known for their energetic creativity, but this time the creativity is handed over to the player as *WarioWare: Do It Yourself* tasks you with making your own micro games. Fortunately, you are not thrown in at the deep end – there are plenty of tutorials on how to produce suitable art, sound and gameplay, all broken down into simple steps, before you are unleashed on the title's full toolset.

As we all know, it takes time to create a really good game, so it is more satisfying when you craft a particularly enjoyable mini-masterpiece that keeps your friends amused. And thanks to the game's cross-compatibility with the Wii, you can even upload your mini games to be played on Nintendo's home console.

And just in case you're not sure of the type of game you want to create, Nintendo have included 90 *WarioWare* micro games (top right) to inspire you.

» **NEW RECORD**
» **UPDATED RECORD**

TRIVIA TRAIL

Nintendo produced two more non-game lifestyle titles in 2010, both aimed at casual gaming DS owners. One is *Art Academy: Learn Painting and Drawing Techniques with Step-by-Step Training* (Nintendo, 2010), which uses simple tutorials to encourage users to improve their artistic skills. The other is *Face Training: Facial Exercises to Strengthen and Relax from Fumiko Inudo* (Nintendo, 2010), which teaches techniques to improve facial tone and well-being, using the DSi camera to ensure players are doing the exercises correctly.

THE LEGEND OF ZELDA: SPIRIT TRACKS

(Nintendo, 2009)

Following on from his adventures in *Phantom Hourglass*, (Nintendo, 2007), Link chugged his way back on to the DS in December 2009, this time as a train engineer in *The Legend of Zelda: Spirit Tracks*, a game that uses the same cel-shaded art style as the earlier *Zelda* DS adventure. This time out, aside from the regular puzzle-solving, Link must also take to the railtracks, shooting enemies with his train's cannon, tooting the horn to persuade livestock off the line and following signposts to get passengers where they want to be.

"AS LONG AS WE'RE ABLE TO CREATE COMPELLING CONTENT THEY CAN ONLY PLAY ON OUR SYSTEMS, THEN PEOPLE WILL WANT TO CARRY OUR DEVICE AROUND WITH THEM."
/NINTENDO'S SHIGERU MIYAMOTO ON WHY THE 3DS CAN HOLD ITS OWN AGAINST THE iPHONE.

POKÉMON HEARTGOLD AND SOULSILVER

(Nintendo, 2010)

As remakes of the original *Pokémon Gold and Silver* games, the latest *Pokémon* titles weren't expected to be quite as successful as they ended up being. By May 2010, the pair had sold over 8.4 million copies, putting them among the best-selling handheld games ever. The added feature that enables players to breed their pokémon undoubtedly added to the game's appeal.

DRAGON QUEST IX: SENTINELS OF THE STARRY SKIES

(Square Enix, 2009)

Japan's cult classic made it to the US and UK in 2010, with Japanese designers Yuji Horii and Akihiro Hino citing western titles such as *The Elder Scrolls IV: Oblivion* (2K, 2006) and *Diablo* (Blizzard, 1997) as inspirations for a game that redefines the long-running series.

Unlike its predecessors, *Dragon Quest IX* is primarily designed as a multiplayer game, and instead of playing established characters, gamers can create their own party members. While the series' traditional turn-based combat remains intact, in this instalment players can also choose which enemies they want to engage in combat as they explore the huge game world. However, the biggest new feature is its Wi-Fi-enabled "Chance Encounter" mode, where users can put their DS on standby and exchange map and character data with each other.

HARDWARE/
BEST OF PSP

SONY'S PORTABLE POWERHOUSE CONTINUED ITS SUCCESS AND WE WERE INTRODUCED TO ITS LITTLE BROTHER.

SYSTEM UPDATE

As the most successful non-Nintendo handheld games console, the PSP remains as popular in the East as ever, its sales neck-and-neck with the DS on a weekly basis. So it's no surprise that Japanese franchises have been making their way to the console, most notably with *Metal Gear Solid: Peace Walker*, considered by Hideo Kojima to be the equivalent of *Metal Gear Solid 5*. Elsewhere, Sony launched a remarkable promotion for the digital-distribution-only PSPgo, with 10 free downloadable games for anyone buying the new console, while a creative new marketing campaign suggested users "step [their] game up" by enjoying the "full fat" gaming experiences PSP has to offer.

EVEN WITH THE PSP'S LONG-TIME PARTNER *MONSTER HUNTER* HAVING MADE THE MOVE TO HOME CONSOLES, SONY'S HANDHELD MANAGED ANOTHER STRONG YEAR IN 2010. FANS OF THE SYSTEM ARE NOW LOOKING TO NEXT YEAR, AS RUMOURS OF A BRAND NEW PSP2 CONTINUE TO CIRCULATE.

METAL GEAR SOLID: PEACE WALKER

(Konami, 2010)
As the first portable *Metal Gear Solid* to be produced and directed by series creator Hideo Kojima (Japan), *Peace Walker* has an incredible pedigree. One of only two handheld *MGS* titles to be considered part of the story canon, the game sees players control Naked Snake four years after the events of PSP title *Portable Ops*. *Peace Walker* cherry-picks the best elements from previous games, with myriad gameplay types that offer arguably the greatest variety of any *MGS* game.

DID YOU KNOW?

In June 2010, Sony held a promotion for UK gamers allowing anyone who bought a PSPgo between April and September to download 10 titles from the PlayStation Store for free. The 10 games were: *Assassins Creed: Bloodlines, Grand Theft Auto: Vice City Stories, Gran Turismo, James Cameron's AVATAR: The Game, LittleBigPlanet, MotorStorm Arctic Edge, NEED FOR SPEED SHIFT, Pursuit Force: Extreme Justice, 2010 FIFA World Cup South Africa* and *WipEout Pure*. The offer was repeated in Australia, while US owners received a voucher to download three free games.

PSPgo

(Sony, 2009)
Launched in 2009, the PSPgo is a leaner and significantly less weighty model than any other PSP, coming in at 56% smaller and 43% lighter than the original PSP-1000. Its screen slides up to reveal the controls, with the analogue nub positioned to the right of the d-pad. The most significant change is the removal of the UMD drive – only digitally distributed games can be played on the go. It features 16 GB of internal flash memory and Bluetooth connectivity, allowing players to control games with a PS3 controller.

TRIVIA TRAIL

Sony made the unusual step of showing off a new marketing campaign at its E3 2010 conference. It stars fictional 12-year-old Marcus Rivers, played by *Role Models* (USA/Germany, 2008) actor Bobb'e J Thompson (USA), who is keen to publicize the PSP. One such advert features *Metal Gear Solid: Peace Walker*, a game Rivers would be unable to play thanks to its teen rating.

HALF-MINUTE HERO

(XSEED Games, 2009)
As the title suggests, you have 30 seconds to save the world, running through the game at high speed with random battles rarely lasting more than a second or two. The game has a number of modes, including an RPG section, an Evil Lord 30 Mode where creatures battle it out in a real-time strategy game, and a Princess 30 Mode, which is a fast-paced shooter.

> "THE ORIGINAL IDEA WAS TO BUILD AN ULTRA-PORTABLE, ALL-DIGITAL DEVICE."
> /SONY'S JOHN KOLLER TELLS OF THE BIG IDEA FOR THE PSPgo.

VALKYRIA CHRONICLES II

(Sega, 2010)
Sony's handheld system proved consistently popular in Japan, as well as more cost-effective in development terms, so it shouldn't have come as a big surprise to see Sega's strategy RPG make the journey from big screen to small. The cult PS3 hit feels comfortably at home on PSP and the game plays similarly to the original, although battles are broken up into smaller chunks to better suit portable play.

BEST OF iPAD/iPHONE

APPLE KEEP THE DESIGN CLASSICS COMING, THIS TIME IN THE FORM OF THE iPAD AND THE iPHONE 4.

SYSTEM UPDATE

Unveiled in January 2010, the iPad promised to revolutionize tablet gaming and was an instant hit, selling 300,000 units on its opening weekend and 2.5 million within its first two months of release. It is available with Wi-Fi-only or Wi-Fi with added 3G functionality, and has a storage capacity of either 16, 32 or 64 GB.

In June, the latest model of the ever-popular iPhone was launched. The iPhone 4 has a stainless steel frame and an improved display with increased pixel resolution known as a "retina display".

September saw the launch of Apple's Game Center, an online multiplayer social network similar to Microsoft's Xbox LIVE. And of course, every new game is available through Apple's record-breaking App Store.

» **NEW RECORD**
» **UPDATED RECORD**

IN 2010, APPLE ESTABLISHED ITSELF AS A MAJOR PLAYER IN THE MOBILE GAMING MARKET WITH THE LAUNCH OF ITS iPAD TABLET AND A NEW ITERATION OF ITS "MUST HAVE" iPHONE. EVEN PEOPLE WHO NEVER CONSIDERED THEMSELVES TO BE GAMERS HAVE BEEN SEDUCED BY APPLE'S TECHNOLOGY.

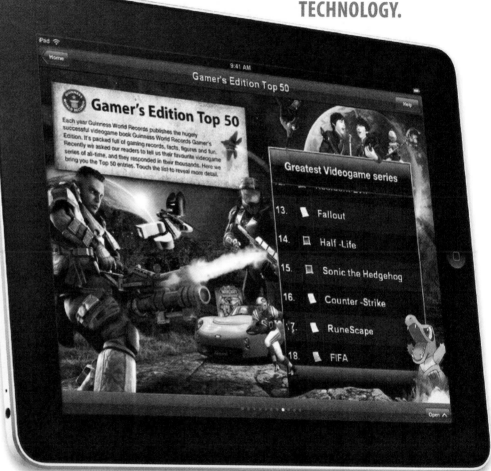

OSMOS

(Hemisphere Games, 2009)
Though previously available on PC, the iPad version of *Osmos* is considered as definitive, mainly thanks to its touchscreen controls. The game is designed to be played with multitouch, offering a tactile satisfaction missing from the PC game. Players guide an organism known as a mote around a series of ambient levels, absorbing smaller motes while staying away from larger ones. A superb electronic soundtrack helps make *Osmos* hypnotically compelling. It's no surprise that many critics claim it to be the best iPad game to date.

{ *"A MERE CHILD LIKE YOU DARES TO CHALLENGE ME? THE VERY IDEA MAKES ME SHIVER WITH MIRTH! VERY WELL, I SHALL SHOW YOU TRUE TERROR AS A NINJA MASTER!"* }

03:15.63
04:15.00

MIRROR'S EDGE

(EA, 2009)

Already a success on PC and Xbox 360, *Mirror's Edge* arrived on iPad in a very different form. Rather than a first-person adventure, this version adopts a 2D side-scrolling approach, with free-runner Faith sprinting across rooftops, and leaping over and sliding under obstacles with simple finger swipes guiding her movement. It makes for a more elegant parkour experience than the original game, with a focus on momentum and the ability to build up a thrilling sense of speed.

The game's simplicity brings to mind *Canabalt* (Armor Games, 2009), though *Mirror's Edge* is blessed with higher production values. Its outdoor environments in particular provide gorgeous backdrops, which aren't obscured by the player's fingers as the intuitive controls simply require you to make the appropriate motions in the corner of the screen. Two multiplayer modes add value to a solid single-player experience, making this an essential iPad download.

"WE WERE CONTACTED BY A BUSINESS MANAGER AT APPLE WHO WAS INTERESTED IN SEEING OSMOS PORTED TO THE iPAD… WE HOPED THAT IF WE COULD PLEASE THE GREAT APPLE GODS, THEY MIGHT FEATURE OSMOS."
/AARON BARSKY OF HEMISPHERE GAMES TELLING GAMEZEBO HOW *OSMOS* MADE IT TO THE iPAD.

FLICK KICK FOOTBALL

(PikPok, 2010)

Sometimes the simplest ideas are the best, and so it proved with the amazingly addictive *Flick Kick Football*. The objective is always the same – kick the ball into the goal – but the distance varies each time, and you're confronted with combinations of defenders and a goalkeeper, who may or may not move around on his line. One miss and it's game over, but you can increase your complement of "lives" by hitting the skill zones in the top corners of the goal. Earn a set number of points, or hit three goals in a row in "Time Attack" mode, and you'll get a burning ball, which powers through any defenders who get in the way of your shot.

TRIVIA TRAIL

On 8 September 2010, Apple launched its new Game Center service, a social gaming network allowing users to interact more effectively in their games. It offered matchmaking services, online achievements and leaderboards, and the ability to invite friends to multiplayer games. Sticking with the classics, the first game available on the service was *Ms. PAC-Man*.

ANGRY BIRDS

(Chillingo, 2009)

A true word-of-mouth phenomenon, *Angry Birds* has consistently topped the App Store chart worldwide since its release in December 2009 (see p.172). The gameplay is simple but addictive – players catapult birds at increasingly complex structures to attack the evil pigs who have stolen their eggs (we said it was simple, not an accurate portrayal of the food chain!). The game has been ported to other mobile devices, and DS and Wii versions are planned for release in 2011.

SCORE
18
HIGHSCORE
84

LIVES

"HMMM. STAY FUZZY, SAVE THE WORLD… CHOICES. OH ALRIGHT FINE! WE'LL SAVE THE WORLD! BUT DO IT QUICKLY BEFORE I CHANGE MY MIND!"

WWW.GUINNESSWORLDRECORDS.COM/GAMERS **035**

MAKING MONEY PLAYING VIDEOGAMES

WANT TO TURN YOUR PASSION FOR GAMING INTO A FULL-TIME PROFESSION? READ ON...

SO THE CAREERS COUNSELLOR HAS TOLD YOU TO CONSIDER A CAREER IN MEDICINE, FINANCE OR LAW BUT ALL YOU WANT TO DO IS PLAY *CALL OF DUTY*? FEAR NOT! THE GAMES INDUSTRY CAN BE AN EXCITING AND WONDERFUL PLACE TO WORK, BUT IT'S A MINEFIELD IF YOU'RE NOT PREPARED. LUCKILY FOR YOU, WE AT *GAMER'S EDITION* HAVE PREPARED THE ESSENTIAL GUIDE TO PLAYING GAMES AND GETTING PAID FOR IT!

GOLD FARMER

It sounds like a glamorous gig, but gold farming is far from it. Basically you and your farming friends spend long days in darkened rooms playing MMOGs to acquire in-game currency. This is then sold on for real cash to lazy, cheating MMO gamers who want to access higher levels without putting in the effort. It's difficult to find any reliable stats on working conditions, but reports suggest that human rights violations in this budding sector are rife, and the pay isn't great either. We'd recommend you avoid gold farming and plough a more fulfilling furrow.

Working day: 10 hours +
Earning potential: Around £30 ($47) per week, with one day off per month.

"WORKING CONDITIONS ARE HARD. WE DON'T GET WEEKENDS OFF AND I HAVE ONE DAY FREE A MONTH."
/CHINESE GOLD FARMER LI HUA EXPLAINS THE RIGOURS OF HIS JOB.

GAMES TESTER

Games testers get to play the latest games before anyone else, and can go online on launch day to "pwn n00bs" before they work out the level layouts – that sounds like a dream, not a job! On the downside, testers don't have a choice when it comes to what they play, so even if they're craving a bit of gentle puzzling they may have to get stuck into the latest ultraviolent shooter instead. The main part of the job is finding and reporting bugs, which means the style of play required is a little different from what most gamers would do: walking into every wall from every level from every angle is enough to make anyone resent in-game physics!

Working day: 8–10 hours
Earning potential: According to *Develop* magazine's salary survey 2010, an entry-level tester takes home around £15,000 ($23,750), with senior testers closer to £19,500 ($30,800).

TOP 10 HIGHEST-EARNING ROLES IN THE UK VIDEOGAMES INDUSTRY

	Role	UK	US Equiv.
1	Studio Head & MD/CEO	£68,750	$108,000
2	COO/CTO/Creative Director	£60,313	$95,000
3	Lead Audio Roles	£46,750	$74,000
4	Lead Producer (Internal)	£44,000	$70,000
5	Lead Artist	£41,125	$65,000
6	Lead Programmer	£40,000	$63,500
7	Lead Designer	£37,500	$59,000
8	Producer (Internal)	£31,500	$50,000
9	Programmer	£31,455	$50,000
10	Artist	£30,441	$48,000

Source: Develop magazine's salary survey 2010

» NEW RECORD
» UPDATED RECORD

"IT HAS BEEN WRITTEN IN THE BOOK OF DIVINE FABRICATIONS THAT THE GREAT GOD OF THE SACRED CROTCH ARKVOODLE CANNOT BE MADE OR UNMADE."

CASH TOURNAMENT PLAYER

Cash competitions spring up all over the world, from small town community gatherings to major organized events in large cities. These competitions have featured on the fighting game scene for many years, and they're the most common way for world-class players to cut their teeth against highly skilled and highly motivated opponents. Entrants pay a fee to take part, and the total prize pot is then divided up between the winners, minus a contribution for the organisers and venue hire. The trick with cash competitions is to find the right fight for your skill level: bigger tournaments have larger prize pots but will attract better players, so be prepared to work for your cash!

Working day: Whatever you can fit in around your regular job – by day, Japan's Daigo Umehara works in a nursing home, but by night he's the world *Street Fighter* champion.

Earning potential: The UK's biggest *Street Fighter* tournament, Super vs. Battle 20X, had over 300 entrants, each of whom paid £10 ($15) to enter. Winner Luffy (France) took home 60% of the takings from a pot of around £1,800 ($2,850).

KOREAN PRO GAMER

The most active and highly paid pro gaming circuit is South Korea's Starleagues. Successful players have full rock-star status, with matches televised on one of two major gaming channels. The road to greatness is littered with failures, though, so make sure you can click a mouse at least 300 times per minute before you buy your ticket to Seoul.

Working day: Up to you, but high-level players in the Starleagues are reported to put in around 12 hours of practise per day.

Earning potential: First prize for the Ongamenet Starleague 2010 was 40,000,000KRW (£22,300; $35,300), which was claimed by Kim "EffOrt"Jung Woo. Top-ranked players can also expect to cash in on some endorsements. Allegations of betting scandals seem to suggest that dishonest gamers can earn even more if they're prepared to throw an important game, though of course that's not something that we condone.

FAQ WRITER

Popular US game guide website GameFAQs.com offers bounties to the first person to write a walkthrough on some games that other users have requested. On average, budding scribes can expect to net a cool $30 (£19) for beating the rush on an in-demand title. It's not easy money, though, particularly if you're writing a guide to a big game: the walkthrough to *Final Fantasy X* by Nick "SinirothX" Henson runs to over 518,000 words – that's 15% longer than *The Lord of the Rings* trilogy!

Working day: Even assuming you already own the game you're writing for, you'll need to put in at least 50 hours to become an expert, plus however long it takes to write the guide itself. Assuming you can type at an average 19 words per minute, you could expect to match SinirothX's oeuvre in around 450 hours.

Earning potential: About £0.04 ($0.06) per hour at that rate.

SHOOTING GAMES

DODGING BULLETS WHILE HITTING MOVING TARGETS, SHOOTING GAMES ARE ALL ABOUT THE GUNS AND GLORY.

»BEST-SELLING CO-OPERATIVE SHOOTER

Holder: *Left 4 Dead 2* **(Valve, 2009)**
With sales of over 3 million since its release in November 2009, *Left 4 Dead 2* easily tops the chart as the best-selling co-operative shooter. The game, set in the aftermath of a viral outbreak that turns humans into the infected (zombie-like beings), is pitched to be almost impossible for a single player to complete, forcing gamers to collaborate to survive successive waves of the infected as they make their way to the next safe house.

"WHAT CAN I SAY? I'M A BAD MAN."

GUINNESS WORLD RECORDS

WHAT ARE THEY?

There's no way around it, from assault rifles to zap guns, ranged weapons play an important role in a rich variety of videogames, and in shooting games firing after foes is particularly pivotal. The genre can trace its origin back to *Spacewar!*, created in 1961 by American MIT students Martin Graetz, Steve Russell and Wayne Wiitane, and has grown in popularity to the point that the launch of a new title can be a worldwide event. The task at hand might be eliminating all enemies, defending a position, capturing an objective or simply survival against overwhelming odds, but the only way you are going to achieve your goal is with some heavy ordinance and plenty of ammunition.

WHO SAYS SO?

Michael French (UK) is Editor-in-Chief of leading games industry publications *MCV*, *Develop* and CasualGaming.biz. He has been a games journalist for over 10 years and his CV includes spells as Reviews Editor for *Official PlayStation 2 Magazine* and Online Editor for *Edge*. Michael has also written for in-flight magazines, newspapers and a host of games magazines including *PSNext GamesMaster*, *Play* and *GamesTM*.

CONTENTS

CALL OF DUTY

CRITICAL HIT!

NOT JUST A SHOOTING GAME, BUT ONE OF THE GREATEST ENTERTAINMENT FRANCHISES OF ALL TIME.

»HIGHEST REVENUE FOR AN ENTERTAINMENT LAUNCH

Holder: *Call of Duty: Modern Warfare 2* **(Activision, 2009)**

Call of Duty: Modern Warfare 2 generated revenue totaling $401,690,771 (£242,424,795) in the 24 hours after its global launch on 11 November 2009, the greatest day-one revenue of any entertainment product.

TRIVIA TRAIL

Completing the single-player mode of *Call of Duty: Modern Warfare 2* unlocks the bonus level, "An Evening with Infinity Ward". Taking the form of a museum featuring scenes from the campaign, it's also the only level in the game where every weapon can be picked up and used.

"LOOKS LIKE HE HIT THE TREE, JIM."

5,565,669: THE ESTIMATED DAY-ONE WORLDWIDE SALES FIGURE FOR *CALL OF DUTY: MODERN WARFARE 2*, RELEASED ON 11 NOVEMBER 2009.

"CALL OF DUTY IS ABOUT THE GUYS IN THE TRENCHES."
/VINCE ZAMPELLA, FORMER CEO OF INFINITY WARD.

» NEW RECORD   » UPDATED RECORD

FIRST TITLE TO SELL 1 MILLION COPIES ON XBOX 360
Holder: *Call of Duty 2* **(Activision, 2005)**
Launch title *Call of Duty 2* was the first Xbox 360 game to sell 1 million copies in the USA. This strong showing for the franchise has continued for all its releases on the Microsoft console, generating sales of 31.36 million and making it the »**biggest-selling series on Xbox 360.**

»MOST DEATHS IN A MULTIPLAYER GAME IN CALL OF DUTY: MODERN WARFARE 2
Holder: Michael Betts (USA)
Going against the usual method of playing the game (i.e. trying to avoid getting killed), Michael Betts undertook the challenge of being killed the most times in an open, ranked multiplayer match on *Call of Duty: Modern Warfare 2* (Activision, 2009). Michael, from Kalispell, Montana, USA, was not allowed to communicate with the other gamers to explain his goal, yet the most times he was killed in one match was 27 times on 24 May 2010.

FIRST OFFICIALLY LICENSED CARD GAME BASED ON AN FPS
Holder: Call of Duty: Real-Time Card Game
Released in 2008 by Upper Deck Entertainment, Call of Duty: Real-Time Card Game is the first officially licensed card game to be based on a first-person shooter.

»FASTEST SEGMENTED SPEED RUN OF CALL OF DUTY 4: MODERN WARFARE
Holder: Sami Reinikainen (Finland)
On 18 January 2009, Sami Reinikainen assembled a segmented speed run (where individual levels of a game are repeated in order to create a "perfect run") on *Call of Duty 4: Modern Warfare* (Activision, 2007) that saw him finish the game in just 1 hr 38 min 59 sec.

»FASTEST-SELLING DOWNLOADABLE CONTENT ON XBOX LIVE
Holder: Stimulus Package
The "Stimulus Package", a collection of five additional maps for *Call of Duty: Modern Warfare 2* (Activision, 2009) costing 1,200 Microsoft points ($15 or £10.20), was downloaded over 1 million times in its first 24 hours on sale on 30 March 2010. The pack sold over 2.5 million downloads in its first week.

MOST PLAYED ONLINE GAME
Holder: *Call of Duty 4: Modern Warfare* **(Activision, 2007)**
Call of Duty 4: Modern Warfare is the most popular online console game, having been played by over 13 million gamers on Xbox Live since its launch in November 2007.

»FASTEST COMPLETION OF "SNIPER FI" ON CALL OF DUTY: MODERN WARFARE 2
Holder: Janner (USA)
US gamer Janner of online community weplaycod.com posted a completion time of 1 min 39.5 sec on the special ops mission "Sniper Fi" on *Call of Duty: Modern Warfare 2* (Activision, 2009) on PC. This is 16 seconds faster than the best time achieved by developers Infinity Ward!

TOP 10 BEST-SELLING *CALL OF DUTY* TITLES BY PLATFORM

	Game	Platform	Sales
1	Call of Duty: Modern Warfare 2 (2009)	Xbox 360	11.56 million
2	Call of Duty: Modern Warfare 2 (2009)	PS3	8.56 million
3	Call of Duty 4: Modern Warfare (2007)	Xbox 360	8.43 million
4	Call of Duty: World at War (2008)	Xbox 360	6.49 million
5	Call of Duty 4: Modern Warfare (2007)	PS3	5.07 million
6	Call of Duty: World at War (2008)	PS3	4.19 million
7	Call of Duty: Finest Hour (2004)	PS2	2.81 million
8	Call of Duty 2 (2005)	Xbox 360	2.47 million
9	Call of Duty 3 (2006)	Xbox 360	2.36 million
10	Call of Duty 2: Big Red One (2005)	PS2	2.35 million

Source: VGChartz

FIRST-PERSON SHOOTERS I

MORE THAN ANY OTHER GENRE, SHOOTERS OFFER A VARIETY OF GAMES THAT AIM TO PLEASE.

► MOST SUCCESSFUL GAMES ENGINE
Holder: Unreal Engine (Epic Games, 1998)
Now in its third iteration, and with 208 games to its name as of September 2010, Epic's Unreal Engine is the most successful licensed games engine. It was first created to power the PC shooter *Unreal* (Epic Games, 1998) and has since been adopted by a variety of FPS developers. Most recently, EA has used a version of the Unreal Engine for the campaign mode of *Medal of Honor* (EA, 2010), with the game's multiplayer mode employing EA's own Frostbite Engine. Perhaps the Unreal Engine's days of dominance are numbered?

TRIVIA TRAIL

One of the most interesting facets to the *MIDI Maze* story (see the record box on the opposite page) is the recent discovery of old prototypes of different Atari machines – both 8-bit consoles and 16-bit computers – that could be connected together to run the game. This feat made *MIDI Maze* a pioneer in the quest to make viable cross-platform and cross-generational multiplayer games.

» **NEW RECORD** » **UPDATED RECORD**

"HERE IS ANOTHER THING... I WANT YOU TO HAVE THIS, TOO. IT'S SHADOW BALL. IT CAUSES DAMAGE AND MAY REDUCE SPECIAL DEFENCE. USE IT IF IT APPEALS TO YOU."

1.666: THE VERSION NUMBER GIVEN TO THE GAME ENGINE FOR THE FIRST RETAIL RELEASE OF *DOOM*, WHICH EARNED IT THE NICKNAME "GAME ENGINE OF THE BEAST".

GUINNESS WORLD RECORDS

»LONGEST-RUNNING FPS SERIES

Holder: *Wolfenstein* **(id Software, 1992 to present)**

With 17 years 102 days between the release of *Wolfenstein 3D* in 1992 and *Wolfenstein* (pictured) on 18 August 2009, the *Wolfenstein* series ranks as the longest-running in the first-person shooter genre. Moreover, *Wolfenstein 3D* enabled id Software to develop the technology and gameplay that was the bedrock of *Doom* (id Software, 1993), the grandfather of the modern shooter.

"THE WEAPONS HAVE TO FEEL GREAT, THE ENEMIES HAVE TO FEEL GREAT TO KILL AND SEEM INTELLIGENT."
/STEVE NIX, DIRECTOR OF BUSINESS DEVELOPMENT AT id.

Kill Put on a Happy Face!

MIDI MAZE FOR THE ATARI ST

»FIRST MULTIPLAYER FIRST-PERSON SHOOTER

Holder: *MIDI Maze* **(Xanth Software F/X, 1987)**

Developed by America's Xanth Software F/X, *MIDI Maze* for the Atari ST exploited the ST's relatively sophisticated MIDI ports to enable multiplayer action. By connecting one computer's MIDI out to the next's MIDI in, it was possible to create a 16-player machine-to-machine network, which was an effective, if rudimentary, basis for multiplayer gameplay. Players in the game were represented as smiley faces and could fire bullet-like dots to take down their fellow gamers.

»FIRST HANDHELD FIRST-PERSON SHOOTER

Holder: *Faceball 2000* **(Bulletproof Software, 1991)**

A reworking of *MIDI Maze* for the Game Boy handheld, *Faceball 2000* lacked the multiplayer functionality of *MIDI Maze* and pitted players against computer-controlled enemies instead. A version for the SNES was also released but the prototyped multiplayer PC version never saw the light of day.

»LONGEST FPS DEVELOPMENT PERIOD

Holder: *Duke Nukem Forever* **(2K, 1998 to present)**

With over 13 years passing since its official announcement in 1997, *Duke Nukem Forever* has languished in development hell for longer than any other first-person shooter. The saga took a sad turn in May 2009 when developer 3D Realms went bust. Publisher Take Two retains the rights and has recently passed them on to its 2K division. The game's latest developer, Gearbox Software, showcased the newest version to gamers at the Penny Arcade Expo in September 2010, where it was announced that *Duke Nukem Forever* is expected to be released in 2011.

FASTEST COMPLETION OF HALF-LIFE 2

Holder: HL2DQ

A team of dedicated speed-runners, the "Half-Life 2 done Quick" crew (HL2DQ) team completed Valve's classic shooter *Half-Life 2* in just 1 hr 36 min 57 sec on 8 March 2006. Their speed run, broken down into 88 segments, is described in detail at speeddemosarchive.com/HalfLife2.html.

TOP 10 MOST CRITICALLY ACCLAIMED SHOOTERS

	Game	Platform	Score
1	Metroid Prime	GameCube	96.30%
2	Halo: Combat Evolved	Xbox	95.58%
3	The Orange Box	PC/PS3/Xbox 360	94.74%
4	Halo 2	Xbox	94.56%
5	Bioshock	PC/PS3/Xbox 360	94.50%
6	Perfect Dark	N64	94.31%
7	Half-Life	PC	94.28%
8	Unreal Tournament	PC	93.57%
9	Half-Life 2	PC/Xbox	93.56%
10	Halo 3	Xbox 360	93.53%

Source: Metacritic

"I'M SORRY, BUT... FROM HERE ON, ONLY THOSE TRAINERS WHO HAVE BECOME CHAMPIONS MAY ENTER. YOU'LL HAVE TO WAIT OUTSIDE WITH PROF. BIRCH."

WWW.GUINNESSWORLDRECORDS.COM/GAMERS **043**

FIRST-PERSON SHOOTERS II

»MOST AUDIO LOGS IN A VIDEOGAME

Holder: *Bioshock 2* **(2K, 2010)**
Collectable audio logs have been a staple of modern first-person shooters for some years, dating back at least as far as *Doom 3* (Activision, 2004), which used the dictated personal diaries of incidental characters to expand on the game's back story. With modern shooters, such narrative devices also serve as an in-game challenge, with rewards if you manage to collect them all. The greatest number of these collectibles in any game is the 189 audio logs scattered around *Bioshock 2*'s underwater city of Rapture, split between its main campaign and the *Minerva's Den* expansion pack.

NEW RECORD
» UPDATED RECORD

»MOST CRITICALLY ACCLAIMED FPS FOR A NINTENDO SYSTEM

Holder: *Metroid Prime* **(Nintendo, 2002)**
With an aggregate score of 96.3% on GameRankings.com, *Metroid Prime* for the GameCube is the most critically acclaimed first-person shooter available for a Nintendo console. Although all GameCube discs are compatible with the Wii, the game was given a makeover as part of the *Metroid Prime Trilogy* collection and adapted for play with the Wii Remote controller.

MOST PROLIFIC TACTICAL SHOOTER FRANCHISE

Holder: *Tom Clancy* **(Red Storm/Ubisoft, 1998 to present)**
Requiring a greater degree of skill and strategy than standard shooters, tactical shooters force players to evalute when best to pull the trigger on an enemy. With 17 tactical shooters and 10 expansion discs for games bearing his name, US author Tom Clancy has endorsed more tactical shooters than any other person or brand. With titles including *Tom Clancy's Rainbow Six* and *Tom Clancy's Ghost Recon*, the author's reputation for military accuracy and technological detail clearly strikes a chord with tactical fans. Clancy has also found significant success within the stealth genre with his iconic *Splinter Cell* series.

"THIS IS CRAZY. A BLIND MAN AND A FOOL, AGAINST THE EMPIRE."

TOP 10 BEST-SELLING CONSOLE FPS TITLES

	Game	Sales
1	Call of Duty: Modern Warfare 2	20.12 million
2	Call of Duty 4: Modern Warfare	13.50 million
3	Halo 3	11.16 million
4	Call of Duty: World at War	10.50 million
5	Halo 2	8.43 million
6	GoldenEye 007	8.09 million
7	Halo: Combat Evolved	6.50 million
8	Medal of Honor Frontline	6.29 million
9	Halo ODST	5.62 million
10	Call of Duty 3	5.39 million

Source: VGChartz

TRIVIA TRAIL

In addition to its standard format, *Bioshock 2* (2K, 2010) was also released in a limited special edition pack containing the game, three posters featuring fictional advertisements from Rapture, a hardbound 164-page book featuring art and concept designs for the series, a CD of the orchestral score for *Bioshock 2* and a similar score from the original *Bioshock* on a vinyl record.

"[BIOSHOCK 2 PUTS] THE PLAYER IN THE DRIVER'S SEAT, ROLLING THEIR OWN SHOOTER…"
/JORDAN THOMAS, CREATIVE DIRECTOR ON *BIOSHOCK 2*.

»FIRST COMMERCIALLY RELEASED FPS
Holder: *Battlezone* **(Atari, 1980)**
While the shooter genre can arguably trace its roots to 1958's *Tennis for Two*, which was adapted from a computer designed to model ballistic missile trajectories (see p.137), it was not until 1980 that the FPS made its commercial debut with Atari's *Battlezone* arcade machine. *Battlezone* featured simple wireframe 3D vector-graphic tanks, which so impressed the US military that they commissioned a modified version, dubbed *Bradley Trainer*, for use in the training of gunners. While only two prototypes of this version were produced, the game went on to great success on Atari's 2600 home console.

»MOST CRITICALLY ACCLAIMED MOVIE SPINOFF
Holder: *GoldenEye 007* **(Nintendo, 1997)**
Videogames that are linked to movies rarely receive critical acclaim, but the N64 classic *GoldenEye 007* is an impressive exception to this general rule, boasting an average rating of 95.35% on reviews aggregate site GameRankings.com. *GoldenEye 007*'s strong single-player campaign was praised by reviewers, but it was the game's peerless four-way multiplayer that really impressed. Popular demand has even led to a "reimagined" version of the game for the Wii complete with updated graphics.

MOST PROLIFIC WWII CONSOLE SHOOTER
Holder: *Medal of Honor* **(Atari, 1980 to present)**
With 12 titles across a total of 13 platforms, the *Medal of Honor* series boasts the record for the most instalments of a shooter series set during World War II. The latest release, *Medal of Honor* (EA, 2010), shifts the setting to the more contemporary conflict of Afghanistan.

»FASTEST COMPLETION OF "AVEC LE BRIQUE" ON TIMESPLITTERS: FUTURE PERFECT
Holder: James Bouchier (Canada)
Proving he doesn't just break records, James "TwIsTeD_ EnEmY" Bouchier smashed every object in sight with a brick to complete the "Avec le Brique" challenge on *Timesplitters: Future Perfect* (Eidos, 2005) in 2 min 17.6 sec on 11 July 2010.

»MOST EXPENSIVE PLAYSTATION 3 SHOOTER
Holder: *Killzone 2* **(Sony, 2009)**
Five years in development and eventually costing an estimated €41 million (£34 million, $52 million) to make, *Killzone 2* is the most expensive shooter developed for the PS3. Hyped as the platform's answer to the *Halo* series, expectations for the game were high, particularly after it achieved an average review of 91% on both GameRankings.com and Metacritic. However, the game, which takes the war against the Helghast to their homeworld, didn't quite reach *Halo* sales levels, shifting around 2.38 million units.

THIRD-PERSON SHOOTERS

FOR THOSE WHO LIKE TO KEEP THEIR CHARACTER IN VIEW AND IN CONTEXT WITHIN THEIR SURROUNDINGS.

»FIRST SHOOTER FOR PLAYSTATION 3

Holder: *Mobile Suit Gundam: Crossfire* **(Namco Bandai, 2006),** *Resistance: Fall of Man* **(Sony, 2006)**

Two shooters, *Mobile Suit Gundam: Crossfire* (pictured) and *Resistance: Fall of Man*, claim the distinction of being the first shooting titles for the Playstation 3, having launched with the console on 11 November 2006. There are over 130 games based on the hit Japanese robo-animé *Gundam Wing* and its many spinoffs.

» NEW RECORD
» UPDATED RECORD

»MOST "F" WORDS IN A VIDEOGAME

Holder: *Mafia II* **(2K, 2010)**

With 397 instances of the "F" word in dialogue in an average 12-hour play through, crime drama *Mafia II* features the highest count of bad language in a game. Gaming community Rooster Teeth suspected the title featured more swearing than previous holder *House of the Dead: Overkill* (Sega, 2009) and compiled a video showcasing 200 of the varied and creative ways in which the game uses the well-known four-letter word. Not surprisingly, the game is rated "M (mature) 17+" by the Entertainment Software Rating Board in the US and "18" by the British Board of Film Classification.

»BEST-SELLING THIRD-PERSON SHOOTER SERIES

Holder: *Gears of War* **(Microsoft, 2006 to present)**

With worldwide sales totalling 11.95 million copies, the *Gears of War* series kerb-stomps its rivals in the third-person shooter genre into submission. Epic's gritty cover-shooter is likely to build on its record with the release of another sequel due in April 2011.

"WELL, KIDDIES, IT'S BEEN MORE FUN THAN A JUMP-SUIT FULL OF WEASELS. NOW KINDLY GET YOUR FREAKISH HIDE OUT OF MY HOME!"

GUINNESS WORLD RECORDS

»LARGEST AUDIENCE FOR A GAME LAUNCH ANNOUNCEMENT

Holder: *Gears of War 3* (Microsoft, 2011)

In a break from the games industry tradition of announcing games via extravagant press conferences, media alerts or the occasional leak on Twitter, designer Cliff Bleszinski (USA) made the first confirmation of the third game in the *Gears of War* series on a US chat show with a nationwide audience of over 6 million viewers. Bleszinski was a guest on *Late Night with Jimmy Fallon* (NBC), where the game's first trailer was premiered and its April 2011 release date was confirmed.

»FASTEST COMPLETION OF MAX PAYNE

Holder: *Nigel Martin (UK)*

On 19 March 2010, Nigel Martin completed *Max Payne* (Rockstar Games, 2001) in 1 hr 1 min 8 sec, an improvement of 21 minutes on his previous record time. The single-segment completion was achieved on the game's hardest setting, "Dead on Arrival". You can check out Nigel's speed runs at http://www.youtube.com/user/1Ridd3r.

»MOST DOWNLOADED THIRD-PERSON SHOOTER DEMO

Holder: *Crackdown 2* (Microsoft, 2010)

Released in June 2010, one month before the game was due to be launched, *Crackdown 2*'s single and multiplayer demo quickly became the most popular game sampler for a third-person shooter on Xbox 360, with more than 500,000 players logging on to play the demo during its first week of availability. Stats released by Microsoft and developer Ruffian say that, collectively, players logged on to kill over 250 million in-game enemies in the space of a week, and cumulatively logged 75 years of gaming time in those seven days. According to sales-tracking website VGChartz, *Crackdown 2* sold 625,000 units in its first 10 weeks on sale.

TRIVIA TRAIL

Although it's known as a colossus of the first-person shooter category, Xbox franchise *Halo* originally started life as a third-person game. It wasn't until Microsoft bought the developer that its perspective changed.

TOP 10 HIGH SCORES ON *GEARS OF WAR 2*, "HORDE" MODE (ALL FATHERS GARDEN)

	Username	Score
1=	Ilx Dr3ad xII	953,402,792
1=	Ilx PaiiN xII	953,402,792
1=	ReignInBlood90	953,402,792
1=	IceGoD RiseN	953,402,792
5	IIArtikBlazeII	909,884,768
6=	MC Adventist RL	429,300,000
6=	x MAX PIKOTTO x	429,300,000
8=	LS EpiCsHoTz v3	390,339,217
8=	XxEcko3xX	390,339,217
10	FlyMonkeyNinja	369,600,000

Source: gearsofwar.xbox.com. Top four entries are a co-op score.

"WHENEVER I SMELL ASPHALT, I THINK OF MAUREEN. THAT'S THE LAST SENSATION I HAD BEFORE I BLACKED OUT; THAT THICK SMELL OF ASPHALT."

WWW.GUINNESSWORLDRECORDS.COM/GAMERS   **047**

2D SHOOTERS

ONE OF THE OLDEST GENRES IN VIDEOGAMES, 2D SHOOTERS ARE STILL PACKING PLENTY OF GAMING HEAT.

DID YOU KNOW?

Whereas bullets in traditional shooters are aimed at the player and are fast but fairly infrequent, bullets in danmaku games tend to be slower, but much greater in numbers, covering the major part of the playing area. They aren't necessarily aimed at the player but can be sprayed indiscriminately, or in patterns that restrict the player's movement.

"FOOTBALLS ARE MADE OF LEATHER!
ARE YOU SAYING ALL FOOTBALLS ARE SUSPICIOUS?!"

GUINNESS WORLD RECORDS

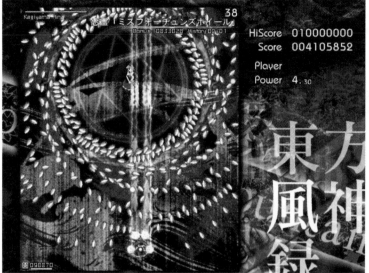

»MOST PROLIFIC DANMAKU SHOOTER DEVELOPER

Holder: Cave (Japan)

In the kingdom of the danmaku (bullet curtain) shooters, Japanese cult developer Cave is clearly king. Cave started out developing for arcades and has released 48 danmaku videogames, including the 2009 Xbox release *Mushihimesama Futari* (pictured left), since they first entered the market with *DoDonPachi* in 1995.

» NEW RECORD » UPDATED RECORD

»FIRST GAME TO FEATURE BOSS WARNINGS
Holder: *Darius* (Taito, 1986)

Now a firm staple of 2D shooters, the first game to feature an alert for an upcoming boss fight was the horizontally scrolling shoot-'em-up *Darius*, with its legendary signal: "WARNING! A HUGE BATTLESHIP… IS APPROACHING FAST". Such alerts have since been adopted by the likes of *Ikaruga* (Treasure, 2001) and now appear on T-shirts and other gaming merchandise.

»HIGHEST SCORE ON RADIANT SILVERGUN
Holder: Jordi Schouteren (Netherlands)

The highest score on the arcade version of *Radiant Silvergun* is 1,067,920 points and was achieved by prolific Dutch record-breaker Jordi Schouteren. Fan-made "superplay" videos featuring footage of skilled shoot-'em-up players exist that show scores over 26,000,000 points. However, the validity of such playthroughs is difficult to authenticate from gameplay footage alone.

»MOST PROLIFIC FAN-MADE SHOOTER SERIES

Holder: *Touhou* series (Team Shanghai Alice, 1996 to present)

With 18 games in its 15-year history, including *Imperishable Night* in 2004 (above), the Touhou project is a series of *doujin* (fan-made) shooters. What is more remarkable is that all of the games in the series were created by one individual – an enigmatic game-maker known only as "ZUN", who handles all aspects of game creation, including artwork, scripting and music duties.

»HIGHEST SCORE ON GRADIUS
Holder: Tom Votava (USA)

On 6 October 2007, Tom Votava managed to rack up a record score of 10,102,000 points on the NES version of the classic shoot-'em-up *Gradius* (Konami, 1985). During the game, Votava was allowed to skip levels by defeating various bosses quickly. As with many classic games, upon completion *Gradius* starts over from the beginning with the player's score intact, enabling them to complete the game multiple times in a single run.

»HIGHEST SCORE ON R-TYPE
Holder: Jason Wilson (USA)

Jason Wilson amassed a score of 251,840 points on the arcade version of *R-Type* (Irem, 1987) on 15 June 1997.

TOP 10 SCORES ON *MUSHIHIMESAMA FUTARI*, ULTRA MODE

	Username	Score
1	tsk1226	3,613,226,235*
2	highmustang	3,355,816,775*
3	yoskq	2,715,239,392*
4	lionmanggg	2,710,461,023
5	huggable pillow	2,415,415,057*
6	CoffeeKIT	2,209,142,489*
7	Ryo 1502	2,207,522,927*
8	mpg sg	1,976,993,192*
9	GMKOK10	1,818,407,499*
10	Legend of HS	1,690,997,762*

*Source: In-game high score table   * failed to complete the game*

»LARGEST ASPECT RATIO FOR AN ARCADE MACHINE

Holder: *Darius Burst* (Taito, 2010)

With an aspect ratio of 32:9 (double the ratio of a standard widescreen TV), *Darius Burst: Another Chronicle* has the widest panoramic display of any arcade game. The side-scrolling shooter was location tested in Akihabara, Tokyo, Japan, in August 2010 ahead of its nationwide roll-out.

"EVEN I COULD RUN FASTER THAN YOU, LANKY. EVEN WHILE CARRYING K. ROOL ON MY BACK!"

WWW.GUINNESSWORLDRECORDS.COM/GAMERS   **049**

ONLINE SHOOTERS

CONNECTIVITY AND COMMUNITIES HAVE BROUGHT HUGE LEVELS OF COMPETITION TO THIS SHOOTING GENRE.

> WE WANT THE GAME TO STAND OUT BY CREATING AN EXPERIENCE THAT VERY FEW STUDIOS WOULD EVEN CONSIDER.
> /ED BYRNE, OF *MAG* CREATORS ZIPPER INTERACTIVE.

»LONGEST VIDEOGAME MARATHON ON A FIRST-PERSON SHOOTER

First-person shooter fans John "WilksboothStyle" Myers, Stephen "Assassin Fury" Millet, Kyle "OneShotBoss" Imeli and Brett "M0UTHforWAR" Bunge (all USA, left to right) played *Left 4 Dead* (Valve, 2008) for 32 hr 20 min at GameStop in Aurora, Ohio, USA, on 25–26 September 2009 to claim the record for the longest videogame marathon on a first-person shooter. Although it may not be immediately obvious from the picture, the quartet played the game dressed as characters from the game.

"ARMED WITH ONLY HIS COURAGE, HE ENTERS THE TELEPORT CHAMBER."

» MOST ONLINE PLAYERS IN A CONSOLE FPS

Holder: *MAG* **(Sony, 2010)**

Sony's PS3 game *MAG*, released in January 2010, boasts the option for 256 people to play a single game online. Online game networks have millions of players connected at once, but when it comes to actual multiplayer games, the number of players online in single games is much lower. Varying connection speeds and server limitations mean that developers usually keep matches to groups of two, four, eight, 16 or 32 depending on match type – sometimes up to 64. This has become a standard for online games, but it's a glass ceiling Sony broke through with new PlayStation 3 FPS *MAG*. In order to properly evoke massive battlefields packed with soldiers, the Sony-owned studio Zipper Interactive developed new server architecture to allow for hundreds to play in a single match together.

» NEW RECORD » UPDATED RECORD

FIRST MMO FIRST-PERSON SHOOTER

Holder: *World War II Online (aka Battleground Europe)* **(Cornered Rat Software, 2001 to present)**

Mistakenly, Sony Online Entertainment's *PlanetSide*, released in May 2003, is often cited as the first massively multiplayer online first-person shooter (MMOFPS), but the first game to get groups of players together into a massively playable environment for shooter fun was was *World War II Online (aka Battleground Europe)* released in 2001. Originally known as *Blitzkrieg*, then as *World War II Online* and re-released in 2006 as *World War II Online: Battleground Europe*, the game pits players in a version of mainland Europe fighting as German, French or British troops. Other games in the MMOFPS genre, including 2002's *Neocron* (CDV Software) and *PlanetSide*, followed soon after.

FIRST 3D SHOOTER ENGINE

Holder: **Quake Engine**

The first genuine 3D engine made for an FPS was the Quake Engine, built for id Software's 1996 release *Quake*. All first-person games up to the release of *Quake* shared a secret – they weren't really 3D. Despite appearing to present real environments with depth viewable from multiple angles, early first-person games really just used scene after scene of sprites – 2D images drawn with 3D perspective points – to create the illusion of 3D. However, *Doom* creator id Software wanted progress when it came to *Quake*, and its engine programmer John Carmack (USA) built the first engine to render environments in actual 3D, using polygons to represent objects instead of sprites, environments pre-made as maps, lighting and the option to add mods.

BEST-SELLING GAME MOD

Holder: *Counter-Strike* **(Valve, 1999)**

Created by Minh "Gooseman" Le (Canada) and Jess "Cliffe" Cliffe (USA), *Counter-Strike* was originally a modification of Valve's *Half-Life* game. It was first unveiled as a public beta on 18 June 1999 and has gone on to sell over 9 million copies on PC and Xbox 360.

MAJOR NELSON'S TOP 10 XBOX LIVE ONLINE SHOOTERS

	Game
1	Halo 3
2	Call of Duty 4
3	Call of Duty: Modern Warfare 2
4	Call of Duty: World at War
5	Gears of War 2
6	Left 4 Dead
7	Halo 3: ODST
8	Resident Evil 5
9	Fallout 3
10	Gears of War

Source: http://majornelson.com/archive/2010/01/10/the-top-20-live-games-of-2009.aspx

» LARGEST MAP IN AN ONLINE SHOOTER

Holder: *World War II Online (aka Battleground Europe)* **(Cornered Rat Software, 2001 to present)**

Maps are the bread and butter of online shooters. Without them there's nowhere to play. The largest by virtual surface area can be found in *World War II Online*, a PC/Mac-only online shooter that throws players into a constant recreation of World War II border skirmish scenarios. Although most play takes place in a 30,000-km² (11,583-mile²) central area where most of the capturable locations are based, the total size of the map is 350,000 km² (135,136 mile²). It currently consists of six giant sectors, which are known as Channel Sector, Holland Sector, Germany Sector, Belgian Front, Maginot Sector and North East France.

LIGHT GUNS

MIXING HARDWARE AND SOFTWARE, LIGHT GUN GAMES MAKE SHOOTING GAMES AS REAL AS THEY CAN BE.

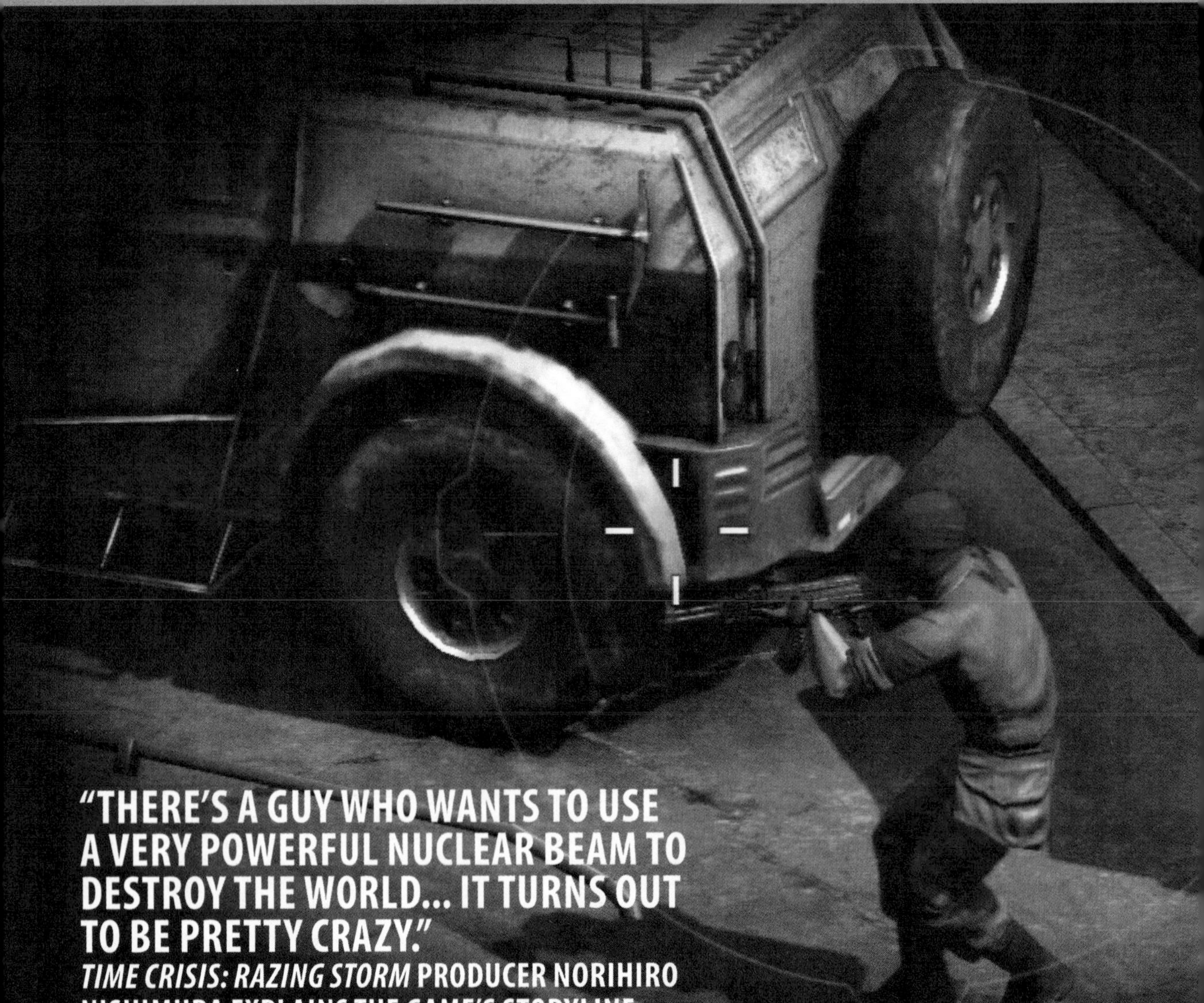

"THERE'S A GUY WHO WANTS TO USE A VERY POWERFUL NUCLEAR BEAM TO DESTROY THE WORLD... IT TURNS OUT TO BE PRETTY CRAZY."
TIME CRISIS: RAZING STORM PRODUCER NORIHIRO NISHIMURA EXPLAINS THE GAME'S STORYLINE.

›HEAVIEST CONSOLE LIGHT GUN

Holder: Silent Scope

Pelican's Xbox sniper rifle, designed for Konami's *Silent Scope* (1999) game and released in 2004, weighs in at 1.5 kg (3 lb 5 oz), which is heavier than any other console light gun. Typically, light guns are light-weight as they need to be held up at the screen for long stretches of time, but the Silent Scope rifle for Xbox throws the rulebook out of the window. The device comes with a detachable barrel, stock and scope, a pump-action moveable reload element and built-in motion sensor that knows when you are leaning in close to look through the scope. It was the first major sniper rifle light gun released for any home console, and one of the first to support use with HDTVs.

›FIRST MATURE-RATED LIGHT GUN

Holder: Innex/Komodo RapidShot

Announced in June 2010, the Innex/Komodo RapidShot for the Wii is the first light gun designed specifically for mature players. Despite their shape, light guns usually look very plasticky and come in bright colours in order to distinguish them from real guns. However, the Innex/

"I HUNGER, COWARD!"

1: THE NUMBER OF LIGHT GUN GAMES RELEASED FOR ATARI'S 1980s CLASSIC 2600 CONSOLE, MAKING IT THE LEAST POPULAR HOME PLATFORM FOR THESE PERIPHERALS.

GUINNESS WORLD RECORDS

»LONGEST-RUNNING LIGHT GUN SERIES

Holder: *Time Crisis*
(Namco, 1995 to present)

Although you can trace the history of the light gun back to 1936 and the Seeburg Ray-O-Lite duck shoot game, it wasn't until the mid-1990s that Namco's *Time Crisis* spawned the genre's longest-running franchise. To date, the 1995 original game has spawned six follow-ups, which are a mix of side-stories and direct sequels. The series shares a symbiotic link with arcade games – the first game debuted as an arcade cabinet but was soon re-released for PlayStation along with the GunCon peripheral. Some sequels have been console exclusives, but others premiered in arcades first, most notably the latest game in the series, *Time Crisis: Razing Storm* (Namco Bandai, 2010, pictured), which has been released for PlayStation 3 and works with the PlayStation Move.

» NEW RECORD » UPDATED RECORD

Komodo RapidShot is so realistic that it's only available for adults to buy. Designed for the Wii, the RapidShot is modelled on gun manufacturer Heckler & Koch's real-life MP5 submachine gun. So while the RapidShot integrates with the Wii Remote, Nunchuck and Motion Plus and has rechargeable batteries, its sleek black finish makes it look just like the real thing.

»MOST POPULAR LIGHT GUN PERIPHERAL
Holder: GunCon range
Technology behind consoles may evolve and shift, but from the original PlayStation onwards, one PlayStation device has remained constant: Namco's GunCon peripheral. The original GunCon model was released in 1995 to coincide with the *Time Crisis* arcade game's port to the PlayStation, and since that time a further two

TOP 10 MILESTONES IN THE HISTORY OF THE LIGHT GUN

	Milestone	Year
1	First home videogame system light gun released for US console Magnavox Odyssey.	1972
2	NES Zapper released in Japan by Nintendo, rolled out around the world the following year.	1984
3	Atari and Sega copy Nintendo with their own XG-1 and Light Phaser guns; meanwhile Taito releases arcade light gun shooter Operation Wolf.	1987
4	While light gun console games waned, they became popular in arcades via the release of video-based games like Mad Dog McCree.	1990
5	Terminator 2 makes the transition to arcades with a striking cabinet complete with Uzi 9-mm light guns.	1991
6	Sega releases the Menacer for the Mega Drive and Nintendo produces the Super Scope.	1992
7	Virtua Cop from Sega debuts in arcades.	1994
8	Time Crisis released in arcades ahead of its transition to PlayStation and the creation of the GunCon device.	1995
9	House of the Dead released by Sega.	1996
10	Capcom releases Resident Evil light gun spin-off series Survivor.	2000

Source: Gamer's Edition

iterations of the light gun have been released, for the PS2 and PS3 respectively. In the 16 years since the first GunCon made its way on to the market, more than 30 home console videogames have been released that use the device.

TRIVIA TRAIL

When first released in Japan, the NES Zapper was shaped like a real revolver hand gun. However, it had to be recoloured grey and orange when released in the US and many other countries due to laws over replica weapons.

»FIRST LIGHT GUN-ONLY HOME CONSOLE

Holder: Action Max
Most light guns are add-ons for existing machines, but one shortlived device was nothing but a console for light gun games. Released in 1987 in the US only, the Action Max was billed as "the first real action system" because it came with its own gun, exclusive game called *Sonic Fury* and headphones to immerse you in the action. The device used VHS tapes for its games and worked by plugging the base unit into your VCR to manipulate the video. When the light gun was "shot" at the TV screen, a red sensor connected to the TV would light up to register a hit.

HALO

CRITICAL HIT!

"REACH REPRESENTS THE CULMINATION OF A DECADE OF HALO AND... [IS] THE DEFINITIVE TITLE IN THE SERIES."
/BRIAN JARRARD, COMMUNITY MANAGER FOR BUNGIE.

»BEST-SELLING SERIES OF BOOKS BASED ON A VIDEOGAME
Holder: *Halo* **(2001 to present)**
With over 1 million copies sold, the *Halo* novels form the most successful series of books based on a videogame. The first book, *The Fall of Reach* (2001), was published as a prequel to *Halo: Combat Evolved* (Microsoft, 2001) before the game's release, and the series has grown in success alongside the videogames that spawned it. The games' creators consider the books, many of which have been written by Bungie staffers, to be part of the series' official backstory – so much so that the first book's content was used to help shape the look and feel of the game *Halo: Reach* (Microsoft, 2010).

»MOST PROLIFIC XBOX FRANCHISE
Holder: *Halo* **(Microsoft, 2001 to present)**
Over the past decade, six full *Halo* games have been released for Microsoft consoles. The first game, *Halo: Combat Evolved*, was a launch title on the original Xbox and, along with *Halo 2* (2004), helped define what a console FPS could be, with its high-end design, refined control and incredible enemy AI. Subsequent sequels for Xbox 360 include *Halo 3* (2007), *Halo: ODST* (2009) and prequel *Halo: Reach* (2010). The biggest departure for the series was the real-time strategy title *Halo Wars* (2009). The series has also seen a range of spin-off toys, comics, books and animated series. There has even been talk of a film adaptation, although this talk has been going on for some time!

»MOST POPULAR VIDEOGAME BETA TEST

Holder: *Halo: Reach* **(Microsoft, 2010)**

Beta-testing is the name given to the process of evaluating a game or a piece of software for any problems before it is sold to the public. As part of their beta testing process, Bungie, the developers of *Halo: Reach*, recruited 2.7 million fans to test a version of the game on Xbox Live, four months before the release of the final version of the game. During the two-week-long beta, testers played 13 million online matches and logged 16 million hours of online play – that's over 1,826 years of total game time. Bungie are hoping that this enthusiasm for the beta will translate into sales of this prequel title, which is set on the doomed world of Reach before the events of the first game, 2001's *Halo: Combat Evolved*.

MOST EXPENSIVE FIRST-PERSON SHOOTER VIDEOGAME EVER PRODUCED

Holder: *Halo 3* **(Microsoft, 2007)**

With a reported budget of $55 million (£27 million), *Halo 3* is the most expensive shooter ever made. The game was in development with Bungie for three years but, in contrast to most other games, *Halo 3*'s production period included intensive user-testing and iteration, in which players were observed playing the game and their progress tracked so that Bungie could refine and tweak the game to perfection.

MOST CRITICALLY ACCLAIMED XBOX GAME

Holder: *Halo: Combat Evolved* **(Microsoft, 2002)**

According to review aggregation site Metacritic, *Halo: Combat Evolved* has a total score of 97% – the highest for any Xbox game. Its closest rival for the title is its own sequel *Halo 2* (2004), which has an aggregate score of 95%.

»FASTEST-SELLING GAME ON A SINGLE CONSOLE SYSTEM

Holder: *Halo: Reach* **(Microsoft, 2010)**

With day-one sales in excess of $200 million (£126 million), the fastest-selling game to be released on one console system is *Halo: Reach*, the latest game in Microsoft's mega-franchise. The game was unleashed on Xbox users on 14 September 2010 and beat the previous record held by *Halo 3,* which managed a still pretty impressive $170 million (£84 million) when released in September 2007.

TRIVIA TRAIL

Halo's press debut was at the 1999 MacWorld expo when Apple CEO Steve Jobs touted the title as a big step for gaming on the Mac. Developer Bungie was bought by Apple's rival Microsoft a year later and the rest is history.

» **NEW RECORD** » **UPDATED RECORD**

TOP 10 MOST POPULAR WEAPONS TO KILL XBOX LIVE'S LARRY HRYB ON *HALO: REACH* MULTIPLAYER

	Weapon	Deaths
1	Plasma Grenade	30
2	Concussion Rifle	27
3	Plasma Pistol	25
4	Melee	24
5	Plasma Rifle	13
6	Shade Turret	12
7	Revenant	7
8	Fuel Rod Gun	6
9=	Plasma Repeater	4
9=	Wraith	4

Source: bungie.net

»LAST ONLINE SESSION OF HALO 2

Holder: *"Apache N4SIR"*

After the introduction of the Xbox 360, Microsoft effectively ran two versions of their online service Xbox Live – one for the new console and one for the original Xbox. When time came to finally turn off the older version, to maximize performance of Xbox 360's Live service, a clutch of die-hard *Halo 2* fans were having none of it and planned to keep the game playable beyond its planned termination date of April 2010. They started playing the game before the original Xbox Live service, along with the game's multiplayer option, was disabled and kept the game "alive" between their machines for 28 days from 15 April to 11 May. The last player out was a gamer known only by his tag of "Apache N4SIR".

SPORTS GAMES

WHETHER YOU PREFER KICKING, CARRYING OR HITTING A BALL, THERE'S LIKELY TO BE A SPORTS GAME FOR YOU.

»MOST PROLIFIC SPORTS GAME DEVELOPER

Holder: Visual Concepts

With development credits on 139 commercially released sports games between 1988 and 2010, Visual Concepts are the most prolific developers in the sports genre. Their credits include work on the *Madden NFL* series from sports game publishing behemoth EA, and they are the current custodians of the 2K Sports brand, which includes titles for all major American sports, including *Major League Baseball 2K10* (pictured).

"GOD, LARRY, YOU'RE PATHETIC. HOW'D YOU EVER GET PAST THE LOVEMASTER 2000? CHEAT?"

GUINNESS WORLD RECORDS

WHAT ARE THEY?

If you can play it in real life, then it's extremely likely you can play it on screen too. Sporting videogames recreate all manner of traditional physical activities from football, cricket and tennis to extreme sports, such as skateboarding. The relationship between sport and videogames has been long. William Higinbotham created *Tennis for Two* in 1958, a game that superficially resembled a tennis simulator (see p.137 for more on this early videogame and its inventor). Nowadays, sports games aim to give players the feel of playing for real. The *FIFA* and *Pro Evolution Soccer* games have realistic players and stadia, while football management games put you in charge. When it comes to sports videogames, it's game on...

WHO SAYS SO?

David Crookes (UK) started his journalistic career as a freelance writer for *Amstrad Action* in 1993. He currently writes for a plethora of magazines and websites, among them *GamesTM*, *Retro Gamer*, *X360* and NowGamer.com. He also produces articles for *The Independent* newspaper and has a games column that runs in several regional newspapers in the UK. David is also the curator of the Videogame Nation touring exhibition, which started in Manchester, UK, in 2009.

CONTENTS

MADDEN NFL

CRITICAL HIT!

FOR THE GRIDIRON CREW, NOTHING ELSE WILL DO. DON'T GET MAD, GET MADDEN...

HIGHEST FIRST WEEK SALES OF AN NFL GAME

Holder: *Madden NFL 07* **(EA, 2006)**

The fastest-selling NFL game is *Madden NFL 07* (pictured), which sold 2 million copies in its first week. By comparison, *Madden NFL 08* (EA, 2007) sold 1.8 million copies and *Madden NFL 09* (EA, 2008) sold 1.6 million. *Madden NFL 10* (EA, 2009) had comparatively modest figures with 1.3 million first week sales.

»LONGEST-RUNNING SPORTS FRANCHISE

Holder: *Madden* **(EA, 1988 to present)**

EA has released an incredible 21 games in the main *Madden* series. The franchise began in 1988 with *John Madden Football*, which featured fictional teams. The current game, *Madden NFL 11*, was released in August 2010 and marks an unbroken run of 20 annual updates for the franchise. Pictured, EA's Phil Frasier receives the certificate celebrating *Madden*'s longevity.

»HIGHEST MARGIN OF VICTORY IN MADDEN NFL 10

Holder: Patrick Scott Patterson (USA)

Patrick Scott Patterson of Denton, Texas, USA, achieved a record 56-point victory margin on *Madden NFL 10* on 19 December 2009. Patterson was playing four seven-minute quarters on the "Pro player" skill level on the Xbox 360.

"JUST A GIRL. GET OUT OF HERE!"

2: THE NUMBER OF NFL PLAYERS ON THE COVER OF *MADDEN NFL 10* (TROY POLAMALU AND LARRY FITZGERALD) – THE FIRST TIME TWO PLAYERS HAVE FEATURED.

TOP 10 BEST-SELLING MADDEN NFL GAMES

	Game	Sales
1	*Madden NFL 2005*	5.77 million
2	*Madden NFL 2009*	5.25 million
3	*Madden NFL 2006*	5.12 million
4	*Madden NFL 2010*	4.90 million
5	*Madden NFL 2007*	4.72 million
6	*Madden NFL 2004*	3.95 million
7	*Madden NFL 2008*	3.61 million
8	*Madden NFL 2003*	3.18 million
9	*Madden NFL 2002*	2.30 million
10	*Madden NFL 2001*	1.21 million

Source: VGChartz

NEW RECORD
UPDATED RECORD

"WE STUMBLED UPON IT. WE'RE STILL GOING. IT JUST GETS BIGGER AND BIGGER."
/FORMER COMMENTATOR JOHN MADDEN TALKS ABOUT THE SECRET OF THE *MADDEN* VIDEOGAME SERIES SUCCESS.

»MOST LINES OF COMMENTARY IN AN NFL GAME

Holder: *Madden NFL 11* **(EA, 2010)**
Madden NFL 11 has a staggering 90,000 lines of commentary in total. It includes play-by-play by Gus Johnson (USA), colour commentary by Cris Collinsworth (USA) and other voice-over throughout the game by players, broadcasters and various actors. Ronnie Morales (USA), EA's speech designer for *Madden NFL 11*, said the number of lines have been increased for this year's release in a bid to make the commentary and overall audio presentation sound more authentic than ever. The first *Madden* game had just 500 lines of dialogue. John Madden (USA) is said to have recorded an estimated 30,000 lines of in-game commentary until his retirement in 2009.

DID YOU KNOW?
There is a Facebook group called "John Madden = worst announcer ever". It asks: "Does anyone ever get tired of hearing John Madden stating the obvious during football games? John Madden is the worst announcer ever, and by that I mean that there is no one worse." Only 14 people have signed up.

18 cities across three countries or via online tournaments on Xbox Live. The winner receives a $25,000 (£15,197) cheque and a voucher for $25,000 for retailer Best Buy.

TRIVIA TRAIL
Professional NFL players get a chance to show off their gaming skills when they take part in the televised Madden Bowl during the Super Bowl weekend. Players choose a team and battle to get to the final, with the winner receiving the Madden Bowl trophy.

»BIGGEST PRIZE FOR AN OPEN MADDEN TOURNAMENT
Holder: EA Sports Madden Challenge
The biggest open-to-all *Madden* videogame tournament is the EA Sports Madden Challenge, which has a first prize worth $50,000 (£30,395). Eric "Problem" Wright (USA) won the 2009 event, which was his second Madden Challenge win in a row. Competitors qualified for the finals of the competition via local tournaments in

»FIRST MADDEN COVER STAR TO BE CHOSEN BY FANS
Holder: Drew Brees (USA)
Drew Brees, the New Orleans Saints quarterback, is the first cover star of a Madden game to have been chosen by fans. He appears on the cover of *Madden NFL 11* (EA, 2010). It followed EA's "Change the Game" campaign, which allowed fans to vote online between 4 February and 15 March 2010. Brees beat Minnesota Vikings' defensive end Jared Allen

and Indianapolis Colts' wide receiver Reggie Wayne (both USA).

"YES, AS I SAID, I AM AN ASSASSIN DROID. IT IS MY PRIMARY FUNCTION TO BURN HOLES THROUGH MEATBAGS THAT YOU WISH REMOVED FROM THE GALAXY..."

WWW.GUINNESSWORLDRECORDS.COM/GAMERS **059**

FOOTBALL

RECREATE GOLDEN GOALS IN THE BEAUTIFUL GAME BY TAKING CONTROL OF YOUR FAVOURITE FOOTBALL TEAM.

»MOST PARTICIPANTS IN A FOOTBALL VIDEOGAME

Holder: *FIFA World Cup 2010 South Africa* **(EA, 2010)**

The most people to take part in a single match in a football videogame is 82, achieved on *FIFA World Cup 2010* in Trafalgar Square, London, UK, on 11 June 2010. To reach that number, each player had to touch the ball at least once before passing the controller on to the next player. The game was part of an event held to mark the opening of the 2010 FIFA World Cup Finals in South Africa.

Emirates

»MOST VIDEOGAMES ATTACHED TO ONE FOOTBALL CLUB

Holder: *Manchester United* **(Krysalis/Codemasters, 1990 to 2004)**

A record seven videogames have been branded with the name of the UK's famous Manchester United Football Club. Krysalis was the first to license the club's name with *Manchester United* (1990). It followed it up with *Manchester United Europe* (1991), *Manchester United: Premier League Champions* (1994) and *Manchester United: The Double* (1995). Codemasters created three games as part of its Club Football series, which focused on 22 different teams. The games were *Manchester United Club Football* (2003), *Manchester United Club Football 2005* (2004) and *Manchester United Manager 2005* (2004). Krysalis also produced the *Manchester United Premier League Champions 1994–95 Season Data Disk* (1994). Two other games have been tied in with Manchester United staff: *Alex Ferguson's Player Manager* (Ubisoft, 2002) and *David Beckham Soccer* (Rage Software, 2002).

Publisher Konami agreed to feature Manchester United in *Pro Evolution Soccer 2009* (2009). The game featured the use of the club crest and kit and has animation for footballers Carlos Tevez (Argentina), Rio Ferdinand (UK), Cristiano Ronaldo (Portugal) and Edwin van der Sar (Netherlands). Finally, the computer board game *Bryan Robson's Superleague* (1985, Paul Lamond) was another Manchester United-inspired release.

"I'VE BEEN LOOKING FOR YOU. YOU'RE THE IBLIS TRIGGER. YOUR ACTIONS WILL CONDEMN US ALL."

TOP 10 *FOOTBALL MANAGER* ACHIEVEMENTS

Achievement	% of players
Signing a player	81.5
Guiding team to competitive victory	80.6
Clean sheet	80.4
Hat-trick	69.6
Scoring in 10 consecutive matches	65.1
Unbeaten in 10 consecutive matches	61.9
Five players named in team of week	56.5
Goal of the month award	56.1
Player in team of the year	52.6
Manager of the month	51.5

Source: steamcommunity.com

»FIRST INTERNATIONAL FIFA FOOTBALL LEAGUE

Holder: Stryxa.com
Stryxa.com became the first international *FIFA* videogame football league when it opened to Xbox 360 and PlayStation 3 players in January 2010. The website was launched with 10 intrepid players attempting to set the world's **longest-running football marathon**. Eight of the 10 players lasted for a record-setting 24 hours, playing *FIFA 10* at London's Victoria Station, UK, on 27 January 2010. Sadly, Stryxa went out of business in June 2010.

DID YOU KNOW?

The *FIFA* soccer videogame franchise has broken many new music acts. *FIFA 03* (EA, 2002) introduced Avril Lavigne to European audiences and Kasabian was among those featured a year later. Acts including Franz Ferdinand, Scissor Sisters, Bloc Party and The Black Eyed Peas have had songs played within a *FIFA* game, making the franchise a hot favourite for music promoters.

»WORST-RATED FOOTBALL VIDEOGAME

Holder: *World Cup Carnival* (US Gold, 1986)
The unfortunate title of the worst-rated football videogame of all time goes to *World Cup Carnival*, which was panned on all the platforms for which it was released. Publisher US Gold acquired the rights to Artic's *World Cup Football* (1984) and re-released the game for the Spectrum, Commodore 64 and Amstrad CPC under the name *World Cup Carnival* in time for the Mexico '86 World Cup tournament.

TRIVIA TRAIL

England goalkeeper David James once blamed getting hooked on playing *FIFA* for a drop in his ball skills. He also claimed that a dreadful performance for Liverpool in April 1997 was due to all-night *Tomb Raider* sessions.

They probably wished they hadn't bothered when *Amstrad Action* magazine gave the game 0%, *Zzap!64* magazine awarded the Commodore version 11% and *Crash* magazine handed the Spectrum version 26%.

FASTEST-SELLING SPORTS GAME

Holder: *FIFA 10* (EA, 2009)
EA's *FIFA 10* sold 1.7 million copies in its first week on sale after its release in October 2009, making it the fastest-selling sports videogame of all time. Publisher Electronic Arts (EA) said the game was the company's biggest ever European launch. The previous game in the series, *FIFA 09* (EA, 2008), sold 1.2 million copies in its first week of release in October 2008 and had been the *FIFA* series' fastest-selling game until *FIFA 10* hit the stores. As well as making an immediate commercial impact, *FIFA 10* also wowed the critics, scoring incredible 91% on Metacritic.

»BIGGEST VIDEOGAME TOURNAMENT

Holder: FIFA Interactive World Cup 2010
FIFA Interactive World Cup 2010, the sixth edition of the world's largest football gaming tournament, attracted a record 775,000 entries from around the globe. The competition, which lasted six months, saw football fans play EA Sports' *FIFA 10* on PlayStation 3 online or at one of the ten live qualifier events held in Australia, Brazil, Denmark, France, Italy, Japan, Poland, Russia, South Africa and the UK. The event culminated in the Grand Final at Port Olympic in Barcelona, Spain, on 1 May 2010, when 11,000 spectators gathered to watch Nenad Stojkovic (USA) beat German opponent Ayhan Altundag 2–1 in the competition's Grand Final. Stojkovic won $20,000 (£13,000) for his efforts.

» NEW RECORD
» UPDATED RECORD

"TELL YOU SOMETHING THERE, JON, A REAL WORM BURNER THAT ONE – RIGHT ALONG THE FLOOR!"

WWW.GUINNESSWORLDRECORDS.COM/GAMERS   **061**

AMERICAN SPORTS

HIGH-OCTANE, HARD-IMPACT SPORTING REALISM THAT TAKES THE US MARKET BY STORM YEAR AFTER YEAR.

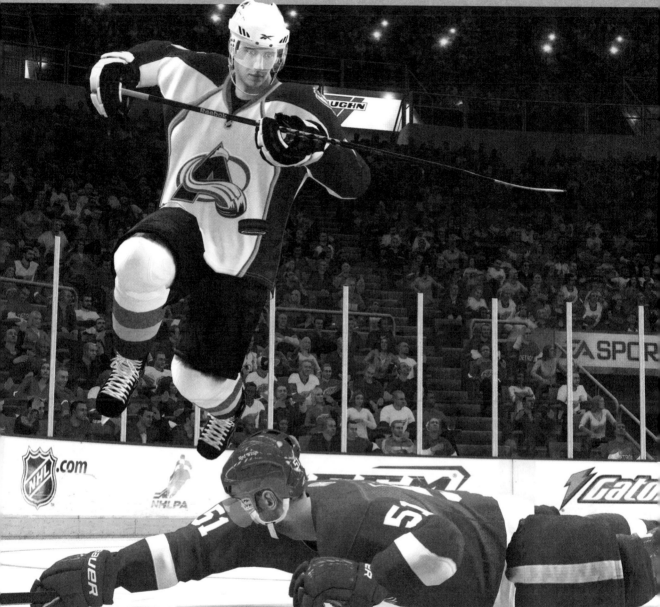

»HIGHEST SCORE FOR HOME RUN PINBALL ON THE BIGS 2

Holder: Chris "dragonangyle" Zupan (USA)

Chris Zupan achieved the highest score for the Home Run Pinball mini game on *The Bigs 2* (2K Sports, 2007) when he reached 1,570,000 points at his home in Tacoma, Washington, USA, on 22 June 2010.

The *Bigs* series gives an intriguing twist to the game of baseball. Greg Thomas, of developers 2K Sports, describes *The Bigs 2* as "Celebrating the most epic moments in Major League Baseball... the dramatic walk-off homeruns, miraculous wall catches and many more incredible plays you'd usually see only in a highlight reel."

»FIRST VIDEOGAME SOUNDTRACK TO REACH PLATINUM STATUS

Holder: *NBA Live 2003*

The first officially released videogame soundtrack to sell 1 million copies, according to the Recording Industry Association of America (RIAA), is *NBA Live 2003*, which was confirmed as having platinum status in March 2003, only six months after its October 2002 launch.

"MAYBE I CAN DEDUCE MY FIST TO YOUR FACE. BET THAT WOULD SHUT YOU UP."

»LONGEST-RUNNING HOCKEY SERIES

Holder: NHL Hockey
(EA, 1991 to present)
EA's NHL series began with *NHL Hockey*, which was released in August 1991 for the Sega Genesis and was considered to be the most realistic hockey game of its time. The game has had 19 annual iterations up to 2010's *NHL 11* (pictured) and the series shows no sign of slowing down.

DID YOU KNOW?

NHL Slapshot is EA Sports' first NHL hockey title for the Wii console. EA claims the Wayne Gretsky-endorsed game's "revolutionary hockey stick controller allows players to shoot, pass and body check just like the pros".

»MOST POINTS IN NBA 2K10

Holder: Cody Redrick and Brandon McJunlain (both USA)
The most points scored in the first half of 2KSports' *NBA 2K10* (playing a four-minute game, one minute per quarter) is 17, which was achieved by both Cody Redrick and Brandon McJunlain at the NBA All-Star Jam Session held in Dallas, Texas, USA, on 12 February 2010.

»HIGHEST WINNING MARGIN IN NHL 2004 FOR PLAYSTATION 2

Holder: Terence O'Neil (USA)
On 10 September 2006, Terence O'Neil thrashed his computer-controlled opponent by a 12-point margin while playing an exhibition mode game in *NHL 2004* (EA, 2003) for PS2.

»MOST ASSISTS IN NBA 2K10

Holder: Andrew Frost and JR Wildly (both USA)
Andrew Frost and JR Wildly both achieved 16 assists playing *NBA 2K10* (2K Sports, 2009) during a four-minute game at the NBA All-Star Jam Session in Dallas, Texas, USA, on 11 February 2010.

» NEW RECORD
» UPDATED RECORD

TOP 10 BEST-SELLING BASKETBALL GAMES

	Game	Sales
1	NBA Street	2.17 million
2	NBA Live 2005	2.12 million
3	NBA Jam	2.05 million
4	NBA Street Vol. 2	1.74 million
5	NBA Live 2004	1.59 million
6	NBA Live 06	1.41 million
7	NBA Live 98	1.40 million
8	NBA Jam	1.39 million
9	NBA Live 2003	1.32 million
10	ESPN NBA 2K5	1.27 million

Source: VGChartz

"CRITICS ARE TAKING NOTICE OF THE INNOVATION WE'RE DELIVERING"
/ PETER MOORE, EA SPORTS.

TRIVIA TRAIL

The NBA All-Star Game is a match between the best players from the Western and Eastern Conferences, as voted by fans online. The NBA Jam Session is a huge fan festival around the game itself, which allows fans of all ages to have some huge basketball fun. As well as breaking Guinness World Records for on-court skills, players and fans alike get the chance to try out their talents on the latest NBA videogames – the resulting records can be found on these pages.

»FIRST PERFECT GAME IN MLB 2K10

Holder: Wade McGilberry (USA)
Wade McGilberry became the first person to achieve a perfect score on *MLB 2K10* (2K Sports, 2010), when he played as the Atlanta Braves and successfully pitched "27-up, 27-down" against the New York Mets at his home in Semmes, Alabama, USA, on 2 March 2010. McGilberry's achievement was officially recognized by the game's publisher Take Two, who rewarded him with an incredible $1,000,000 (£670,000) payday!

EUROPEAN SPORTS

GOLF, TENNIS, RUGBY, CRICKET... OK, THEY'RE PLAYED ALL OVER THE WORLD, BUT THEY STARTED IN EUROPE.

»LONGEST-RUNNING CONSOLE GOLF SERIES

Holder: *Tiger Woods PGA Tour* **(EA, 1998 to present)**

The console golf game with the longest lifespan is *Tiger Woods PGA Tour,* which has been running for 12 years. In the latest iteration of the game, *Tiger Woods PGA Tour 11* (EA, 2010), young European golf ace Rory McIlroy (UK, pictured) shares cover star status with US legend Woods.

FIRST 10 GOLF GAMES RELEASED

Game	System	Year
Cassette 27: Golf	*Interton VC4000*	1978
Computer Golf	*Magnavox Odyssey*	1978
Miniature Golf	*Atari 2600*	1979
Golf	*Atari 2600*	1980
Golf	*Intellivision*	1980
Birdie King	*Taito Arcade*	1982
Golf	*BBC Micro*	1982
3D Golf Simulation	*MSX*	1983
Abrasco Golf	*Commodore 64*	1983
Birdie Barrage	*BBC Micro*	1983

»BEST-SELLING GOLF GAME SERIES

Holder: *Tiger Woods PGA Tour* **(EA, 1998 to present)**

Since its inception in 1998, *Tiger Woods PGA Tour* has racked up sales of 21.8 million units worldwide. According to videogame sales tracking specialists VGChartz (www.vgchartz.com), the top-selling game in the series is *Tiger Woods PGA Tour 07* (EA, 2006), which has racked up impressive worldwide sales of 3.01 million to date.

»HIGHEST WINNING MARGIN IN EA SPORTS RUGBY

Holder: Andrew Mee (UK)

The highest winning margin in the game *EA Sports Rugby* (EA, 2001) was 38–0, achieved by Andrew Mee, from Rhyl, Wales, UK, on 14 April 2007. Mee reached his score playing a friendly game on the PAL version of *Rugby* on a half length of six minutes and with injuries turned on.

Five *Rugby* games were released by EA between

2001 and 2007. Although they were well received critically, sales of the oval ball game failed to match the US equivalent *Madden NFL* series.

» NEW RECORD » UPDATED RECORD

"GET YOURSELF DOWN HERE BILL. YOU KNOW YOU AIN'T MAN ENOUGH TO STOP ME!"

DID YOU KNOW?

EA claims that the Wii version of *Tiger Woods PGA Tour 11* provides a "truly authentic interactive golf experience". EA also reckons that the combination of fully enhanced swing mechanics courtesy of the Wii MotionPlus accessory and True View, an all-new first-person camera view, will help you "play like a pro".

»MOST REALISTIC TABLE TENNIS GAME

Holder: *Rockstar Games Presents Table Tennis* (**Rockstar Games, 2006**)
Table tennis has had a long history in videogame development. Way back in 1972, Atari's seminal *Pong* was based on the sport, and most recently Nintendo's *Wii Play* has used MotionPlus technology to simulate gameplay. But as far as visual authenticity is concerned, Rockstar Games have crafted the most realistic version of the game with 2006's *Rockstar Games Presents Table Tennis,* which was the first to use the Rockstar Advanced Game Engine, subsequently employed for *Grand Theft Auto IV* in 2008.

»LONGEST-RUNNING CRICKET MANAGEMENT SERIES

Holder: *International Cricket Captain* (**Childish Things, 1998 to 2009**)
International Cricket Captain, a game that allows players to take control of their favourite side from English county, International or Australian domestic cricket, is the longest-running cricket management series on record. First released in 1998, there have been 12 games in the series over 11 years.

»FIRST PGA-LICENSED VIDEOGAME

Holder: *Mattel's PGA Golf* (**Mattel, 1980**)
The first videogame to be officially licensed by the Professional Golfer's Association (PGA) was *Mattel's PGA Golf,* which was released for Intellivision in 1980. The game was played from a basic top-down view and allowed up to four players to compete against each other.

"YOU DON'T WANT TO SET IN PLACE A BAR WHEREBY THE ONLY PEOPLE WHO CAN ENJOY YOUR GAME ARE THOSE WHO KNOW THE DIFFERENCE BETWEEN A TOP SPIN AND A SLICE."
/ TOBY ALLEN OF SUMO DIGITAL TALKS ABOUT THE PHILOSOPHY BEHIND *VIRTUA TENNIS 3.*

FIRST 3D TENNIS GAME

Holder: *Virtua Tennis* (**Sega, 1999**)
The 1999 arcade version of racket sport classic *Virtua Tennis* was the first tennis game to use 3D graphics.

The game provided a far more realistic and enjoyable simulation of tennis than its competitors, thanks to the realism of the player movements and the use of complicated ball physics.

»FIRST CRICKET VIDEOGAME TO OFFER ONLINE PLAY

Holder: *Brian Lara International Cricket 2007* (**Codemasters, 2007**)
Codemasters' *Brian Lara International Cricket 2007* became the first cricket videogame to offer extensive online play when it was released in March 2007. Cricket fans playing on Xbox 360 and PC could take part in tournaments and leagues as well as exhibition and warm-up matches.

TRIVIA TRAIL

The developers of *Brian Lara International Cricket 2005,* Swordfish Studios, added model Lauren Pope in the game as a streaker. Whenever Lara hit a boundary, the streaker would appear. But publisher Codemasters spotted this and Pope was removed before the game hit the stores.

EXTREME SPORTS

FOR WHEN YOU JUST HAVE TO PUSH YOURSELF THAT LITTLE BIT FURTHER AND FLIRT WITH TRUE DANGER...

DID YOU KNOW?

Ubisoft internal data shows that producing one ton of paper used in Ubisoft's game manuals consumes an average of two tons of wood from 13 trees, with a net energy of 28 million BTU's (equivalent to average heating and energy for one home in a year), greenhouse gases equivalent of over 2,721 kg (6,000 lb) to CO_2, and wastewater of almost 56,781 litres (15,000 gal).

»FIRST ENVIRONMENTALLY FRIENDLY GAME

Holder: *Shaun White Skateboarding* **(Ubisoft, 2010)**

In April 2010, Ubisoft announced that *Shaun White Skateboarding* would be the first game in its environmental initiative to eliminate paper game manuals, replacing them with an in-game digital manual for all titles on PlayStation 3 and Xbox 360. According to Ubisoft, as well as helping to combat global warming, this first initiative of its kind in the videogame industry will offer the player easier and more intuitive access to game information.

NEW RECORD
» UPDATED RECORD

"I HAVE ACHIEVED ULTRA-SPEED BY TRAINING, AND TRAINING, AND TRAINING, ALL WHILE WEARING 100-TON BOXERS!"

2: THE NUMBER OF TIMES *720°* (ATARI, 1986) WAS PORTED TO THE COMMODORE 64 – A UK VERSION BY US GOLD IN 1987 AND A US VERSION PRODUCED BY MINDSCAPE IN 1988.

GUINNESS WORLD RECORDS

BIGGEST SOUNDTRACK FOR AN EXTREME SPORTS GAME

Holder: *Amped 3* **(2K Sports, 2005)**
The snowboarding game with the greatest number of songs as part of its soundtrack is *Amped 3*, which has more than 300 new indie music tracks. The game claims to have "more fresh tracks than any other game", some of which featured on an exclusive *Amped 3* soundtrack CD that was released as a promotional item at major retailers.

»**MOST PORTED EXTREME SPORTS TITLE**
Holder: *California Games* **(Epyx, 1987)**
California Games, which is a mini game selection themed around sports popular on the USA's West Coast, has appeared on 16 machines over 23 years, making it the most ported extreme sports title ever. The game was originally created for the Apple II and Commodore 64 but it has since been ported to the Amiga, Apple IIGS, Atari 2600, Atari ST, Atari Lynx, DOS, Sega Mega Drive, Amstrad CPC, ZX Spectrum, Nintendo Entertainment System, MSX, Sega Master System and Java mobile phones. The Commodore 64 version has also appeared on the Wii's Virtual Console. The game is also due for release on the PlayStation 3.

»**LARGEST GAME WORLD IN A SKATEBOARD GAME**
Holder: *Tony Hawk's Proving Ground* **(Activision, 2007)**
The largest environment for a skating game is in *Tony Hawk's Proving Ground* (Activision, 2007). The game allows you to skate around three North American cities: Philadelphia, Baltimore and Washington D.C. But sheer size didn't help it ward off competition from new game on the block *Skate* (EA, 2007), which outsold *Tony Hawk* by two to one.

»**HIGHEST SCORE ON *720°* (MAME)**
Holder: Rasmus K Enoksen Holt (Greenland)
The highest score ever achieved on the MAME version of *720°* (Atari, 1986) is 18,870 points, set by Rasmus K Enoksen Holt on 12 December 2009. The **highest score on *720°* (arcade version)** still stands at 527,100 points. It was set by Ron Perelman (USA) on 17 June 1987 at Camelot Arcade in Anaheim, California, USA.

"I JUST COULDN'T WAIT FOR THE GAME TO GET OUT, SO NOW I CAN SKATE WITH MY HOMIES."
/*SKATE 3* PRODUCER CHRIS PARRY LOVES HIS OWN GAME.

»**MOST EXPENSIVE SKATEBOARD GAME**
Holder: *Tony Hawk: RIDE* **(Activision, 2009)**
The most expensive skateboard game is *Tony Hawk: RIDE,* which retailed in the UK for £99 ($151). The game was expensive because it was the first to include a motion-sensing skateboard controller peripheral, which allowed hands-free gaming. The Wii Fit board has been used by other extreme sports games, but this was the first time a dedicated skateboard had been produced.

»**LONGEST-RUNNING SKATEBOARDING SERIES**
Holder: *Tony Hawk* **(Activision, 1999 to present)**
With 13 games released since 1999, the *Tony Hawk* series is the longest-running skateboard videogame franchise. *Tony Hawk* games have sold more than 30 million units worldwide, according to industry analyst Anita Frazier at the NPD Group research firm. Including ports, there have been 80 *Tony Hawk* games in the last decade.

TRIVIA TRAIL

The first internally developed title by publisher and developer Electronic Arts (EA) was *Skate or Die!* (1987), the title was taken from the catchphrase of another game, *720°* (Atari, 1986). Since its initial release, *Skate or Die!* has been produced for the Commodore 64, Apple IIGS, ZX Spectrum, Amstrad CPC, Nintendo Entertainment System, PC, Atari ST and the Nintendo Wii Virtual Console.

»**MOST CRITICALLY ACCLAIMED SKATEBOARDING GAME**
Holder: *Tony Hawk's Pro Skater 2* **(Activision, 2000)**
According to review aggregation website Metacritic, the highest rated skateboarding game ever is *Tony Hawk's Pro Skater 2*. Reviewers claimed that the second game in the *Pro Skater* franchise was the joint top best game of the Noughties with 98%, tying for top spot with *Grand Theft Auto IV*

(Rockstar Games, 2008). *Tony Hawk's Pro Skater 3* (Activision, 2001) was rated 97% and claimed fifth place through the same period.

TOP 10 *SKATE 2* REPLAYS
AS CHOSEN BY EA

	Player
1	??
2	Ibsoloaded
3	HollowTip82
4	Will713
5	Teri_Yakimoto
6	Cydrid
7	jamesg123
8	Pothocket
9	Hobosaniac
10	GldnState

View them at www.shacknews.com/onearticle.x/59895

"HE NOW HAD HIS PRIZE, BUT FOR SOME UNKNOWN REASON COVETED THE DAGGER AS WELL. WELL, I WOULD GIVE HIM WHAT HE SOUGHT. I WOULD PLUNGE IT INTO HIS FOUL AND TREACHEROUS HEART!"

WWW.GUINNESSWORLDRECORDS.COM/GAMERS   **067**

THE 3D REVOLUTION

IT'S NOT ALL ABOUT ADDING DEPTH TO GAMEPLAY – DEVELOPERS WANT TO ADD DEPTH TO THE VISUALS TOO.

THE ABILITY TO GIVE A 3D EFFECT TO A 2D VIDEOGAME HAS BEEN WITH US FOR SOME TIME, BUT THE RESULTS HAVE BEEN FAR FROM SATISFACTORY. NOW NEW TECHNOLOGY IS ABOUT TO CHANGE THE WAY WE VIEW OUR GAMES.

FIRST 3D CONSOLE GAME
Holder: *3-D WorldRunner* **(Square, 1987)**
The very first console release to support stereoscopic 3D was *3-D WorldRunner*, released on the Famicom in Japan and the NES in North America. The game is a shooter that views the player's character from behind, walking towards the horizon, from which enemies appear to try to halt his progress. It supported a "3D mode" that uses anaglyph red/green glasses to enhance the effect of the 3D world. The 3D mode was optional, and since the glasses were made from flimsy cardboard, very few complete examples of the game are known to be in circulation.

So, how does 3D work? Well, the principle behind 3D games and movies is stereoscopy. This is a process whereby a different image is sent to each eye in such a way that the brain interprets them as one image. This tricks the brain into perceiving one 3D scene rather than two 2D ones. You can see the basic idea behind stereoscopy by looking at your hand with one eye open, and then the other eye. The image you see should be slightly different from each eye. This is caused by their position in your head and it's what allows you to see in three dimensions.

EARLY YEARS
Stereoscopic technology first came to movies in the 1950s with the likes of Columbia Pictures' *Man in the Dark* (USA, 1953), the first 3D film by a major studio. The relatively simple system projects an anaglyph image,

"LADIES AND GENTLEMEN, BOYS AND MORONS, I GIVE YOU... RUSSELL! RUSSELL, GO SORT HIM OUT FOR THE NASTY THINGS THAT HE SAID ABOUT YOUR MOM AND FARMYARD ANIMALS."

» NEW RECORD » UPDATED RECORD

FIRST CONSOLE GAME TO SUPPORT DIGITAL 3D GRAPHICS

Holder: *Invincible Tiger: The Legend of Han Tao* **(Blitz Arcade/Namco Bandai, 2009)**
On its release for the Xbox Live Arcade and PlayStation Network in August 2009, *Invincible Tiger: The Legend of Han Tao* earned the title of first console game to support digital 3D graphics. The game, which is a take on the scrolling beat-'em-up genre, supports eclipse, polarized and the several variations of anaglyph technology.

system was also offered as a little-known feature of the Build Engine that was used to power the aptly-titled *Duke Nukem 3D*.

More recently, the arrival of 3D-ready TVs has cleared the way for 3D gaming to enter the mainstream, which we'll see much more of as developers learn to exploit the 3D display capabilities of the modern consoles. Rather than old-style anaglyph glasses, Sony's system uses eclipse technology, which uses powered glasses (see main picture) containing LCD shutters that blink about 60 times per second, alternating which eye can see the screen. The glasses synchronize with the display to provide different images to each eye, and the shutter effect is so fast that the brain interprets them as one image, just as with anaglyph glasses. PC users have had access to this kind of technology for a while now with NVidia's 3D Vision system, which behaves in much the same way.

EYE SPY

Perhaps the most exciting development in 3D gaming over the last 12 months was Nintendo's unveiling of the 3DS (below), which allows players to experience 3D gaming without the need for glasses. It does this using a parallax barrier – a series of extremely fine slits that are placed in front of the LCD screen – which sends different images to each eye using only the angle of the light. Televisions and computers have been built using the same technology but fall victim to its main drawback: a relatively small viewing angle, which is far less of a problem on a handheld device like the 3DS.

which is composed of red and green layers. Viewers wear coloured glasses with one red and one green lens, which filter the image so that each eye sees a slightly different view. The brain interprets the two images as one 3D visual.

Since early videogames only worked in black and white, games developers couldn't start experimenting with 3D technology until full colour displays were commonplace. One of the first examples was *3-D WorldRunner*, a 1987 console game from developers Hironobu Sakaguchi, Nobuo Uematsu (both Japan) and Nasir Gebelli (Iran-USA) at Square. The team would later go on to greatness outside of the 3D shooter genre as creators of the *Final Fantasy* series.

GETTING ACTIVE

Later games to use anaglyph 3D include *Magic Carpet* (Bullfrog, 1994), and the

RACING GAMES

THE WORLD OF SPEED HAS BECOME SO REAL AND SO DYNAMIC, YOU CAN ALMOST SMELL THE BURNING RUBBER.

»MOST CARS IN A RACING GAME

Holder: *Gran Turismo 5* **(Sony, TBC)**
The racing game that features more cars than any other is *Gran Turismo 5*, which has a staggering 1,000 licensed vehicles from the world's top manufacturers. It beats the previous record-holder, *Gran Turismo 4* (Sony, 2004), which had 721 cars available. All of the 1,000 cars for *Gran Turismo 5* are included on the game disc.

"NO ONE LIVES IN THE SLUMS BECAUSE THEY WANT TO. IT'S LIKE THIS TRAIN. IT CAN'T RUN ANYWHERE EXCEPT WHERE ITS RAILS TAKE IT."

WHAT ARE THEY?

From *Gran Track 10* (Atari, 1974) to *Gran Turismo 5* (Sony, TBC), racing games have been thrilling gamers throughout the history of videogaming. Whether gameplay is top down or 3D, first- or third-person, in cars, on boats, on motorbikes or astride futuristic vehicles, variety has always been the key to the genre's success. Sometimes players have to race against the clock, sometimes they have to race against opponents. They can opt for arcade racers that give exhilarating rides, often defying the rules of physics, or choose an ultra-realistic simulation that looks like a high-def TV stream straight from one of the world's greatest race tracks. At the heart of all racing games, though, is speed and the need to get from A to B in the fastest possible time.

WHO SAYS SO?

David Crookes (UK) started his career as a freelance writer for *Amstrad Action* in 1993. He currently writes for a plethora of magazines and websites, among them *GamesTM*, *Retro Gamer*, *X360* and NowGamer.com. He also produces articles for *The Independent* newspaper and has a games column that runs in several regional newspapers in the UK. David is also the curator of the Videogame Nation touring exhibition, which started in Manchester, UK, in 2009.

CONTENTS

MARIO KART

CRITICAL HIT!

IT'S HIM! THE MOUSTACHIOED PLUMBER! HURTLING AROUND A KART TRACK AT BREAKNECK SPEEDS!

"ALMOST EVERYONE HAS THE EXPERIENCE OF USING SOME KIND OF STEERING WHEEL, FROM RIDING TOY CARS WITH PEDALS AS CHILDREN, TO DRIVING GO-KARTS AT A THEME PARK." /NINTENDO'S SHIGERU MIYAMOTO GIVES THE REASON FOR DEVELOPING THE Wii WHEEL FOR *MARIO KART Wii*.

FASTEST-SELLING KART GAME

Holder: *Mario Kart Wii* **(Nintendo, 2008)**
In its first week on sale in April 2008, *Mario Kart Wii* sold an incredible 2,372,441 units worldwide, making it the fastest-selling kart game of all time. The title continued to sell at a phenomenal rate after those first seven high-octane days, racking up sales of 4,534,256 copies after just four weeks, and has now become the best-selling racing game ever (see record on opposite page).

"WAIT... I'M A HUMAN."

MOST CRITICALLY ACCLAIMED KART GAME
Holder: *Super Mario Kart* **(Nintendo, 1992)**
The kart game that has charmed the most critics is *Super Mario Kart*, which has an average review score of 94% on Gamerankings.com. The venerable racer beats *Mario Kart Super Circuit* (Nintendo, 2001), which has 91.79%; *Crash Team Racing*'s (SCEA, 1999) 91.73%; *Mario Kart DS* (Nintendo, 2005), which racked up 91.19%; and *Diddy Kong Racing* (Nintendo, 1997), which comes in with 89.11%.

FASTEST LAP TIME ON MARIO KART'S MOST DIFFICULT TRACK
Holder: Michael Jongerius (Netherlands)
Mario Kart ace Michael Jongerius raced around Rainbow Road on *Mario Kart 64* (Nintendo, 1996) in a record time of 1 min 57.790 sec on 28 June 2005. Rainbow Road is historically the final and toughest track in *Mario Kart* games, and the *Mario Kart 64* version is also the **longest track in the *Mario Kart* series** at 2 km (1.6 miles). Rainbow Road's legendary difficulty has earned it a place in the broader lexicon of gaming, including a recent cameo in *Scott Pilgrim vs. the World: The Game* (pictured).

TRIVIA TRAIL
Mario is not the only kart racer to be released on a Nintendo console. Diddy Kong lent his name to *Diddy Kong Racing* (Nintendo, 1997) on the Nintendo 64 and *Diddy Kong Racing DS* (Nintendo, 2007). The Nintendo 64 game was produced by Rareware and sold 800,000 copies in its first two weeks on sale, which made it the world's fastest-selling videogame at that point.

»LONGEST-RUNNING KART GAME FRANCHISE
Holder: *Mario Kart* **(Nintendo, 1992 to 2008)**
The *Mario Kart* series started life in 1992 with *Super Mario Kart*, which was the **first console kart-racing game**. The latest release in the mega-successful Nintendo franchise was 2008's *Mario Kart Wii*, which hit the stores 15 years 225 days later, making it the longest-running kart game series. Of the eight games released over the years, Hideki Kommo (Japan), who is credited as a producer on *Mario Kart Wii*, has worked directly on every game except *Super Circuit* and *Double Dash!!*, on which he took an advisory role.

»LARGEST KART GAME TOURNAMENT IN THE UK
Holder: Grand Wii
Held between 5 and 12 April 2008, the largest kart game tournament in the UK was a *Mario Kart Wii* preview event called the Grand Wii. The tournament, which was run by retailer GAME, featured 30 regional events held in stores across the UK. Each regional winner went forward to the final on 12 April, where they battled it out for the top prize: a Mario-themed VW Beetle.

»FASTEST LAP OF AIRSHIP FORTRESS ON MARIO KART DS
Holder: Jake Ruggier (UK)
Jake Ruggier completed the Airship Fortress track on *Mario Kart DS* (Nintendo, 2005) in 39.516 seconds in Poole, UK, on 18 May 2010.

»BEST-SELLING RACING GAME
Holder: *Mario Kart Wii* **(Nintendo, 2008)**
With worldwide sales of over 23 million copies as of October 2010, *Mario Kart Wii* has improved upon its own record of 15.4 million copies sold, which we featured in last year's *Gamer's Edition*. The series continues to defy traditional sales performance by selling millions of copies years after the games are released. Another of the franchise's heavyweight titles, *Mario Kart DS*, has also shifted an extra 3 million units in the last 12 months, bringing its total sales to 18.5 million and maintaining its place as the **»best-selling handheld racing game**.

TOP 10 BEST *MARIO KART 64* PLAYERS

	Name	Standard	AF	Course & Lap Totals
1	Michael Jongerius (Netherlands)	God	1.406	[32'19"21 , 10'28"88]
2	William Lacey (Ireland)	God	4.438	[32'24"22 , 10'30"26]
3	Karlo Tomazelli (Brazil)	God	4.312	[32'25"95 , 10'29"99]
4	Marcelo Almeida dos Reis (Brazil)	God	5.156	[32'25"60 , 10'30"36]
5	Zoran Tintor (Croatia)	God	8.000	[32'29"37 , 10'30"74]
6	Vincent Tolhuis (Netherlands)	God	9.281	[32'31"20 , 10'31"40]
7	Trystan Pugh (UK)	Legend +	10.000	[32'31"53 , 10'31"13]
8	Jeffrey Gutierrez (USA)	God	10.125	[32'30"21 , 10'31"83]
9	Michael Fried (USA)	Legend +	14.062	[32'33"65 , 10'32"07]
10	Sami Cetin (UK)	Legend +	14.594	[32'32"18 , 10'32"66]

Source: Mario Kart 64 Players' Page rankings at http://www.mariokart64.com/mk64/pl.cgi
Ranks are calculated using a combination of factors, including average finish (AF), total times and the number of world records achieved.

» UPDATED RECORD » NEW RECORD

SIMULATION RACING

FOR THOSE THAT WANT TO KEEP IT REAL WHEN IT COMES TO THEIR VIDEOGAME DRIVING, SIM IS THE THING.

»LONGEST-RUNNING SIMULATOR RACING WEBSITE
Holder:
www.theuspits.com
Launched on 19 November 2005, www.theuspits.com, created by Neil "Jed" Jedrzejewski (UK), started out as a site hosting a utility that fixed problems with a demo of the game *Indycar Racing II* (Papyrus Design Group, 1995). Over the years the site has grown and grown and now hosts the first complete mod for the racing simulator *The Pits Touring Car*.

TRIVIA TRAIL

Mark Cale, the boss of videogame publisher System 3, is a huge fan of Italian supercar manufacturer Ferrari. His company has published a series of games based on Ferraris including *Ferrari Challenge: Trofeo Pirelli* (System 3, 2008). Cale currently owns four Ferraris himself and has owned a staggering 57 of the cars in his lifetime.

» NEW RECORD   » UPDATED RECORD

"BLAOW!"

DID YOU KNOW?

In February 2010, Dan Greenawalt, the lead game designer for *Forza Motorsport 3*, reported that the game's Automagic physics engine was so realistic that the flaws its simulations revealed in the Ferrari Enzo's handling replicated the problems that the car had in real life.

»MOST POLYGONS PER CAR IN A RACING GAME
Holder: *Gran Turismo 5* **(Sony, TBC)**
Gran Turismo 5 boasts a record 400,000 polygons per vehicle, 100 times greater than the number present on the vehicles featured in *Gran Turismo 4* (Sony, 2004), which had 4,000 polygons per car. By comparison, rival simulation racing title *Forza Motorsport 3* (Microsoft, 2009) has 300,000 polygons per car.

»FASTEST TIME TRIAL IN GRAN TURISMO 5
Holder: *"Gc_under_01"* **(Canada)**
The *GT5* Time Trial Challenge was a competition held on the PlayStation Network in December 2009 to find North America's fastest driver on a demo version of *Gran Turismo 5*. Entrants submitted course times for a set track in both tuned and untuned cars. The winner of the event was a Canadian known only by his gamer tag of "Gc_under_01", who achieved times of 1 min 47.676 sec in a normal car and 1 min 35.569 sec in a tuned one, giving him an overall time of 3 min 23.245 sec. The next fastest combined run was by American Carl Posey with a time of 3 min 23.251 sec.

	TOP 10 FASTEST TIMES ON *FUEL*'s FROZEN SPIRAL TRACK	
	Name	**Time**
1	KmKB Slash	3:00:088
2	MoE QuAsTe	3:02:010
3	MoE paN	3:04:041
4	X51TopHerx05X	3:04:073
5	Skyliner GTR 34	3:04:094
6	MEGA NG MAN	3:05:018
7	Massai ZePhiR	3:05:053
8	topius fin	3:05:056
9	PATRICK 02	3:05:070
10	IJSheerCRISTYAN	3:05:075
	Sources: Xbox 360 leaderboard	

»MOST TRACKS IN A SIMULATION RACING GAME

Holder: *Forza Motorsport 3* **(Microsoft, 2009)**
Microsoft's *Forza Motorsport 3* boasts a total of 100 race tracks, more than any other simulation racing game. Of those 100 circuits, more than 60 are based on real-life venues. For authenticity, the game's developers, Turn 10 Studios, visited all the real tracks in person, measuring them and taking thousands of reference photographs.

»MOST EXPENSIVE RACING GAME DEVELOPMENT
Holder: *Gran Turismo 5* **(Sony, TBC)**
The most expensive racing game in terms of development is *Gran Turismo 5*, which racked up costs of more than $60 million (£38 million) during its four years in production. The game, which is a PlayStation 3 exclusive, also provides users with online play for the first time in the main *Gran Turismo* series, as well as mechanical and external damage modelling on all featured cars.

LONGEST DRAW DISTANCE IN A SIMULATION RACING GAME
Holder: *FUEL* **(Codemasters, 2009)**
Codemasters' *FUEL* boasts a draw distance of 40 km (24.8 miles), the longest in a simulation racing game. *FUEL*'s racing environment is inspired by the North American wilderness and allows gamers breathtaking views of recognizable landmarks including Death Valley and Mount Rushmore. The landscape, which is modelled from satellite data and rendered by the game engine, is battered by weather effects including blizzards, tsunamis and tornadoes.

»BEST-SELLING PLAYSTATION 3 RACING GAME
Holder: *Gran Turismo 5 Prologue* **(Sony, 2007)**
With sales of 4.65 million units, *Gran Turismo 5 Prologue* (Sony, 2007) is the best-selling PlayStation 3 racing game, although *Gran Turismo 5* is expected to take the record upon its release. *GT5 Prologue*'s sales are still some way short of earlier games in the series. The first *Gran Turismo* (Sony, 1997) for the original PlayStation sold 10.85 million units, but in pole position is *Gran Turismo 3: A-Spec* (Sony, 2001), which sold 14.88 million copies on the PlayStation 2, making it not only the **»best-selling racing game on any Sony platform** but also the **»best-selling simulation racing game ever**.

ARCADE RACING

HIGH-SPEED, HIGH-ADRENALINE RACING FUN THAT BLURS THE BOUNDARY BETWEEN REALITY AND FANTASY.

≫ FIRST RACING GAME TO INTEGRATE WITH A SOCIAL NETWORK WEBSITE

Holder: *Blur* **(Activision, 2010)**

Activision's arcade racer *Blur* features a "Share" button, which players can use to share their in-game achievements with their Facebook friends, making it the first racing game to integrate with a social network website. The game also enables players to challenge their friends to a race via Facebook and post in-game photos, unlockable items and racing statistics to the site.

≫ NEW RECORD
≫ UPDATED RECORD

≫ BEST-SELLING SCI-FI RACING GAME

Holder: *Star Wars Episode I: Racer* **(LucasArts, 1999)**

With worldwide sales of 3.12 million according to VGChartz, the N64 classic *Star Wars Episode 1: Racer* is the best-selling futuristic racing game of all time, leaving the likes of PlayStation favourite *WipEout* and Nintendo stablemate *F-Zero* in a cloud of space dust.

The game is based on the pod-racing scene from the movie *Star Wars Episode I: The Phantom Menace* (USA, 1999) and according to review website Gamespot, the game is "even better than the scene that inspired it, and that's a big compliment indeed".

≫ HIGHEST SCORE ON OUT RUN (ARCADE)

Holder: Richard Jackson (USA)

Richard Jackson from Austin, Texas, USA, scored an incredible 52,897,690 points playing *Out Run* (Sega, 1986) on 21 February 1987. The record was verified by Twin Galaxies' referee Walter Day (USA) in the year after the game was released, and has now stood for over 23 years.

"PRESIDENT RONNIE HAS BEEN KIDNAPPED BY THE NINJAS. ARE YOU A BAD ENOUGH DUDE TO RESCUE RONNIE?"

GUINNESS WORLD RECORDS

"THE PR PEOPLE DON'T REALLY LET ME SAY THIS, BUT BLUR IS LIKE AN ADULT MARIO KART."
/BEN WARD, *BLUR* EXECUTIVE PRODUCER.

»FIRST FILM RELEASED WITH A RACING GAME

Holder: *Stealth* **(Columbia Pictures, 2005)**
Columbia Pictures' 2005 movie *Stealth*, an action thriller about US Navy pilots, became the first film to be accompanied by a racing game when it was released together with the first three levels of sci-fi racer *WipEout Pure* (Sony, 2005). The film and game came on a single Universal Media Disc (UMD), Sony's proprietary format for the PlayStation Portable.

STEALTH

»FIRST RACER TO FEATURE A 3D POLYGON DRIVING ENVIRONMENT
Holder: *Hard Drivin'*
(Atari, 1988)
Hard Drivin' achieved two record-breaking firsts – not only was it the first racing game to feature a 3D polygon environment, it was also the **first racer to feature true force feedback**.

TRIVIA TRAIL

Ridge Racer (Namco, 1994) started with a game of classic arcade alien shooter *Galaxian* (Namco, 1979). You could ignore the game and wait for the racing title to start, but if you killed all of the on-screen aliens, it would unlock eight extra cars. This didn't include the black "Devil" car, however, which was unlocked by beating the game on the Time Trial race mode after winning four Grands Prix.

»LOWEST-RATED NINTENDO 64 RACING GAME
Holder: *Carmageddon 64*
(Stainless Games, 2000)
Having been ported to the Nintendo 64 from PC, *Carmageddon 64* was widely panned by the critics on its release in 2000 and became holder of the unfortunate record for the lowest-rated N64 game. *N64* magazine awarded *Carmageddon 64* just 8%, which made it the lowest-rated Nintendo racing game at that time. The game is also the lowest-ranking release on Gamerankings with 28.5%. Gamespot awarded it 2.1 out of 10 and said: "*Carmageddon 64* has absolutely nothing going for it." The main issue for reviewers was that the ported game had sucked all the fun from the PC original.

TOP 10 FASTEST TIMES ON *HYDRO THUNDER HURRICANE*, "AREA 51" TRACK

	Gamertag	Boat	Time
1	Kobendwyane	RAD HAZARD	1 min 19.54 sec
2	insane cl0wn987	RAD HAZARD	1 min 19.70 sec
3	Legit Magicz	RAD HAZARD	1 min 21.70 sec
4	The Scrivenater	RAD HAZARD	1 min 22.69 sec
5	MadX FlAmEr x	RAD HAZARD	1 min 23.14 sec
6	strikebowler585	RAD HAZARD	1 min 23.30 sec
7	iDuRaCeLL x	RAD HAZARD	1 min 23.42 sec
8	LilReed17	RAD HAZARD	1 min 23.80 sec
9	phizicL	RAD HAZARD	1 min 25.25 sec
10	i SoAp v	RAD HAZARD	1 min 25.64 sec

Source: In-game leaderboard

STREET RACING

ZOOMING DOWN THE HIGH STREET IS NOT ADVISABLE IN REAL LIFE, BUT IN A VIDEOGAME, ANYTHING GOES!

LONGEST-RUNNING RACING FRANCHISE

Holder: *Test Drive*
(Accolade/Atari, 1987 to present)
The *Test Drive* series began in 1987 and is still going strong today, more than 23 years later, making it the longest-running racing franchise of all time. There have been 10 main racing games in the series as well as four off-road games and five spin-off titles. The latest game is Atari's *Test Drive Unlimited 2* (pictured), released in 2010.

»FIRST OPEN WORLD STREET RACING GAME
Holder: *Midtown Madness* **(Microsoft, 1999)**
Midtown Madness did away with predefined circuit tracks, which were previously seen as standard for racing games, to give players free rein to explore the streets of an open world recreation of the city of Chicago, Illinois, USA. At the game's launch in 1999, Microsoft described the first open world street racing game as giving "an unprecedented degree of freedom to drive around in a virtual city".

TRIVIA TRAIL

Eventually released by THQ in 2005, street racing title *Juiced* was originally due to be released by rival publisher Acclaim in 2004. Unfortunately, Acclaim went bankrupt before the game could reach the shelves. THQ bought the rights to the game and gave it some tweaks of their own before final release. MobyGames described the final version as "[a game] that embraces the lifestyle and culture of street racing and tuning, similar to *Need for Speed Underground*, with slick, fully customizable cars, fast races, gaining respect and betting".

"BEHOLD THE IDOLS THAT STAND ALONG THE WALL... THOU ART TO DESTROY ALL OF THEM. BUT THOSE IDOLS CANNOT BE DESTROYED BY THE MERE HANDS OF A MORTAL."

»MOST RACING GAMES IN A SERIES IN DEVELOPMENT SIMULTANEOUSLY

Holder: *Need for Speed* **(EA, 1994 to present)**
In January 2009, plans were announced for four racing games in EA's *Need for Speed* franchise. Each game is pitched at a slightly different racing game audience: *Need for Speed: Shift* (EA, 2009) focuses on simulation racing, *Need for Speed: Nitro* (EA, 2009) is a casual title and *Need for Speed: World Online* (EA, 2010, above) is a free-to-play online street racing game. The fourth street-racing title is being considered for 2011.

»MOST POLICE VEHICLES DAMAGED ON NEED FOR SPEED: MOST WANTED

Holder: **Chris Zupan (USA)**
Chris "dragonangyle" Zupan of Tacoma, Washington, USA, demonstrated a complete and utter lack of respect for virtual authority when he wrecked a record total of 54 police cars, along with a range of other vehicles, in *Need for Speed: Most Wanted* (EA, 2005) on 3 June 2010.

»MOST POPULAR SOCIAL NETWORK RACING GAME

Holder: *Car Town* **(Cie, 2010)**
Produced by social network games company Cie, the driving-based title *Car Town* claimed an all-time high of 840,909 daily active users as of September 2010. The popular Facebook game enables players to collect and customize a wide variety of cars and trucks and then race them against friends in drag races.

»LONGEST VIDEOGAME MARATHON PLAYING A RACING GAME

Holder: **Sebastian Giessler and Marcus Wiessala (both Germany)**
Two gamers with a definite need for speed, Sebastian Giessler and Marcus Wiessala lasted 30 hours playing *Need for Speed: Shift* (EA, 2009) at "Dez Kassel" shopping centre in Kassel, Germany, from 19 to 20 February 2010.

»MOST DEVELOPER-PRODUCED TRACKS IN A RACING GAME

Holder: *Metropolis Street Racer* **(Sega, 2000)**
The Dreamcast title *Metropolis Street Racer* featured a total of 262 developer-produced tracks for players to race around. Many of these tracks are not available at the beginning of the game, but are unlocked, along with new areas of the city of Metropolis, as the challenging single-player game progresses.

»NEW RECORD   »UPDATED RECORD

FIRST 10 GAMES IN THE *TEST DRIVE* SERIES

	Name	Year
1	Test Drive	1987
2	The Duel: Test Drive II	1989
3	Test Drive III: The Passion	1990
4	Test Drive 4	1996
5	Test Drive 5	1998
6	Test Drive 6	1999
7	TD Overdrive	2002
8	Test Drive: Eve of Destruction	2004
9	Test Drive Unlimited	2006
10	Test Drive Unlimited 2	2010

Source: Accolade/Atari

MOST CRITICALLY ACCLAIMED STREET RACING GAME

Holder: *Burnout 3: Takedown* **(EA, 2004)**
With a rating of 93.32% from 56 reviews on the aggregate ratings website Gamerankings.com and 93% from 52 reviews on Metacritic, *Burnout 3: Takedown* is streets ahead of its rival street racing games when it comes to critical acclaim. Shortly after its release, the game, widely regarded as the best in the *Burnout* series, garnered numerous awards including the Golden Joystick for best racing game and the BAFTA for Best Game on the PS2.

KART RACING

GETTING THE FEELING OF THE WIND IN YOUR HAIR WITH DEVIL-MAY-CARE DRIVING.

»MOST CUSTOMIZABLE KART RACING GAME

Holder: *ModNation Racers* **(Sony, 2010)**

ModNation Racers is the first kart racing game that allows users to modify the entire game. In its first three months, 1.1 million unique user-generated creations were available through the game's robust community features – that's 15,000 mods uploaded every day.

»LOWEST-RATED KART GAME

Holder: *M&M's Kart Racing* **(Destination Software, 2008)**

Spluttering over the finish line in last place in the race to achieve critical acclaim is *M&M's Kart Racing*, which garnered a ranking of just 22.5% on GameRankings.com. The title was bestowed with the ignominious "Flat-Out Worst Game" award in the GameSpot 2008 videogame awards.

The game's nearest "rival" is *Shrek Swamp Kart Speedway* (TDK Mediaactive, 2002), which was awarded 26.4% by GameRankings.com.

»MOST BRAND-HEAVY KART GAME

Holder: *Club Kart* **(Sega, 2000)**

Sega's *Club Kart* features more recognizable consumer brand names than any other kart racer. The game is populated with more than 50 brand names, all of which are integrated into the gameplay. By successfully completing a series of races, the companies will look to sponsor you and your kart. Among the names are Castrol, FedEx, BP and Sega's own console, Dreamcast.

»MOST REAL-LIFE DRIVERS IN A KART RACING GAME

Holder: *NASCAR Kart Racing* **(EA, 2009)**

NASCAR Kart Racing boasts 14 real-life racing drivers, which is more than any other kart racer. The game includes US NASCAR drivers Jeff Burton, Kevin Harvick, Kyle Busch, Jimmie Johnson, Dale Earnhardt, Jr., Kasey Kahne, Carl Edwards, Matt Kenseth, Jeff Gordon, Elliott Sadler, Denny Hamlin, Tony Stewart and two mystery drivers. There are 10 other fictional characters.

»FIRST RACING GAME TO BE SOLD IN A FAST-FOOD RESTAURANT

Holder: *PocketBike Racer* **(King Games, 2006)**

In 2006, *PocketBike Racer* became the first racing game to be sold in a fast-food restaurant, when it retailed for $3.99 (£2.04) when purchased with a value meal at Burger King outlets in the USA. The game, described as a "*Mario Kart*" clone, can be played on Xbox and Xbox 360. Two other games, *Big Bumpin'* and *Sneak King*, were also available.

"JASON!"

»MOST PLAYED ONLINE KARTING GAME

Holder: *Crazyracing Kartrider* **(Nexon, 2004)**

Crazyracing Kartrider has attracted more than 30 million players, making it the most played online karting game of all time. It is estimated that one in four Koreans has played the game. At the moment, the game is available in Asia and attempts to bring it to an English-speaking audience appear to have been abandoned following beta testing in 2007 and 2008. The game is known as *PopKart* in China.

DID YOU KNOW?

The Xbox 360 version of *Sonic & Sega All-Stars Racing* (Sega, 2010) is the only iteration of the game to include Rare Software's characters Banjo and Kazooie. To reflect the addition of these non-Sega characters, the game's name was slightly altered to *Sonic & Sega All-Stars Racing with Banjo-Kazooie* (Sega, 2010). In the Wii version of the game, players can go head-to-head with the hedgehog and his friends using their own Mii avatar.

"WE TRY TO ALLOW THE USER TO EXPRESS THEMSELVES AND CREATE SOME REALLY COOL EXPERIENCES."
UNITED FRONT'S DAN SOCHAN DISCUSSING *MODNATION RACERS* WITH *EDGE* MAGAZINE.

TRIVIA TRAIL

A mini-game was included in *Mortal Kombat: Armageddon* (Midway, 2006) called *Motor Kombat*. It was not only possible to play online but also as one of a number of classic *Mortal Kombat* characters (Scorpion, Sub-Zero, Bo' Rai Cho, Jax, Baraka, Raiden, Kitana, Mileena, Cyrax and Johnny Cage), complete with some truly evil karts that reflected the respective personalities of the characters.

» NEW RECORD
» UPDATED RECORD

»FASTEST LAP ON CRASH NITRO KART

Holder: Alex Herrera (USA)

On 31 May 2010, Alex Herrera achieved a record fast lap of 37.77 seconds on the "Jungle Boogie" level of *Crash Nitro Kart* (Universal, 2003). Karting king Alex set his superfast time on the bandicoot-based racer at his home in Lilburn, Georgia, USA.

TOP 10 CRITICALLY ACCLAIMED KART RACING GAMES

	Name	Rating
1	Super Mario Kart (Nintendo, 1992)	94.00%
2	Mario Kart Super Circuit (Nintendo, 1992)	92.00%
3	Crash Team Racing (Sony, 1999)	91.73%
4	Mario Kart DS (Nintendo, 2005)	91.21%
5	Diddy Kong Racing (Nintendo, 1997)	89.11%
6	Mario Kart: Double Dash!! (Nintendo, 2003)	86.96%
7	Mario Kart 64 (Nintendo, 1997)	86.85%
8	Wacky Races (Infogrames, 2000)	84.12%
9	ModNation Racers (Sony, 2010)	83.85%
10	Konami Krazy Racers (Konami, 2001)	82.07%

Source: GameRankings.com

PARTY GAMES

YOUR OPPORTUNITY TO LIVE OUT YOUR DREAMS AS A GUITAR HERO, A SINGING SENSATION OR A DANCING QUEEN.

»HIGHEST SCORE FOR A SINGLE TRACK ON GUITAR HERO III (FEMALE)

Holder: Annie Leung (USA)

On 30 September 2010, at her home in San Francisco, California, USA, Annie Leung achieved the highest score on *Guitar Hero 3: Legends of Rock* by a female gamer when she racked up 789,349 points playing "Through the Fire and Flames" on the "Expert" setting.

Annie has been playing videogames since she was a kid, but got seriously into gaming in 2004 when she got hooked on *Unreal Tournament* (GT Interactive, 1999). Since that time, Annie has moved on to the *Guitar Hero* series and has a mission to get more women involved with competitive gaming.

{ *"PREJUDICED? I'M NOT PREJUDICED! BY THE NINE HELLS, I EVEN TRAVEL WITH A BACK-STABBING TIEFLING OF ALL THINGS, AND YOU KNOW HOW HER KIND ARE!"* }

WHAT ARE THEY?

With more and more people enjoying gaming as a social activity, games have moved out of the bedroom and into the living room in recent years. One consequence of this shift in gaming habits is that party games have become more popular than ever. Most of them have simplistic controls, making them easy to pick up and play, and many are played with special controllers designed to be intuitive to use. From karaoke and music titles to sports and mini-game collections, there's a party game to suit all tastes, ages and levels of experience. So pick the one that's right for you, invite some friends round and get ready to party!

WHO SAYS SO?

Ellie Gibson (UK) has worked in the games industry for 10 years, but she's been a gamer for a lot longer than that. She started out writing manuals for PlayStation games and is now deputy editor of Eurogamer.net. Ellie's favourite game of all time is *Tomb Raider* but she also loves party titles, especially *Guitar Hero* and *Just Dance*. Ellie loves *SingStar* too – her signature tune is "Total Eclipse of the Heart".

CONTENTS

"PLEASE TURN OFF ALL CELL PHONES, GAUSS RIFLES, EMPS, PSIONIC WAVEFORM EMITTERS, AND PLASMA-BASED PERDITION FLAMETHROWERS. THANKS, AND HAVE A GREAT FLIGHT!"

WWW.GUINNESSWORLDRECORDS.COM/GAMERS   **083**

Wii SPORTS

WHETHER IT'S Wii SPORTS, SPORTS RESORT OR PLAY, THIS SERIES GUARANTEES SPORTS-BASED FAMILY FUN.

DID YOU KNOW?

Strangely, it is possible to bowl a 91-pin strike in *Wii Sports*... In the final Power Throws training exercise, move your Mii to the right-hand side of the lane, as close to the barrier as possible. Adjust the angle of your throw two clicks to the right. Throw the ball as hard and straight as you can. Your ball should roll along the top of the barrier. You'll then hear a "sonic boom" and see all 91 pins fall over.

›› BEST-SELLING GAME OF ALL TIME

Holder: *Wii Sports* **(Nintendo, 2006)**
The best-selling videogame of all time is *Wii Sports*, which comes bundled with the Wii console. By July 2010, 63.78 million copies of the game were in homes around the globe. If you add in sales of 16.18 million for *Wii Sports Resort* (pictured) and 27.49 million for *Wii Play* (see record on opposite page), you get a total sales figure for the series of an incredible 107.45 million units.

"BEFORE Wii SPORTS WAS RELEASED, WE HAD ABSOLUTELY NO IDEA HOW WELL IT WOULD SELL... THE REALITY TURNED OUT TO GO SO FAR BEYOND ANYTHING WE HAD PREDICTED."
/NINTENDO'S ZENICHI YAMASHITA, CO-CREATOR OF THE BASEBALL AND BOXING GAMES IN *Wii SPORTS*.

›› NEW RECORD
›› UPDATED RECORD

[*"ZEUS, IS THIS HOW YOU FACE ME? COWARD! I AM THROUGH DOING THE BIDDING OF THE GODS, COME DOWN AND FACE ME RIGHT NOW."*]

TRIVIA TRAIL

In June 2010, the University of Delaware, USA, carried out research on a group of senior citizens playing *Wii Sports*. The study showed that golden oldies playing individual bowling burned up to 176 calories in 30 minutes, those playing baseball used up to 144 calories, while team bowling consumed up to 89 calories and tennis up to 72.

»FIRST MOTIONPLUS-COMPATIBLE GAME
Holder: *Wii Sports Resort* (Nintendo, 2009)
The first game to work with the MotionPlus accessory for the Wii remote was *Wii Sports Resort*. MotionPlus is designed to give players more precision control when using the Wii remote. The accessory comes bundled with copies of *Wii Sports Resort*, which was released in summer 2009. Like its predecessor, the game was a huge hit. In the first week after launch, a copy of the game was sold every 1.5 seconds in the USA. Within two months, sales had passed the 1 million mark in the USA, Europe and Japan.

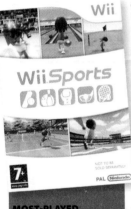

BEST-SELLING NON-BUNDLED GAME
Holder: *Wii Play* (Nintendo, 2006)
Of games which do not come bundled with a console, *Wii Play* is the best-selling game of all time. More than 27.49 million copies of the game had been sold by July 2010. Although *Wii Play* does not come with a console, it does come packaged with a Wii remote, which helps to explain its popularity. In the first two years after the game's release, 10 million copies were sold in North America alone.

MOST-PLAYED Wii GAME
Holder: *Wii Sports* (Nintendo, 2006)
According to the Nintendo Channel, *Wii Sports* is the game most played by European Wii owners. As of June 2010, they had spent a total of 26,014,439 hours with the game over the course of 21,782,040 playing sessions. On average, *Wii Sports* players had booted up the game 32.82 times and played for a total of 39 hours and 11 minutes. The figures for *Wii Sports Resort* were 2,532,327 total hours and 15,471,148 playing sessions, with an average playtime of 20 hours and 55 minutes and 12.78 sessions per person.

»MOST Wii PLAY TABLE TENNIS VOLLEYS
Holder: Kevin Conner (USA)
The record for the most volleys in a game of *Wii Play* Table Tennis is held by Kevin Conner who fired off 285 volleys on 16 July 2009. Conner was playing the NTSC version of the game. The record for the PAL version is 178 volleys, achieved by John Eden (UK) on 12 October 2009.

»LARGEST Wii SPORTS BOWLING TOURNAMENT
Holder: TexanPlus (USA)
An impressive 436 people took part in a record-breaking *Wii Sports* bowling tournament held at the Reliant Center, Houston, Texas, USA, on 1 October 2009. The tournament was organized by US medical insurance provider TexanPlus as part of a health fair that also provided health advice to senior citizens.

»FIRST GAME TO FEATURE Mii CHARACTERS
Holder: *Wii Sports* (Nintendo, 2006)
Nintendo's special brand of avatar – known as a Mii – was first featured in *Wii Sports* in November 2006. The option to customize your Mii to look like yourself proved highly popular; however, the plan wasn't always to feature them in *Wii Sports*. "At one point during development, we did try using Mario characters," legendary designer Shigeru Miyamoto (Japan) revealed. But people preferred Miis, so Nintendo went with them instead.

»MOST iPOINTS AMASSED IN Wii SPORTS RESORT FLYOVER
Holder: Andrew Mee (UK)
On 2 January 2010, Andrew Mee collected 51 iPoints in five minutes flying over the *Wii Sports Resort* island.

TOP 10 *Wii SPORTS/Wii SPORTS RESORT* RECORDS (PAL VERSION)

	Game & Record	Score	Player (nationality)	Date
1	Archery – highest score	106 points	Ronnie Dalbianco (USA)	26 December 2009
2	Baseball – biggest blowout	9 points	John Eden (Australia)	14 February 2009
3	Bowling – highest score	300 points	Kimberley Sanders (UK)	31 July 2009
4	Golf – best score	4 under par	John Eden (Australia)	14 January 2010
5	Tennis – highest skill level	158 points	Jordi Schouteren (Netherlands)	15 August 2008
6	Canoeing – highest score	462.09 points	Andrew Mee (UK)	26 September 2009
7	Cycling – fastest time	15 min 32.89 sec	Andrew Mee (UK)	28 September 2009
8	Power Cruising – highest score	208.8 points	Andrew Mee (UK)	17 August 2009
9	Sky Diving – highest score	241 points	Pekka Luodeslampi (Finland)	24 March 2010
10	Table Tennis – highest score	1,484 points	Kristian Farnan (UK)	19 January 2010

Source: www.twingalaxies.com

MINI GAMES

IF SHORT, SHARP BURSTS OF MULTIPLAYER FUN ARE WHAT YOU'RE AFTER, MINI GAMES ARE THE ANSWER.

DID YOU KNOW?

Only four characters appear in every *Mario Party* game: Mario, Luigi, Princess Peach and Yoshi the dinosaur. Special guest stars include Wario and Donkey Kong. *Mario Party 8* marked the first occasion where players could get in on the action themselves, using their own customized Mii avatars as playable characters.

»LONGEST-RUNNING MINI GAME SERIES

Holder: *Mario Party*
(Nintendo, 1998 to 2007)
A videogame take on the classic boardgame format, the *Mario Party* series tasks players with taking turns at a variety of mini games as they send their chosen Mario character around a virtual board. The first game in the series hit Japan on 14 December 1998 and there have been seven further main *Mario Party* games and two handheld titles since.

"HEY ROMEO, REMEMBER WHEN I TOLD YOU TO SHUT YOUR MOUTH?
CONSIDER THAT A STANDING ORDER."

»FASTEST COMPLETION OF MONKEY SNOWBOARD

Holder: Troy Whelan (USA)

The fastest time for completing Monkey Snowboard Course 1 in *Super Monkey Ball: Banana Blitz* is 1 min 34 sec, set by Troy Whelan in Mechanicsville, Virginia, USA. Released in November 2006, *Banana Blitz* expanded the mini game repertoire from earlier *Super Monkey Ball* games, which had mainly featured platform gameplay. Other featured mini games included in the seminal simian title were Monkey Darts, Monkey Bowling and Monkey Squash.

»BEST-SELLING CHARACTER CROSS-OVER

Holder: *Mario & Sonic at the Olympic Games* (Nintendo, 2008 to present)

Since 2008, long-time rival characters Mario and Sonic, both mascots for their respective rival companies Nintendo and Sega, have co-starred together in the Olympic-themed sports mini game series *Mario & Sonic*. The two titles in the series so far, *Mario & Sonic at the Olympic Games* and *Mario & Sonic at the Olympic Winter Games*, have combined worldwide sales of more than 18 million units. The original game, tied to the 2008 Olympic Games in Beijing, China, marked the first time that Mario and Sonic had appeared in a videogame together.

»FIRST VOICE-CONTROLLED MINI GAME COMPILATION

Holder: *Kimi no Tame nara Shineru* (Sega, 2004)

Released in November 2004 for the launch of Nintendo's DS handheld, *Kimi no Tame nara Shineru* was the first mini game compilation to use the device's microphone as a way of controlling the game, with players being encouraged to speak and blow into it as part of the gameplay. Titled *Feel the Magic: XY/XX* in the US and *Project Rub* in Europe, the compilation's overall plot tasks the player with impressing a young girl with the aid of a performance group known as the "Rub Rabbits".

»FIRST OFFICIALLY RELEASED DIY MINI GAME COMPILATION

Holder: *WarioWare: Do It Yourself* (Nintendo, 2009)

The first official game designed around the creation and distribution of user-generated mini games was *WarioWare: Do It Yourself*, first released in Japan on 29 April 2009. Mini games have long been a hallmark of the *WarioWare* series, but *WarioWare: Do It Yourself* was the first title to put players in the driving seat, designing everything from the gameplay and graphics to the soundtrack. Players could even share their creations and download mini games designed by others online.

»BEST-SELLING MAT-BASED MINI GAME SERIES

Holder: *Family Trainer/ Active Life* (Namco Bandai, 2008 to present)

The two titles in the *Family Trainer* series, known as the *Active Life* series in the USA, have sold more than 1.6 million copies worldwide to date. In Japan, the series takes its name from the first floor mat peripheral, also called *Family Trainer*, released for NES in 1986.

TOP 10 BEST-SELLING Wii MINI GAME COLLECTIONS

	Game	Sales
1	Wii Sports	63.78 million
2	Wii Play	27.49 million
3	Wii Sports Resort	16.18 million
4	Mario & Sonic at the Olympic Games	7.63 million
5	Mario Party 8	7.14 million
6	Mario & Sonic at the Olympic Winter Games	3.44 million
7	Carnival Games	3.20 million
8	WarioWare: Smooth Moves	2.26 million
9	Game Party	2.21 million
10	Rayman Raving Rabbids: TV Party	1.78 million

Source: VGChartz

TRIVIA TRAIL

As the title suggests, the original *Rayman Raving Rabbids* (Ubisoft, 2006) mini game collection starred Ubisoft mascot Rayman. However, the Rabbids ended up outshining him with their mischievous antics, and by the time the fourth instalment, *Rabbids Go Home*, was released, Rayman had been dropped from the series.

»NEW RECORD
» UPDATED RECORD

LIFESTYLE GAMING

WANT TO GET FIT, TRAIN YOUR BRAIN OR BECOME A MASTER CHEF? THEN THERE'S A GAME OUT THERE FOR YOU!

»MOST SUCCESSFUL PHYSICAL FITNESS SERIES

Holder: *Wii Fit* **(Nintendo, 2007)**
By July 2010, more than 22.55 million copies of *Wii Fit* had been sold, along with over 12.85 million copies of the 2009 follow-up *Wii Fit Plus*. With combined sales of 35.4 million copies, *Wii Fit* is the most successful physical fitness series.

»NEW RECORD
UPDATED RECORD

】 "THERE SHE IS, WILLAMETTE, COLORADO. POPULATION 53,594." 【

20: THE BEST POSSIBLE BRAIN AGE SCORE YOU CAN ACHIEVE IN *BRAIN TRAINING*. THIS IS BECAUSE DR KAWASHIMA BELIEVES THE BRAIN STOPS DEVELOPING AT THE AGE OF 20.

DID YOU KNOW?

In October 2009, it was reported that US Homeland Security was conducting experiments with the Wii Balance Board. Researchers were investigating to see if the Board could be used to detect fidgeting, and thereby to expose nervous terrorists. It was thought that use of the Board might speed up the security screening process at places such as sports stadiums and airports.

»FIRST GAME TO LET PLAYERS WEIGH THEIR PETS

Holder: *Wii Fit Plus* **(Nintendo, 2009)**
Legendary designer Shigeru Miyamoto (Japan) was pleased with the success of the first *Wii Fit*, but felt there was something missing. "I did go through a period when I regretted the fact that users couldn't weigh their dogs," he said. "Dogs are the classic pet, after all." So for the sequel, *Wii Fit Plus*, Miyamoto implemented a feature that allows users to weigh their pets by holding them and standing on the Wii Balance Board.

»MOST PROLIFIC COOKING MAMA RECORD BREAKER

Holder: William Willemsteyn III (USA)
The most prolific record-breaker for the *Cooking Mama* series is William Willemsteyn III, who holds nine records in total. All of Willemsteyn's achievements were made using the original DS version of the game. They include the records for cracking eggs, peeling shrimps and stuffing cabbages.

»BEST-SELLING THIRD-PARTY NINTENDO DS SERIES

Holder: *Cooking Mama* **(Majesco, 2006)**
By November 2009, more than 2.5 million *Cooking Mama* games had been purchased in Europe, while the sales figure for the USA was 4 million, which combined to make *Cooking Mama* the best-selling third-party game series for the Nintendo DS. The series has proved so popular that publisher Majesco decided to produce a series of spin-offs, including *Gardening Mama*, *Crafting Mama* and *Babysitting Mama*.

TRIVIA TRAIL

In November 2008, pro-vegetarian group PETA lashed out at *Cooking Mama* for featuring recipes which included meat. A spoof game, titled *Cooking Mama Kills Animals*, can be found at www.peta.org/cooking-mama/index.asp

»MOST CRITICALLY ACCLAIMED FITNESS GAME

Holder: *EA Sports Active* **(EA, 2009)**
According to aggregator Gamerankings.com, the most critically acclaimed physical fitness game ever is *EA Sports Active*, which has an average review score of 81.85%.

TOP 10 *Wii FIT* RECORDS (PAL VERSION)

	Game & Record	Score	Player (Country)	Date
1	Free Jogging – 30 minutes	16,484 metres	Pekka Luodeslampi (Finland)	22 June 2008
2	Ski Jump – farthest distance	358 points	Andrew Mee (UK)	26 December 2008
3	Soccer Heading – advanced	438 points	Jordi Schouteren (Netherlands)	14 August 2008
4	Rhythm Kung Fu – advanced	840 points	Noora Suoniemi (Finland)	18 March 2010
5	Penguin Slide	99 points	Julie Mee (UK)	11 January 2009
6	Rhythm Boxing – 3 minutes	338 points	Andrew Mee (UK)	22 August 2008
7	Balance Bubble – advanced	29.75 seconds	Jordi Schouteren (Netherlands)	20 September 2008
8	Agility Test	18 points	Andrew Mee (UK)	26 December 2008
9	Ski Slalom – advanced	38.23 seconds	Jordi Schouteren (Netherlands)	15 August 2008
10	Tightrope Tension – advanced	44.2 seconds	Andrew Mee (UK)	21 August 2008

Source: Twin Galaxies

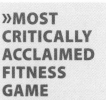

RHYTHM GAMES: KARAOKE

SING WHEN YOU'RE WINNING... AND IF YOU'RE NOT WINNING, SING MORE ACCURATELY!

»MOST SUCCESSFUL SINGING GAME SERIES

Holder: *SingStar*
(Sony, 2004 to present)
Sony Computer Entertainment Europe's *SingStar* has become the most successful singing videogame series of all time, having sold more than 17.5 million copies worldwide.

P1
P1
No plea - sure cruise
I con - si - der it a chal - lenge

TIME

TOP 10 MOST DOWNLOADED *SINGSTAR* TRACKS

	Game
1	"Total Eclipse of the Heart" – Bonnie Tyler
2	"Torn" – Natalie Imbruglia
3	"Eye of the Tiger" – Survivor
4	"Take On Me" – A-Ha
5	"Suspicious Minds" – Elvis Presley
6	"The Final Countdown" – Europe
7	"…Baby One More Time" – Britney Spears
8	"Girls Just Wanna Have Fun" – Cyndi Lauper
9	"Just Like a Pill" – P!nk
10	"American Pie" – Don McLean

Source: Singstar Store

»MOST PEOPLE TO SING TO A KARAOKE VIDEOGAME

A crowd of 10,490 people gathered for Los Premios 40 Principales at Palacio de Deportes de la Comunidad de Madrid, in Madrid, Spain, on 11 December 2009 to sing along to tracks on *Lips: Canta en Español* (Microsoft, 2009).

»FIRST HIP-HOP KARAOKE GAME

Holder: *Get On Da Mic* **(Eidos, 2004)**
The first karaoke game to exclusively feature hip-hop tracks was *Get On Da Mic*, released by Eidos for PS2 in October 2004. *Get On Da Mic* had an impressive song roster, with hits from high-profile artists such as Snoop Dogg, Jay-Z, Public Enemy, Missy Elliott and Kanye West. But the game failed to impress the critics – according to review aggregator Metacritic, the average review score was 49%. In April 2010, 4mm Games announced plans to produce a superior hip-hop karaoke game titled *Def Jam Rapstar*. "Internally, we used *Get On Da Mic* as the architectural model of how *not* to do this game," said boss of 4mm Games Paul Coyne.

TRIVIA TRAIL

Welsh pop star Duffy showed up at Microsoft's E3 2008 conference to demo new karaoke game *Lips*. "I really like the ethic of the game," she told the BBC. "I'm not a real fan of violent games, I'm a bit of a wuss, so I like the fact this is interactive and no one gets hurt... unless you hit them with the microphone!" Duffy sang "Mercy", one of her own songs, but failed to get a perfect score.

"DWAYNE, WHICH QUESTIONS WOULD YOU LIKE IN THE NEXT ROUND?"

DID YOU KNOW?

The first instalment in the *SingStar* series was released for PS2 in May 2004 and a series of sequels followed, based around themes such as Pop, Rock, R'n'B and Disney. The PS3 version, released in December 2007, was the first *SingStar* game to let players download tracks and upload videos of their performances. Special editions of the game based entirely around the music of ABBA, Queen (pictured) and Take That have since been released.

»MOST EXPENSIVE KARAOKE GAME PERIPHERAL

Holder: Crystal Roc
Fancy showing off some bling while you sing? Then check out the limited edition Swarovski-crystal-studded microphones released for *Lips*. The mics were designed by Crystal Roc, a company that also produces sparkly instruments for stars such as Rihanna, Kylie and Leona Lewis. Only 100 sets of the *Lips* mics were manufactured. Each pair features more than 1,000 Xilion-Rose-cut crystals and carries a price tag of $680 (£430).

HARDEST UNLOCKABLE ACHIEVEMENT IN LIPS

Holder: *I'm Kind of a Big Deal*
The hardest Xbox 360 Achievement to unlock in *Lips* is titled *I'm Kind of a Big Deal*.

To unlock the Achievement you must earn the ranking of Infinity by getting Cool in all pages and winning all six medals. As a reward, you will receive 40 Gamerpoints. *Lips* experts recommend exploiting the Vibrato feature to get a higher score.

> ## "THE MUSIC INDUSTRY TAKES US VERY SERIOUSLY NOW... GAMES HAVE HAD A POSITIVE IMPACT ON THEIR FINANCES IN THE LAST COUPLE OF YEARS."
> /*SINGSTAR* PRODUCER DAVE RANYARD.

»MOST POPULAR ONLINE KARAOKE NETWORK

Holder: My SingStar Online (Sony, 2007)
With more than 1.1 million registered users as of June 2010, the world's most popular online karaoke network is My SingStar Online. According to *SingStar* publisher Sony, more than 7,000 new *SingStar* players sign up for the service each week. Over 200,000 videos of player performances have been uploaded since My SingStar Online launched in December 2007, and there have been in excess of 23,740,000 videos viewed in that time.

»MOST SUCCESSFUL KARAOKE TRACK STORE

Holder: SingStore
With 11 million songs downloaded to date, the most successful videogame karaoke track store is *SingStar*'s SingStore. As of June 2010, there were nearly 2,000 songs available in the SingStore.

Interestingly, while *Singstar* releases various region-specific titles such as *Singstar Deutsch Rock Pop*, English-language songs still top their downloads chart.

»LONGEST-RUNNING SINGING GAME SERIES

Holder: *Karaoke Revolution* (Konami, 2003 to present)
The longest-running series of karaoke games is Konami's *Karaoke Revolution*, the first instalment of which was released in Japan and North America in November 2003. Since then, *Karaoke Revolution* has also appeared on more platforms than any other karaoke game, with versions released for the PS2, PS3, GameCube, Wii, Xbox and Xbox 360. Special editions have included *American Idol* and country-music-themed versions of the game.

» **NEW RECORD**
» **UPDATED RECORD**

RHYTHM GAMES: INSTRUMENT

WHETHER YOU'RE A GUITAR HERO OR A ROCK BAND LEGEND, PLAYING MUSIC HAS NEVER BEEN SO MUCH FUN.

TOP 10 MOST DOWNLOADED *GUITAR HERO* TRACKS

	Game
1	"Twilight of the Thunder God" – Amon Amarth
2	"(I Can't Get No) Satisfaction (Live)" – The Rolling Stones
3	"Laser Cannon Deth Sentence" – Dethklok
4	"Dream On" – Aerosmith
5	"Lycanthrope" – +44
6	"Almost Easy" – Avenged Sevenfold
7	"The Day that Never Comes" – Metallica
8	"We Are the Champions" – Queen
9	"What's My Age Again?" – Blink-182
10	"NJ Legion Iced Tea" – A Day to Remember

Source: Guitar Hero Store

»LONGEST-RUNNING INSTRUMENT RHYTHM GAME SERIES

Holder: *Guitar Freaks* **(Konami, 1999 to Present)**
The longest-running series of instrument based games is *Guitar Freaks*, which first appeared in arcades in 1999. The most recent version, *Guitar Freaks V7*, released in March 2010, was the 19th instalment in the series and features 500 songs.

»SMALLEST DRUM KIT PERIPHERAL

Holder: *Band Hero DS* **(Activision, 2009)**
Fitting over the lower screen of the DS Lite, the Drum Grip peripheral released for *Band Hero DS* is the smallest videogame drum kit. The grip, made of silicone rubber, fits over the Lite's 133 mm by 73.9 mm (5.2 in x 2.9 in) frame, but is not compatible with the original DS or DSi. To play the kit, you tap the grip's miniature drum pads with your fingers. Developer Vicarious Visions said the idea was to make playing the drums on the DS more fun.

"TRANSCENDING HISTORY AND THE WORLD, A TALE OF SOULS AND SWORDS, ETERNALLY RETOLD."

»BEST-SELLING SINGLE-BAND INSTRUMENT GAME

Holder: *Guitar Hero: Aerosmith* **(Activision, 2008)**

Guitar Hero: Aerosmith, released in June 2008, has sold over 3.2 million copies worldwide, a figure that, perhaps surprisingly, beats the 2.9 million sales of *The Beatles: Rock Band*.

DID YOU KNOW?

For the 2008 NASCAR Sprint Cup race at the New Hampshire Motor Speedway, USA, Dario Franchitti's #40 Dodge Charger sported a *Guitar Hero: Aerosmith* paint job. Sadly, his car didn't take him "Head First" over the finish line.

»LONGEST SONG FEATURED IN A RHYTHM GAME

Holder: "2112"(Rush, 1976)
The prize for the longest commercially released song to be featured in a rhythm game goes to veteran Canadian rockers Rush, whose 20-min 23-sec 1976 track "2112"features as the final number in *Guitar Hero: Warriors of Rock* (Activision, 2010).

»BEST-SELLING RHYTHM GAME SERIES

Holder: *Guitar Hero* **(RedOctane, 2005 to present)**
Since making its debut, the *Guitar Hero* franchise has seen global sales of over 49 million units up to July 2010. When it was released, Charles Huang, co-founder of RedOctane, was told to expect sales of 150,000 units.

TRIVIA TRAIL

The idea for *The Beatles: Rock Band* came from Dhani Harrison, the son of the Fab Four's George Harrison. Joining Dhani in the game's development was the offspring of another Beatles icon, Giles Martin, the son of the band's legendary producer Sir George Martin.

»FIRST RELIGIOUS MUSIC GAME

Holder: *Guitar Praise* **(Digital Praise, 2008)**
Bringing a spiritual theme to rhythm gaming, *Guitar Praise* was first published by Digital Praise in September 2008. Priced at $100 (£55), the game comes with a wireless guitar peripheral and works on Mac or PC. It works in the same way as titles like *Guitar Hero* and *Rock Band*, but features songs by Christian recording artists such as Stryper, Hawk Nelson and Whitecross, and also lacks on-screen avatars. According to recent MTV reporting, demand for *Guitar Praise* exceeded the number of guitars being produced within a month of release.

»LONGEST GUITAR HERO WORLD TOUR MARATHON

Part of Finland's thriving demoscene, which melds programming, gaming and music, the Assembly Winter 2009 event held in Tampere, Finland, on 21 February 2009 saw a record 24-hr 2-min *Guitar Hero World Tour* marathon featuring Finns Simo Piispanen, Aku Valmu, Jaakko Kokkonen and Simo-Matti Liimatainen.

» **NEW RECORD**
» **UPDATED RECORD**

»FIRST RHYTHM GAME TO REACH $1 BILLION SALES

Holder: *Guitar Hero III* **(Activision, 2007)**
At the 2009 Consumer Electronics Show in Las Vegas, USA, Activision revealed that *Guitar Hero III* had reached $1 billion (£650 million) in sales.

»LARGEST LIVE AUDIENCE FOR A VIDEOGAME

Holder: Jon Edney and Matt Beadle (both UK)
On 11 June 2010, Activision's John Edney and *ZOO Magazine*'s Matt Beadle (below, left to right) achieved what countless bedroom DJs dream of when they played Activision's DJ Hero in front of a crowd of 16,000 people at the Isle of Wight Festival, Newport, Isle of Wight, UK.

GAMER'S EDITION

RHYTHM GAMES: DANCING

DANCING GAMES ARE A GREAT WAY TO GET INTO THE GROOVE AND SHOW OFF YOUR MOVES!

»YOUNGEST GAMER TO ACHIEVE A PERFECT SCORE ON DANCE DANCE REVOLUTION

Holder: Ryota Wada (Japan)
Aged just 9 years 288 days, Ryota Wada achieved a perfect "AAA" rating on *Dance Dance Revolution* (Konami, 1998) dancing to the song "Hyper Eurobeat" on the "Expert" difficulty setting at his home in Tokyo, Japan, on 29 August 2010. Ryota was first able to beat his dad at *DDR* at the tender age of five, but had always missed out on the elusive "AAA" rating because the mat kept slipping under his feet. All it took for him to reach a perfect score was a non-slip surface and the record was his.

LONGEST DANCE DANCE REVOLUTION MARATHON

Holder: Airy Peterson (USA)
Dance master Airy Peterson recorded the longest ever *Dance Dance Revolution* session on 3 September 2006, when he played *Dance Dance Revolution: Extreme (8th Mix)* for 13 hr 9 min 40 sec. Peterson's incredible achievement was verified by Twin Galaxies, which sets strict rules for those undertaking *Dance Dance Revolution* marathons. For the first five hours of the marathon, players must select "Light" difficulty or higher. They must then pick "Standard" difficulty or higher for the next five hours. After 10 hours of dancing, players must select "Heavy" difficulty. Players are warned that they take part at their own risk.

TRIVIA TRAIL

In May 2010, Ubisoft launched the *Just Dance* Talent Search, an exclusive contest open to fans of the game in France, the UK and the USA. Auditions were held in each country, during which judges picked the most talented dancers. The winners, Liana (USA), Mandy (UK) and Sam (France), were invited to Ubisoft's Paris studio, where their choreography was recorded to feature in *Just Dance 2*. Everyone who attended an audition was promised a free demo disc in advance of the sequel's release.

»FIRST CONTROLLER-FREE DANCING GAME

Holder: *EyeToy: Groove* **(Sony, 2003)**
While the arrival of Kinect and Move has brought about a new era in camera-based gaming, the first controller-free dancing game predates the current generation by several years. Sony's *EyeToy: Groove* used the PlayStation 2's webcam accessory to track

"YOU CAN 'WAX ON, WAX OFF' ALL YOU LIKE – I'M STILL KICKING YOUR ASS."

And girls they want to have fun
O-oh girls just want to have fun

BEST-SELLING THIRD-PARTY Wii GAME

Holder: *Just Dance* (Ubisoft, 2009)
Released in November 2009, Ubisoft's *Just Dance* racked up sales of 4.1 million copies around the world by October 2010, making it the best-selling third-party game on the Wii. *Just Dance* is also the fastest-selling new intellectual property from a third-party publisher on Wii, with 2 million copies shifted in the game's first four months on sale. All of which makes *Just Dance* the most successful Wii game Ubisoft has ever released.

"AFTER SEEING THIS GAME, I HAD AN EPIPHANY OF WHAT MOTIVATED HUMANS TO START STANDING."
/DDR SOUND DIRECTOR "WAC", EXPLAINING WHAT HE THINKS OF *DDR HOTTEST PARTY*.

the player's movements as they bopped along to hits by pop acts including Las Ketchup and The Cheeky Girls, who were popular when the game launched in November 2003.

»FIRST FULL-BODY MOTION DDR GAME
Holder: *Dance Dance Revolution Hottest Party* (Konami, 2007)
The first *Dance Dance* *Revolution* game to evaluate players' full-body movements was *Dance Dance Revolution Hottest Party* (known as *Dancing Stage Hottest Party* in some regions), which was released by Konami in 2007. Like other instalments in the *DDR* series, *Hottest Party* was played using a dance mat. However, the game also registered upper body movements, which players performed by holding a Wii remote while moving their arms in time with the arrows on screen.

» **NEW RECORD**
» **UPDATED RECORD**

»LONGEST-RUNNING DANCE MAT SERIES
Holder: *Dance Dance Revolution* (Konami, 1998 to present)
Dance Dance Revolution was first released in Japan in November 1998 and the series is still going strong today. *Dance Dance Revolution*, often abbreviated to *DDR*, was previously known as *Dancing Stage* in Europe and North America. There have been dozens of *DDR* games released in the arcades and many more for home consoles. There have even been some for the Game Boy Color – instead of a dance mat, they came with a special thumb pad that fits over the handheld's buttons.

TOP 10 DDR UNIVERSE 3 PLAYERS

RANK	NAME	SKILL	AAA SCORES
1	PP1_OTL	753,831	418
2	cryle_1102	656,710	324
3	kay0ss	620,967	311
4	lzam22	582,708	232
5	hlavco	557,580	118
6	Silvercube	536,371	8
7	RDRAGON	517,781	24
8	lynnku511	428,685	121
9	HillySweetie	377,591	1
10	omfg007	371,581	53

Source: DDRonline commuity.com/leaderboards

A TOUCH OF CLASS

A BRIEF HISTORY OF THE TOUCHSCREEN, THE MOST IMPORTANT GAMING TECHNOLOGY OF THE 21ST CENTURY.

A MERE SEVEN YEARS AGO, VIDEOGAMES WERE HAPPILY GOING ABOUT THEIR BUSINESS WITH BUTTONS AND JOYSTICKS AND NOT A CARE IN THE WORLD. THEN, IN 2004, NINTENDO RELEASED A HANDHELD CONSOLE WITH A TOUCHSCREEN TO A SCEPTICAL PUBLIC. THAT HANDHELD WAS THE DS, AND THE TOUCHSCREEN GAMING REVOLUTION HAD BEGUN.

TRIVIA TRAIL

This image, called "Discovering iPad", is by French comic book artist Mathieu Reynès. The incredible thing about the picture is that it was created entirely on an iPad, using an application called Autodesk Sketchbook Pro. It's a great example of how the touchscreen revolution is opening up opportunities in all sorts of artistic and creative fields.

In May 2010, Nintendo announced that the DS had become the **best-selling handheld console of all-time**, beating the original Game Boy, which had spent 15 years at the top, into second place. Also in 2010, Apple's iPhone 4 became the **fastest-selling mobile device** in history, the iPad took the world by storm and a host of tablet computers emerged on to the marketplace.

The technology that links these record-breaking devices is the touchscreen. It has been the catalyst for a new kind of interactive gaming that is, literally, hands on. It has enabled games designers to bring a new immediacy to gaming that brings players into the action in an exciting and intuitive way.

FIRST CONTACT
The first touchscreen, as we understand them today, was developed in 1974 at the University of Kentucky, USA, by Dr Sam Hurst and produced by his company, Elographics. While it was comparatively crude by

"LET'S GO, SCALETTA. THOSE TOILETS AIN'T GONNA CLEAN THEMSELVES."

» NEW RECORD » UPDATED RECORD

"ITS LARGE, 360-DEGREE, HORIZONTAL USER INTERFACE OFFERS A UNIQUE GATHERING PLACE." /MICROSOFT'S ERIC HAVIR SEES THE SURFACE AS A PLACE TO HANG OUT.

modern standards, Hurst's touchscreen nonetheless found use in a variety of research, educational and industrial applications.

TOUCHING DESTINY
The potential of touchscreen gaming wasn't fully realized until Nintendo took a gamble on the launch of the DS. The dual-screen handheld (above) came at a time when the Japanese giant needed a sales success to revitalize its struggling fortunes. The DS did exactly that. It enabled developers

to experiment with new gameplay ideas and the result was a massive influx of innovative, must-have titles.

A consequence of the touchscreen's simple, intuitive controls was that the DS opened up gaming to groups of people, young and old, who hadn't felt comfortable with gaming before. And the release of titles such as Nintendo's own *Brain Training* (2005) attracted people who were looking for a pastime that mixed self-improvement with entertainment.

FIVE FINGERS OF FUN
The Nintendo DS, and its successors the DS Lite and DSi, stood unchallenged as the ruling dynasty in handheld gaming for three years, but upheaval was just around the corner. When Apple's iPhone and iPod Touch arrived in 2007 the impact on gaming was minimal, but eight months later its App Store was unveiled and the face of mobile entertainment was irreparably changed.

The 500 apps available for download on the App Store's launch on 10 July 2008, featured 145 games, which was the **largest launch line-up of any gaming system**.

PADDING IT OUT
The incredible success of the multi-touch iPhone and its App Store allowed Apple to take the touchscreen to the next level and popularize the tablet computer.

While other companies had been experimenting with keyboard-free touchscreen computers since the early 2000s (Microsoft's Windows XP Tablet PC Edition was released in 2001), Apple's iPad was an immediate success with tech geeks and gamers alike. The system's compatibility with Apple's existing App Store meant many iPhone mega hits, including *Angry Birds* (Chillingo, 2009), could

be played on the iPad and many received hi-def remixes to make use of the tablet's bigger screen.

BELOW THE SURFACE
So how far can the touchscreen go? Are we heading for a *Minority Report*-style world? Microsoft has offered glimpses of the future of touchscreen technology with its Surface system: a multi-touch computer built into a table with the screen as the table top. Games have been demonstrated in action on the system, but due to its cost of over $12,000 (£7,500) for a basic system, so far its main applications are in commercial locations such as restaurants and shops.

Such prohibitive costs suggest that large-scale touchscreen gaming is some way off for most of us, but with hundreds of new games hitting app stores every week it seems that the touchscreen will stay conveniently handheld for some time to come.

» FIRST TOUCHSCREEN GAMES CONSOLE

Holder: Game.com (Tiger, 1997)
It wasn't until September 1997 that the first touchscreen games console was released, in the form of Tiger's Game.com. While it was certainly impressive for the time, its monochrome LCD screen was difficult to see in low-light and with a catalogue of fewer than 30 games available it quickly became another console casualty. Highlights of Game.com's limited releases included an in-built version of *Solitaire* and a near-unplayable port of *Duke Nukem 3-D*.

ACTION-ADVENTURE GAMES

FIGHTING, SHOOTING, PUZZLES, STEALTH, EXPLORATION, COLLECTING – ACTION-ADVENTURE'S GOT IT ALL!

»MOST MAGAZINE COVER FEATURES FOR A VIDEOGAME

Holder: *Assassin's Creed II*
(Ubisoft, 2009)

It's been a busy year for the Florentine nobleman Ezio Auditore da Firenze. Aside from his normal duties assassinating various villains in Renaissance Italy as the main character in the action-adventure title *Assassin's Creed II*, he also appeared as cover star and lead story on 127 different magazines in 32 different countries worldwide between April 2009 and April 2010! (If you look closely you can spot the covers in this picture.)

"THE SKUNK OVER HERE WILL BRING YOU LUCK."

WHAT ARE THEY?

Action-adventure is the most varied genre in gaming, encompassing a wide range of titles with every kind of narrative gameplay from linear plot-driven adventures to sandbox games where the player virtually creates their own stories. In fact, variety is the key to the whole genre, with the best examples relying not on any one single stylistic, narrative or gameplay technique, but a combination of several. Many modern action-adventures force players to vary their style of play at various points throughout the game. Branching story paths, as seen in *Heavy Rain* (Sony, 2010), are the latest thing, but expect further innovations as the action-adventure genre continues to evolve.

WHO SAYS SO?

Chris Schilling (UK) is an experienced videogames writer whose work has featured in *The Daily Telegraph*, *The Observer*, Eurogamer.net and *GamesTM*. He has been an avid fan of videogames since the age of five, and has more consoles than he can play. Chris is a fan of action-adventures of any kind, but particularly likes 3D platformers, and his current favourite is *Super Mario Galaxy 2* (Nintendo, 2010).

CONTENTS

"NOW, LOGIC WOULD DENOTE THAT ANYONE WHO DRINKS THAT... IS GONNA GET THE SCREAMIN' SQUITS!"

WWW.GUINNESSWORLDRECORDS.COM/GAMERS   **099**

THE LEGEND OF ZELDA

THE LEGENDARY SERIES CREATED BY SHIGERU MIYAMOTO IS THE STANDARD FOR MULTIFACETED GAMEPLAY.

»MOST VALUABLE GAME TRAILER

Holder: *The Legend of Zelda: Twilight Princess* **(Nintendo, 2006)** On 25 March 2010, an anonymous buyer paid $301.78 (£200) on the internet auction site eBay for a rare DS cartridge carrying a video trailer of *The Legend of Zelda: Twilight Princess* – far more than the cost of the full game! The cartridge was originally handed out, complete with a standard DS case, to attendees at Nintendo's E3 press conference in 2006. It is estimated that only 500 such cartridges are in existence.

"AXEL. SKATE. ZAN. WHAT ARE WE GOING TO DO?"

CRITICAL HIT!

GUINNESS WORLD RECORDS

THE LEGEND OF ZELDA LINK'S AWAKENING

TRIVIA TRAIL

Veteran videogame director Eiji Aonuma (Japan) has overseen the creation of many *Zelda* titles, most notably as director of the hugely celebrated *Ocarina of Time*. He also leads a 40-strong musical ensemble of Nintendo employees, which takes its name from another *Zelda* game – the group is called The Wind Wakers.

»BEST-SELLING HANDHELD NARRATIVE ADVENTURE GAME

Holder: *The Legend of Zelda: Link's Awakening* **(Nintendo, 1993)**
The most successful portable *Zelda* game is *The Legend of Zelda: Link's Awakening*, which sold a total of 6 million copies worldwide. The title is unusual in that it is one of very few *Zelda* games that does not take place in the land of Hyrule, nor does it feature Princess Zelda, who gives the series its name. The game was remade for the Game Boy Color five years later, featuring compatibility with the Game Boy Printer peripheral.

»FASTEST COMPLETION OF THE LEGEND OF ZELDA: TWILIGHT PRINCESS

Holder: Daniel Hart
With a single-segment time of 3 hr 56 min, Daniel "Jiano" Hart holds the record for the fastest completion of *The Legend of Zelda: Twilight Princess*. His time was achieved using the GameCube version of the game, with Hart exploiting several sequence breaks and glitches to finish so quickly. By contrast, the average recorded play time for *Twilight Princess* on the Wii's Nintendo Channel is more than 45 hours.

»HIGHEST LETTER-SORTING SCORE IN THE LEGEND OF ZELDA: THE WIND WAKER

Holder: Pierre Barthod (France)
The 2002 GameCube title *The Legend of Zelda: The Wind Waker* contains a number of mini-quests, one of which is a letter-sorting challenge held on Dragon Roost Island. This tasks players with matching the seals on letter slabs with the symbols on the shelf within a tight 30-second time limit. Pierre Barthod takes top prize at this with a score of 36 matches, a feat that requires split-second timing.

» NEW RECORD
» UPDATED RECORD

»MOST CRITICALLY ACCLAIMED VIDEOGAME OF ALL TIME

Holder: *The Legend of Zelda: Ocarina of Time* **(Nintendo, 1998)**
With a review average of 97.48% on Gamerankings.com, and a near-perfect 99% on Metacritic, *The Legend of Zelda: Ocarina of Time* tops the list of the most critically acclaimed games ever. The game even scored a coveted 40/40 from the Japanese gaming magazine *Famitsu*.

TOP 10 MOST CRITICALLY ACCLAIMED TITLES IN THE *LEGEND OF ZELDA* SERIES

	Game	Platform	Score %
1	*Ocarina of Time (1998)*	N64	97.48%
2	*Twilight Princess (2006)*	GameCube/Wii	94.73%
3	*The Wind Waker (2002)*	GameCube	94.53%
4	*A Link to the Past (1991)*	SNES	92.78%
5	*Oracle of Ages (2001)*	Game Boy Color	91.92%
6	*Majora's Mask (2000)*	N64	91.89%
7	*Oracle of Seasons (2001)*	Game Boy Color	91.50%
8	*Link's Awakening (1993)*	Game Boy	91.23%
9	*The Minish Cap (2004)*	Game Boy Advance	90.22%
10	*The Phantom Hourglass (2007)*	DS	88.91%

Source: Gamerankings.com

»HIGHEST SCORE FOR THE LEGEND OF ZELDA THEME ON DONKEY KONGA

Holder: Kevin M LaLonde (USA)
The bongo-controlled music title *Donkey Konga* (Nintendo, 2003) features a number of Nintendo theme songs including *The Legend of Zelda Theme*. Kevin M LaLonde of Texas, USA, tapped out a score of 132,652 points on this theme at the "Gorilla/Expert" difficulty in June 2009.

"TAKE HEART FELLOW ADVENTURERS, FOR YOU HAVE CURRIED THE FAVOUR OF BOO, THE ONLY MINIATURE GIANT SPACE HAMSTER IN THE REALM!"

WWW.GUINNESSWORLDRECORDS.COM/GAMERS **101**

OPEN WORLD

»BEST-SELLING WESTERN-THEMED VIDEOGAME

Holder: *Red Dead Redemption* **(Rockstar Games, 2010)**
Having roped in an incredible £10 million ($15.6 million) in sales within just two days of its UK release on 21 May 2010, *Red Dead Redemption* went on to herd sales of more than 6.15 million units worldwide by October 2010. These figures easily trump those of the game's 2004 predecessor *Red Dead Revolver*, as well as a posse of its Western rivals, including Ubisoft's *Call of Juarez* series.

TRIVIA TRAIL

Reflecting the electricity superpower of main character Cole MacGrath, Sony's 2009 open worlder *inFAMOUS* employs an innovative electronic soundtrack by renowned Brazilian musician Amon Tobin. The music was crafted using several non-traditional instruments, such as metal refuse bin lids, flowerpots, metal shelves and even a bungee cord, to evoke the game's unusual urban soundscape. With plans for a sequel reportedly featuring characters with different powers, we can't wait to see what Tobin will create for *inFAMOUS 2*.

»LARGEST IN-GAME SOUNDTRACK
Holder: *Grand Theft Auto IV* **(Rockstar Games, 2008)**
The fully expanded version of *Grand Theft Auto IV*, including downloadable expansion packs *The Lost and Damned* and *The Ballad of Gay Tony*, features 340 commercially released songs. The retail release of the two expansion packs, called *Episodes from Liberty City*, contains 48 tunes that are not in the downloadable version but omits many of the tracks originally featured in the main game.

The PC version of *GTA IV* also features an additional radio station called Independence FM, which plays any music files placed in the User Music folder in the game's directory – enabling gamers to create their own playlists.

LONGEST SURVIVAL ON A 6-STAR WANTED LEVEL ON GRAND THEFT AUTO IV
Holder: Henrik Lindholm (Denmark)
Defying police and federal agents aplenty, Henrik Lindholm managed to survive *GTA IV*'s 6-star wanted level for 16 min 16 sec at the Copenhagen E-Sports Challenge, in Copenhagen, Denmark, on 13 April 2009.

"I'M STONEHEAD, THE THIRD HENCHMAN OF THE KING."

TOP 10 BEST-SELLING *GRAND THEFT AUTO* CONSOLE GAMES

	Game	Sales
1	GTA: San Andreas	20.3 million
2	Grand Theft Auto IV	14.3 million
3	Grand Theft Auto: Vice City	14.2 million
4	Grand Theft Auto III	11.6 million
5	GTA: Liberty City Stories	6.0 million
6	GTA: Vice City Stories	4.5 million
7	Grand Theft Auto II	3.4 million
8	Grand Theft Auto	2.3 million
9	GTA: Episodes from Liberty City	1.9 million
10	GTA: Chinatown Wars	1.5 million

Source: VGChartz

DID YOU KNOW?

Hollywood film director John Hillcoat turned his hand to machinima (film-making using videogames) with *The Man from* *Blackwater*, a 30-minute-long account of *Red Dead Redemption* protagonist John Marston tracking down his former friend, the outlaw Bill Williamson.

"WE WANT [IT] TO BE ABOUT GAME PLAY FREEDOM, THE PLAYER SHOULD PLAY THE GAME THE WAY HE WANTS..." /*JUST CAUSE 2* DIRECTOR MAGNUS NEDFORS ON THE JOY OF HIS GAME'S SANDBOX FORMAT.

»LARGEST PLAYABLE ENVIRONMENT IN AN OPEN-WORLD VIDEOGAME

Holder: *Just Cause 2* (**Square Enix, 2010**)

The fictional tropical island of Panau in *Just Cause 2* is the largest playable environment in an open world action-adventure videogame, with a total area of 1,035 km² (400 miles²). The map for *Just Cause 2* is only slightly larger than the original game, though developer Avalanche has filled it with more things to see and do as well as a fair few Easter eggs, such as an island in the north-west styled on the television series *Lost* (ABC), complete with a crashed plane and a mysterious hatch.

» **NEW RECORD**   » **UPDATED RECORD**

»LONGEST VIDEOGAME MARATHON

Dutch gamers Renzo Bos, Maykel Leest, Sven de Vries, Robbie van Eijkeren, Marcel van Waardenburg and Edward Leest (pictured, left to right) won €1,000 (£840, $1,290) each in prize money for playing *Red Dead Redemption* (Rockstar, 2010) for an epic 50 hours at the Twistdock Endurance Gaming Challenge in Rotterdam, the Netherlands, from 16 to 18 July 2010. Renzo also clocked up the »**fastest 100% single-player completion on *Red Dead Redemption*** with a 41-hr 10-min 50-sec speed run.

NARRATIVE ADVENTURE

BLENDING PLOT WITH PLAY, THE NARRATIVE ADVENTURE IS A UNIQUELY INTERACTIVE WAY TO TELL A STORY.

TRIVIA TRAIL

Ubisoft's 2003 narrative adventure *Beyond Good and Evil* was a commercial failure but picked up a significant cult following, to the extent that a teaser trailer for a potential sequel released in August 2008 was greeted with great excitement among the gaming community. Since then, little has been heard about any follow-up title, causing some to speculate that it has been cancelled. Ubisoft itself has sent out mixed messages, with the company's North American President Laurent Detoc saying "whether or not it comes out remains to be seen".

»MOST CHANGES MADE TO A GAME BETWEEN US AND EUROPEAN RELEASE

Holder: *Ico* **(Sony, 2001)**
With five significant post-completion additions and numerous additional tweaks to the overall level design, *Ico* incurred more gameplay changes between its US and European/Japanese release dates than any other game. According to its developers, Team Ico, the US version of the game was rushed out for a September 2001 launch. A number of additions were thereafter prepared for the later Japanese and European releases, including a two-player mode, an extra ending, a lightsaber-esque weapon, dialogue translation and extra film grain effects. There were also a number of minor design adjustments made to the game's castle environment.

»MOST SUCCESSFUL STUDENT-DEVELOPED VIDEOGAME

Holder: *de Blob* **(THQ, 2008)**
With sales of over 800,000 units, the student-made videogame *de Blob* has become a key franchise for publisher THQ. Originally created by a group of students from the Utrecht School of the Arts (Netherlands) as a

"THE OX KING'S DAUGHTER, HUH? YEAH… I NEVER LIKED THAT GUY."

»MOST CRITICALLY ACCLAIMED PS3 EXCLUSIVE

Holder: *Uncharted 2: Among Thieves* **(Sony, 2009)**

With an average score of 96% on review aggregate website Metacritic and a total of 110 awards, Sony's *Uncharted 2: Among Thieves* is the most critically acclaimed game that is exclusive to the PlayStation 3 platform. The sequel to 2007's *Uncharted: Drake's Fortune*, *Uncharted 2* built on the original title's success commercially and critically, taking an unprecedented ten awards from the Academy of Interactive Arts and Sciences in 2010, including Game of the Year and Outstanding Achievement in Game Play Engineering.

»FIRST 3D REMASTER FOR CONSOLE

Holder: *Batman: Arkham Asylum* **(Eidos, 2010)**

Released in March 2010, the Game of the Year Edition of *Batman: Arkham Asylum* featured a key difference from the version released in 2009 – an enhanced 3D mode that has the action popping out of the screen. This new mode was achieved using TriOviz 3D, a process that adds a visual depth to the images for those wearing 3D glasses. The effect was most noticeable in the "detective mode" sequences, where certain objects are highlighted in orange, and enemies are seen as blue 3D skeletons.

TOP10 MULTIPLAYER MONEY-EARNERS ON *UNCHARTED 2: AMONG THIEVES*

	Game	Amount
1	gloomcool	$396,487,000
2	Hi-Tech-Hate	$258,720,950
3	Skw1shE	$257,345,400
4	ScRaMB59	$239,696,150
5	Racheldavid	$228,520,200
6	budylove54	$227,843,150
7	DeejayNoise	$220,116,150
8	T_A_I_W_A_N_2008	$219,570,350
9	Z5116304	$217,643,350
10	Solaire2010	$212,490,000

Source: In-game leaderboard

»MOST-VIEWED VIRAL CAMPAIGN FOR A NARRATIVE ADVENTURE

Holder: *Shadow of the Colossus* **(Sony, 2005)**

Game developers Team Ico estimate that 25 million people have seen the viral marketing campaign for *Shadow of the Colossus*. The viral took the form of a blog charting the remains of colossal giants from the game around the world.

free downloadable title for the PC, *de Blob* requires players to literally paint the town with a variety of colours. The quality of *de Blob*'s innovative gameplay impressed the folks at THQ so much that they purchased the rights to publish the game on Nintendo's Wii and DS platforms. THQ has also released a version for the iPhone, along with the sequel *de Blob: Underground*.

»FIRST PAX 10 WINNER

Holder: *The Maw* **(Twisted Pixel, 2009)**

Organized by the people responsible for the popular webcomic of the same name, the Penny Arcade Expo (PAX) began recognizing excellence in independently developed games in 2008 with the inaugural PAX 10 Audience Choice award, voted for by PAX attendees. The winner that year was *The Maw*, a game where players guide a little blob around as he slowly eats his way through the universe.

» **NEW RECORD**
» **UPDATED RECORD**

STEALTH

STAYING HIDDEN FROM ENEMIES CAN BE A HARD TASK, BUT HIDE AND SNEAK IS HOW YOU PLAY STEALTH GAMES.

≫FASTEST-SELLING HANDHELD STEALTH GAME

Holder: *Metal Gear Solid: Peace Walker* **(Konami, 2010)**
With 445,138 copies sold in its first week of release in April 2010, *Metal Gear Solid: Peace Walker* for the PSP easily ranks as the fastest-selling stealth game for a handheld console. Its global sales of 1.21 million units as of October 2010 also marks it out as the ≫ **best-selling handheld stealth game**, just nudging past the previous record of 1.07 million units sold by the PSP title, *Metal Gear: Portable Ops.*

≫ **NEW RECORD**
≫ **UPDATED RECORD**

≫ FIRST STEALTH-BASED ADVERGAME

Holder: *Sneak King* **(King Games, 2006)**
Advergaming, the process of advertising things in the form of a videogame, dates back to at least 1983, when Coca-Cola commissioned *Pepsi Invaders*, a *Space Invaders*-style game that poked fun at its main cola rival. The first stealth-based console advergame is *Sneak King*, sold in outlets of Burger King across North America for $3.99 (£2) in November 2006. The game had the chain's mascot "The King" sneak around to deliver burgers without being spotted.

≫LONGEST CUTSCENE IN A VIDEOGAME

Holder: *Metal Gear Solid 4: Guns of the Patriots* **(Konami, 2008)**
Whether you love them or fast forward through them, "cutscenes" – the animated sequences in a game that advance the plot and give the gamer a break from the ongoing tension – are a staple of the modern game. The longest example of the form occurs in Konami's classic stealth title *Metal Gear Solid 4: Guns of the Patriots*, which contains a single scene cutscene that is 27 minutes long. The **longest cutscene sequence**, which strings a number of non-interactive cutscenes together, is 71 minutes from the same game. This mini-movie represents the culmination of the game's narrative.

"YOURS IS A FACE ONLY A MOTHER COULD LOVE, AND ONE THAT I COULD NEVER FORGET"

DID YOU KNOW?

Solid Snake, the star of much of the *Metal Gear* series, has made appearances in various games for other companies including *Super Smash Bros. Brawl* and *LittleBigPlanet*.

»MOST GAMES HEADLINED BY AN INDIVIDUAL

Holder: Tom Clancy (USA)

Tom Clancy, the spy fiction novelist extraordinaire, has a staggering 127 commercially released games based on characters and concepts he originated as of August 2010. Pictured is the latest entry in the stealth series, *Tom Clancy's Splinter Cell: Conviction*, which features the latest adventures of his stealth hero, Sam Fisher.

"I WANTED THE PLAYER TO FEEL LIKE A PANTHER, NOT A GRANDMOTHER"
/UBISOFT'S MAXIME BELAND ON SAM FISHER'S NEW DIRECTION IN *SPLINTER CELL: CONVICTION*.

»FIRST STEALTH GAME

Holder: *005* (Sega, 1981)

While the original *Metal Gear* (Konami, 1987) popularized the stealth genre, Sega's arcade title *005* pioneered the form way back in 1981. In the game, players take control of a spy, who must deliver a briefcase to a helicopter while avoiding enemies.

»LONGEST UK BAN FOR A STEALTH GAME

Holder: *Manhunt 2* (Rockstar Games, 2007)

Originally refused a certificate by the British Board of Film Classification (BBFC), preventing it from being released in the UK, Rockstar resisted calls to tone-down *Manhunt 2* for 500 days before submitting a revised final cut that was passed for release.

TRIVIA TRAIL

Now best known as the writer of *Thor* for Marvel and his own *Phonogram* comics and graphic novels, Kieron Gillen (UK) started out as a videogames journalist renowned for his verbosity and passionate, almost obsessive, love for the medium. Among his most fondly remembered gaming articles was an incredibly detailed 10-page dissection of *The Cradle*, a single, particularly creepy, level from the stealth game *Thief: Deadly Shadows* (Eidos, 2004), which was published in the March 2005 edition of the UK magazine *PC Gamer*.

TOP 10 BEST-SELLING STEALTH GAMES

	Game	Sales
1	Metal Gear Solid (1998)	5.59 million
2	MGS 2: Sons of Liberty (2001)	5.58 million
3	Tom Clancy's Splinter Cell (2002)	5.35 million
4	MGS 4: Guns of the Patriots (2008)	4.77 million
5	MGS 3: Snake Eater (2004)	4.07 million
6	Hitman 2: Silent Assassin (2002)	3.87 million
7	Tom Clancy's Splinter Cell: Pandora Tomorrow (2004)	2.37 million
8	Tom Clancy's Splinter Cell: Chaos Theory (2005)	1.92 million
9	Tom Clancy's Splinter Cell: Double Agent (2006)	1.46 million
10	Tom Clancy's Splinter Cell: Conviction (2010)	1.10 million

Source: VGChartz

SURVIVAL HORROR

FIGHT FOR YOUR LIFE AGAINST HEAVY ODDS IN THIS MOST NERVE-SHREDDING OF GENRES.

»LONGEST DEVELOPMENT PERIOD FOR A SURVIVAL HORROR VIDEOGAME

Holder: *Alan Wake*
(Microsoft, 2010)
Having been in production for over five years, *Alan Wake* holds the record for the longest gestation period for a survival horror game. Initial planning for *Alan Wake* started way back in 2001, when the psychological action thriller was set for release on PC as well as Xbox 360, and was an open-world game. When it was finally released in 2010, the game was an Xbox 360 exclusive.

» NEW RECORD » UPDATED RECORD

»MOST PLAYABLE CHARACTERS IN A SURVIVAL HORROR VIDEOGAME
Holder: *Eternal Darkness*
(Nintendo, 2005)
Eternal Darkness allows the player to control 12 different characters – the most ever in a survival horror game. The story of *Eternal Darkness* spans millennia, with characters ranging from a Roman Centurion in the year 26 BC and a 15th Century Franciscan monk to the main protagonist Alexandra Roivas, a present day student. It's not the only survival horror to utilize multiple player characters – the first two *Siren* games each feature a cast of 10 different characters.

»FIRST SURVIVAL HORROR GAME
Holder: *Haunted House*
(Atari, 1981)
The term "survival horror" was coined upon the release of the original *Resident Evil* in 1996, but many earlier games share the key elements of horror and survival. Released in 1981, Atari's *Haunted House* is widely regarded as the first ever survival horror videogame. In *Haunted House*, the player controls a character whose eyeballs are the only visible part of its body, and who explores a maze-like mansion using a magical sceptre to keep himself safe from enemies.

A re-imagining of the Atari classic is set for release in late 2010, with players taking on the roles of the grandchildren of the original game's character who disappeared in the evil mansion 30 years before.

"YOU CAN'T GIVE IT UP! TRIUMPH OR DIE"

TOP 10 SURVIVAL HORROR GAMES AT GAMETRAILERS.COM

	Game	Downloads
1	Resident Evil 5 (2009)	26.0 million
2	Dead Space (2008)	8.0 million
3	Alone in the Dark (2008)	7.0 million
4	Silent Hill: Homecoming (2008)	4.1 million
5	Resident Evil: Umbrella Chronicles (2007)	4.0 million
6	Resident Evil Retrospective (2009)	2.5 million
7	Resident Evil 4 (Wii) (2007)	2.4 million
8	Dead Space 2 (2010)	2.0 million
9	Resident Evil Degeneration (2008)	1.8 million
10	SAW (2009)	1.4 million

Source: Gametrailers.com

»BEST-SELLING SURVIVAL HORROR SERIES

Holder: *Resident Evil* **(Capcom, 1996 to present)**
With over 40 million copies sold, *Resident Evil* tops the chart as the best-selling survival horror franchise. To date, 26 games have been released in the *Resident Evil* series, across more than 15 different formats. Among the seven entries in the main series, the biggest sales success has been *Resident Evil 2* on the PlayStation, which sold 5.82 million units.

> "I'M KINDA PROUD THAT I THINK WE MIGHT HAVE BEEN THE FIRST KISSING SCENE BETWEEN TWO POLYGONAL CHARACTERS RENDERED IN REAL-TIME."
> /DIRECTOR HIDEKI KAMIYA ON *RESIDENT EVIL 2*.

»WIDEST VARIETY OF PLAYER DEATH ANIMATIONS

Holder: *Resident Evil 4* **(Capcom, 2005)**
With at least 47 unique ways for protagonist Leon S Kennedy to die, Capcom's 2005 smash *Resident Evil 4* has the widest variety of player death animations seen in a videogame.

Boasting a Metacritic aggregate review score of 96%, *Resident Evil 4* is one of the most critically acclaimed videogames of all time. The game is well-known for the incredible attention to detail of its animation, particularly the vast number of ways in which Leon S can meet his gory demise: he can be decapitated, drowned, stabbed, crushed, torn in half, eaten, set on fire and even shot by an ally.

»FASTEST COMPLETION OF RESIDENT EVIL

Holder: Brandon "Ekudeht" Armstrong (USA)
According to speeddemosarchive.com, the fastest completion of the original PlayStation version of *Resident Evil*, which was released in 1996, is 1 hr 9 min 17 sec set by Brandon Armstrong. With multiple endings and the post-game "Arrange" mode, *Resident Evil* has a number of different speedrun possibilities. Armstrong's time was achieved playing as Jill Valentine, without obtaining the game's "good" ending. The time was achieved on the NTSC version of the game, which is faster than the PAL version.

TRIVIA TRAIL

The *Fatal Frame* series (known as *Project Zero* in Europe) has enjoyed a cult following since the release of the original game in 2001, and is considered by its fans to be one of the scariest videogame franchises ever. Despite being the fastest selling game of the series, Wii title *Fatal Frame IV: Mask of the Lunar Eclipse* was never released in the West – Japanese publisher Nintendo passed up the opportunity to localize the game. Fortunately, a group of fans have created an unofficial translation patch for the game, which was released in January 2010.

»FIRST USE OF PLAYER-CONTROLLED SECOND-PERSON PERSPECTIVE IN A VIDEOGAME

Holder: *Siren* **(Sony, 2003)**
The original *Siren*, which was developed for PlayStation 2 by Sony's Japan studio and released in Japan in 2003, was the first survival horror game to use a player-guided second-person perspective. Known as *Forbidden Siren* in Europe and Australia, the title allowed players to "sight-jack" enemies. Using this method, players could see the action through their enemy's eyes, allowing them to move past unseen when the enemy's back is turned or they have moved to another location. Other games (such as 1991's *Battletoads*) have used the second-person perspective in boss battles, for example, but *Siren* was the first game to make it a central gameplaying feature.

2D PLATFORMERS

FROM DONKEY KONG TO NEW SUPER MARIO BROS. Wii, THE SIDE-SCROLLING RUN-AND-JUMP IS A GAMING STAPLE.

TOP 10 BEST-SELLING 2D MARIO PLATFORMERS

	Game	Sales
1	Super Mario Bros. (1985)	40.24 million
2	New Super Mario Bros. (2006)	21.94 million
3	Super Mario World (1990)	20.61 million
4	Super Mario Land (1989)	18.14 million
5	New Super Mario Bros. Wii (2009)	14.49 million
6	Super Mario Land 2: 6 Golden Coins (1992)	11.18 million
7	Super Mario All Stars (1993)	10.55 million
8	Super Mario Bros. 2 (1988)	7.46 million
9	Super Mario World 2: Yoshi's Island (1995)	4.12 million
10	Super Mario Bros. 2: The Lost Levels (1986)	2.65 million

Source: VGChartz

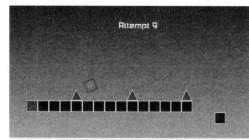

Attempt 9

»SHORTEST CONSOLE PLATFORMER

Holder: *The Impossible Game* **(FlukeDude, 2009)**
At exactly 90 seconds long if completed successfully, *The Impossible Game* is the shortest commercially available 2D platformer. Despite its brevity, this Xbox Live indie game is also one of the most difficult in its genre, with deadly obstacles appearing almost every second, and one mistake sending you right back to the start. A version has been made for the iPhone and iPod Touch.

»FASTEST COMPLETION OF SUPER MARIO BROS. 2: THE LOST LEVELS

Holder: Andrew Gardikis (USA)
The Japanese version of *Super Mario Bros. 2* is widely regarded among fans as being far more difficult than the first game in the series, and arguably one of the toughest platformers ever commercially released. This hasn't stopped gifted gamer Andrew Gardikis steaming through it in just 8 min 34 sec. Andrew recorded this run on the Wii Virtual Console after training exclusively on the SNES version of the game.

»MOST PROLIFIC VIDEOGAME CHARACTER

Holder: Mario
With 207 games to his name as of August 2010, Nintendo's very own Mario is the most prolific videogame character. Making his arcade debut in *Donkey Kong*, when he was initially called Jumpman, he has appeared on 14 different platforms, including the ill-fated Philips CD-i and Nintendo's first 3D portable console, the Virtual Boy. His most recent game, *Super Mario Galaxy 2*, launched in 2010.

TRIVIA TRAIL

While many 3D platform franchises began life in 2D, one series is particularly notable for making the journey in reverse, moving from 3D to 2D. First-person parkour-action title *Mirror's Edge* (EA, 2008) appeared in three dimensions on PC before being converted to a 2D side-scrolling format for the iPad and iPhone in April 2010, to much critical acclaim.

"YOU THINK THE SPEED OF YOUR FINGERS CAN MATCH THE STRENGTH OF MY FISTS?"

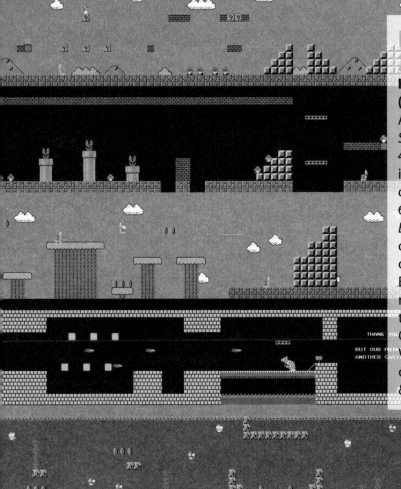

BEST-SELLING 2D PLATFORMER

Holder: *Super Mario Bros.*
(Nintendo, 1985)
A classic among 2D platformers, *Super Mario Bros.* has sold 40.24 million copies since its debut in 1985. Until the recent release of *Wii Sports*, which has now sold 63.78 million copies, *Super Mario Bros.* was the best-selling videogame of all time. Originally available on the Famicom and Nintendo Entertainment System, it has been remade and re-released several times, with versions on the N64, the Game Boy Advance and the Wii's Virtual Console. A version was even created for Nintendo's original Game & Watch handhelds.

»LONGEST WAIT FOR A VIDEOGAME SEQUEL
Holder: *The Legend of Kage*
(Taito, 1985 to 2008)
The 2D platformer The *Legend of Kage* was originally released in Japanese arcades in 1985, but fans had to wait until March 2008 to pick up the sequel on Nintendo DS – a gap of 23 years.

»FASTEST COMPLETION OF LEVEL 1 ON SONIC 2
Holder: Justin Towell (UK)
Justin Towell (UK) completed Emerald Hill, Zone 1 of the Xbox Live Arcade version of *Sonic the Hedgehog 2* (Sega, 1992) in just 21 seconds in London, UK, on 30 October 2009.

»HIGHEST SCORE ON SONIC THE HEDGEHOG
Holder: Michael Sroka (USA)
Many gamers compete for speed run records on *Sonic the Hedgehog* (Sega, 1991), but Michael Sroka is one of the few who have the staying power to attempt the record for highest score. Sroka's concentration proved up to the challenge and his tally of 404,980 points, achieved on 28 May 2010, beat the previous record by more than 120,000 points.

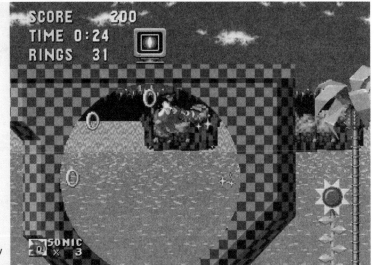

» NEW RECORD   » UPDATED RECORD

3D PLATFORMERS

NO GLASSES REQUIRED – AN EXTRA DIMENSION ADDS DEPTH TO THE PLATFORM GENRE.

»HIGHEST-GROSSING VIDEOGAME MOVIE

Holder: *Prince of Persia: The Sands of Time* **(USA, 2010)**

With a worldwide box-office gross of over $326,813,000 (£211,841,000) and rising, the film adaptation of *Prince of Persia* surpasses rival 3D platform series *Tomb Raider* as the biggest game-to-movie box-office success. While the film, starring Jake Gyllenhaal (USA, pictured) in the title role, could only manage second place in the US and UK charts on its first week of release, its staying power, combined with substantial revenues in international markets, enabled the Prince to take the Guinness World Records crown.

»MOST CRITICALLY ACCLAIMED PLATFORMER

Holder: *Super Mario Galaxy* series **(Nintendo, 2008 to present)**

With an average online rating of 97% on review aggregator site Metacritic, *Super Mario Galaxy 2* equals *Super Mario Galaxy*'s score as a near-flawless game. Both titles picked up perfect 10 scores from the notoriously critical games magazine *Edge*. Of Mario's four 3D platform adventures, only *Super Mario Sunshine*, Mario's platform debut title for the GameCube, failed to elicit a 10 from *Edge*. Thankfully, with the *Mario Galaxy* games it looks like the franchise is back on top form.

»MOST SUCCESSFUL VIDEOGAME HEROINE

Holder: Lara Croft

With global sales for the *Tomb Raider* series in excess of 28 million units, Lara Croft beats out Bayonetta, chops down Chun-Li and minces Ms Pac-Man to claim the title of gaming's most successful heroine. Lara is now such a recognizable pop-cultural figure that she has even appeared in TV adverts endorsing soft drinks.

"OUR CITIZENS ARE ONCE AGAIN SAFE FROM THE HOSTILE ENEMY ALIENS WHOSE ATTEMPTS TO INVADE AND DESTROY OUR WORLD HAVE BEEN FOILED. YOU LOOK... TIRED"

DID YOU KNOW?

In *Prince of Persia: The Sands of Time*, the titular Prince is named Dastan, which is the Azerbaijani word for "story". Azerbaijan once formed part of the Persian Empire.

»MOST PROLIFIC 3D PLATFORM SERIES

Holders: *Tomb Raider* series **(Eidos, 1996 to present)** and *Ratchet & Clank* series **(Sony, 2002 to present)**

Sharing the honours, the *Tomb Raider* and *Ratchet & Clank* series both boast nine games, not including compilations, spin-offs or expansions. *Tomb Raider* misses out on claiming the title exclusively because the latest adventure, *Lara Croft and the Guardian of Light*, is not a 3D platformer. The most recent addition to the *Ratchet & Clank* canon, *Ratchet & Clank Future: A Crack in Time*, completes the "future" trilogy and sees the gameplay innovation of the Chronosceptor, a device that can slow time.

TRIVIA TRAIL

The Xbox Live Arcade releases of *Banjo-Kazooie* and *Banjo-Tooie* finally made good on a promise that developer Rare had made in 2000. The idea way back then was a feature called "Stop 'N' Swop", whereby players would load up their original *Banjo-Kazooie* cartridge on their N64 and then swap it with a *Banjo-Tooie* cartridge to unlock secret Banjo content. Sadly, owing to hardware revisions, this feature never materialized on the N64. Luckily the Xbox Live Arcade versions of the two games introduced a revised "Stop 'N' Swop II" feature on *Banjo-Tooie* that unlocks various new achievements. In addition, the XBox Live Arcade version of *Banjo-Kazooie* unlocks bonus vehicle parts in the retail version of *Banjo-Kazooie: Nuts & Bolts*.

»FASTEST COMPLETION OF THE GALAXY'S GREATEST WAVE

Holder: Troy Whelan (USA)

Widely regarded as the trickiest level on *Super Mario Galaxy*, the *Galaxy's Greatest Wave* stage sees Mario ride a manta ray through a Mobius strip of water, which requires the gentlest of tilts to the Wii Remote. The steady hands of Troy Whelan of Mechanicsville, Virginia, USA, did it in 60.07 seconds.

FIRST SEAMLESS 3D WORLD ON A CONSOLE

Holder: *Jak & Daxter: The Precursor Legacy* **(Sony, 2001)**

Thanks to developer Naughty Dog's advanced "streaming" technology, the game world in *Jak & Daxter: The Precursor Legacy* could be explored freely without loading times slowing down gameplay. Now seamless worlds are common in 3D games.

»FASTEST COMPLETION OF BANJO-KAZOOIE

Holder: Alex Penev (Australia)

The record for the fastest speed run on the N64 original version of *Banjo-Kazooie* (Nintendo, 1998) belongs to Australia's Alex Penev, who was able to guide Banjo the bear through the game in 3 hr 32 min 45 sec on 20 February 2000.

A classic title for the N64, *Banjo-Kazooie* is now experiencing a new lease of life, having been released on Xbox Arcade Live in 2008.

» NEW RECORD
» UPDATED RECORD

TOP 10 BEST-SELLING 3D PLATFORMERS

	Game	Sales
1	*Super Mario 64 (1996)*	11.89 million
2	*Super Mario Galaxy (2007)*	8.66 million
3	*Super Mario 64 DS (2004)*	8.36 million
4	*Tomb Raider II (1997)*	7.23 million
5	*Tomb Raider (1996)*	6.36 million
6	*Super Mario Sunshine (2002)*	6.28 million
7	*Donkey Kong 64 (1999)*	5.27 million
8	*Sonic Heroes (2003)*	5.19 million
9	*Tomb Raider III (1998)*	4.85 million
10	*Banjo-Kazooie (1998)*	3.65 million

Source: VGChartz

"YOU'RE A NINJA, RIGHT? A WHILE BACK THERE WERE A LOT OF NINJAS DRESSED LIKE YOU RUNNING AROUND HERE, BUT THEY DISAPPEARED AS OF LATE. I WONDER IF THEY WERE ALL KILLED?"

WWW.GUINNESSWORLDRECORDS.COM/GAMERS **113**

GRAPHIC ADVENTURE

POINT 'N' CLICK, PICK UP AND USE – YOU NEED TO SOLVE THE PUZZLES TO PROGRESS THE STORY.

DID YOU KNOW?

At E3 2006, David Cage, CEO of Quantic Dream, the developer behind *Heavy Rain* (Sony, 2010), presented a brief animation dubbed "The Casting" on an early version of the PlayStation 3. His aim was to demonstrate the performance-capture expertise of his studio, as well as the impressive abilities of the then-unreleased PS3. As its title suggests, the demo takes the form of a casting tape in which virtual actress "Mary Smith" is auditioning for a role in *Heavy Rain*.

»LONGEST WAIT FOR A DIRECTOR'S CUT

Holder: *Broken Sword: The Shadow of the Templars: The Director's Cut* **(Ubisoft, 2009)**

Released 13 years after the PC original, the Wii and DS versions of Charles Cecil's (UK) seminal adventure game *Broken Sword: The Shadow of the Templars* represent the longest-ever wait for a director's cut of a videogame. The new versions of the game added a brand new opening section featuring female protagonist Nicole Collard, as well as new puzzles and original character art from *Watchmen* artist Dave Gibbons (UK). In 2010, *The Director's Cut* was also released for the iPhone and iPad.

»FIRST TEXT ADVENTURE ENGINE FOR iPHONE

Holder: *Frotz* **(Craig Smith, 2008)**

The precursors to modern graphic adventures, text adventures use many of the same gameplay traditions as their more aesthetically appealing progeny. The first app to allow players to experience these gaming relics on the iPhone was *Frotz*, released to the App Store on 11 August 2008.

"WHY DO YOU HIDE, STUPID ALIENS? MR ZURKON ONLY WISHES TO KILL YOU."

»LONGEST SCRIPT FOR A GRAPHIC ADVENTURE

Holder: *Heavy Rain* **(Sony, 2010)**
Running to over 2,000 pages and with more than 40,000 words of dialogue, the script for *Heavy Rain* easily ranks as the longest ever written for a graphic adventure. In creating this immersive, visually driven game, which is often described as an "interactive movie", director David Cage (France) oversaw the work of 70 actors and stuntmen over a period of nine months to record all the motion-capture footage it required. The hard work was undoubtedly worth it – having sold more than 1.4 million copies, *Heavy Rain* is also the **»best-selling graphic adventure on the PlayStation 3.**

»FIRST AUDIO COMMENTARY FOR A DOWNLOADABLE CONSOLE GAME

Holder: *Monkey Island 2: LeChuck's Revenge: Special Edition* **(LucasArts, 2010)**
The special edition of *Monkey Island 2: LeChuck's Revenge* has a number of bonus features, including a significant visual upgrade (see images above), improved sound and the inclusion of concept art. But arguably the most notable addition is a DVD-style scene commentary, featuring series creators Ron Gilbert, David Grossman and Tim Schafer (all USA), which is the first audio commentary for a downloadable console game.

"THIS RENAISSANCE OF [GRAPHIC] ADVENTURE GAMES IS REALLY EXCITING AND I THINK THE NEXT FEW YEARS ARE GOING TO BE AMAZING."
/BROKEN SWORD CREATOR CHARLES CECIL ON THE RE-EMERGENCE OF THE GRAPHIC ADVENTURE.

»MOST CRITICALLY ACCLAIMED THIRD-PARTY Wii EXCLUSIVE

Holder: *Zack & Wiki: Quest for Barbaros' Treasure* **(Capcom, 2007)**
Boasting a review average of 87% on aggregator site Metacritic, the most critically acclaimed third-party Wii exclusive title is *Zack & Wiki: Quest for Barbaros' Treasure*. The game was praised for its innovative use of the Wii remote as well as its puzzle design and striking art style. Sadly for publisher Capcom, the critical acclaim did not translate into sales success, with under 300,000 copies of the game sold – a figure that Chris Kramer (USA) Capcom's Senior Director of Communications and Community called "abysmal".

»LONGEST-RUNNING EPISODIC ADVENTURE SERIES

Holder: *Sam & Max* series **(Telltale Games, 2006 to present)**
Running for four years and three seasons, the *Sam & Max* series is the longest-running episodic adventure series in videogames. *Sam & Max: Season One* was released on PC in October 2006. The third season, *The Devil's Playhouse*, arrived in April 2010.

»MOST WIDELY PORTED GAME ENGINE

Holder: SCUMM **(LucasArts, 1987)**
Having been ported to 14 different platforms, LucasArts' SCUMM scripting language has appeared on more formats than any other single game engine. Many adventure games of the 8- and 16-bit era used SCUMM – including *Maniac Mansion*, for which the system was developed.

FIRST 10 GRAPHIC ADVENTURE GAMES TO USE THE SCUMM SCRIPT-CREATION UTILITY

	Game	Year
1	*Maniac Mansion*	*1987*
2	*Zak McKracken and the Alien Mindbenders*	*1988*
3	*Indiana Jones and the Last Crusade*	*1989*
4	*Loom*	*1990*
5	*The Secret of Monkey Island*	*1990*
6	*Monkey Island 2: LeChuck's Revenge*	*1991*
7	*Indiana Jones and the Fate of Atlantis*	*1992*
8	*Maniac Mansion: Day of the Tentacle*	*1993*
9	*Sam & Max Hit the Road*	*1993*
10	*Full Throttle*	*1995*

Source: LucasArts

» NEW RECORD   » UPDATED RECORD

FIGHTING GAMES

FIGHT! IT'S AS SIMPLE AS IT SOUNDS – TWO PLAYERS ENTER THE GAME, BUT ONLY ONE CAN LEAVE VICTORIOUS.

» BEST-SELLING 3D FIGHTING GAME SERIES

Holder: *Tekken*
(Namco Bandai, 1995 to present)
A perennial favourite of virtual pugilists everywhere, *Tekken* is the clear champion of the 3D fighter genre with 31.2 million copies sold worldwide since its debut in 1995 (2009's *Tekken 6* pictured). This figure is more than triple that of its closest rivals, including its Namco Bandai stablemate the *Soul* series (8.03 million copies), Sega's *Virtua Fighter* (6.54 million copies) and Tecmo's *Dead or Alive* (4 million copies, not including the *Xtreme Beach Volleyball* sub-series).

"HOW DARE YOU ADDRESS ME LIKE A COMMON PAPERBACK!"

WHAT ARE THEY?

Kick, punch, it's all in the mind… There are few competitive videogames as pure as the fighting game, a genre that tests players' reactions, dexterity and ability to read their opponent's playing style in a series of close-combat bouts. Since the early 1990s, fighting games have introduced many of the features seen in real life combat, including blocking, counter-attacks and the stringing together of attacks into "combos". Born in the arcades, fighting games, with their short match lengths, are perfectly suited to competitive play and today there are numerous tournaments staged across the world.

WHO SAYS SO?

Simon Parkin's (UK) career in videogame journalism began in 2002 as a freelancer for British games bible *Edge*. Over the past eight years he has continued to write for the magazine as well as a wide variety of British and American websites including Yahoo, Offworld and Gamasutra. Simon now primarily works for Eurogamer. net, where he does the majority of his work writing thoughtful reviews, interviews and features. Additionally, Simon works as a game designer and producer at Littleloud, a boutique developer based in Brighton, UK. His writing is collected on the gaming blog www.chewingpixels.com.

CONTENTS

STREET FIGHTER

CRITICAL HIT!

THE MOST FAMOUS FIGHTING SERIES OF ALL, WITH AN ONGOING ARRAY OF UPDATES, SEQUELS AND SPIN-OFFS.

DID YOU KNOW?

Making his debut in 2009's *Super Street Fighter IV*, Hakan (pictured above) is a Turkish oil wrestler who is billed as "president of the world's leading edible oil manufacturer".

TRIVIA TRAIL

In the 1993 kung-fu movie *City Hunter* (Hong Kong/Japan), actor Jackie Chan (Hong Kong) is at one point smashed into an arcade machine running *Street Fighter II*, an event that causes him to take on the attributes of the *Street Fighter* characters E. Honda, Chun-Li, Guile and Dhalsim. But while Chan parodied the *SFII* characters, the game's M. Bison was originally intended as a parody of real-life boxer Mike Tyson (USA). In order to avoid a potential lawsuit, Capcom rotated the names of three of the boss characters for different international versions of the game.

FIRST PLAYABLE FEMALE CHARACTER IN A FIGHTING GAME
Holder: Chun-Li
Ex-Interpol agent Chun-Li was the first playable female character in a fighting game. She made her debut in *Street Fighter II: The World Warrior* in 1991 and has appeared in every major *Street Fighter* title since. Chun-Li means "Beautiful Spring" in Mandarin Chinese and her character enjoys the distinction of being the **first fighting game character to star in a movie spin-off**, namely *Street Fighter: The Legend of Chun-Li* (Canada/India/USA/Japan, 2009).

"IT'S THE STENCH OF BETRAYAL. THE ODOUR OF THAT ACCURSED SPARDA! I WILL ANNIHILATE EVERY LAST BLOOD RELATION OF SPARDA!"

82: THE NUMBER OF PLAYABLE CHARACTERS THAT HAVE FEATURED IN THE VARIOUS FLAVOURS OF *STREET FIGHTER* SINCE THE GAME'S INITIAL RELEASE IN 1987.

MOST PROLIFIC FIGHTING GAME SERIES

Holder: *Street Fighter* **(Capcom, 1987 to present)**
With 133 commercially released games in the series across all platforms, *Street Fighter* is the most prolific fighting game franchise. This accolade is aided by publisher Capcom's habit of releasing numerous *Street Fighter* remixes with additional characters and added adjectives in their titles. The longest of these is 2000's *Super Street Fighter II X for Matching Service: Grand Master Challenge*, a Japanese Dreamcast port that supports online play.

»MOST EXPENSIVE GAME-LICENSED FIGHTING STICK

Holder: Mad Catz Arcade FightStick: Tournament Edition
With an RRP of £149.99 ($229), *Street Fighter IV*'s Arcade FightStick: Tournament Edition, a licensed controller manufactured by Mad Catz, is certainly expensive, but that's because it uses the same premium quality Sanwa Denshii components as Capcom's arcade cabinets. Weighing a solid 3 kg (6 lb 8 oz), this competition-standard stick has proven particularly popular among *Street Fighter* pro-gamers, who often customize the main panel artwork for live events.

»LONGEST RUN OF WINS AGAINST HUMAN OPPONENTS IN STREET FIGHTER IV
Holder: Ryan Hart (UK)
Playing as Sagat, Ryan Hart remained undefeated for 169 straight matches of *Street Fighter IV* (2008) at GAME in the Prospect Centre, Hull, UK, on 27 March 2010. His fastest victory was a 7-second defeat of Chun-Li.

»MOST ARCADE CABINETS SOLD
Holder: *Street Fighter II* (Capcom, 1991)
Since its release in 1991, *Street Fighter II* has sold 6.3 million coin-operated arcade cabinets. An early arcade title for Capcom's CPS hardware, it was designed by Akira Nishitani (aka Nin-Nin) and Akira Yasuda (aka Akiman) (both Japan).

»MOST PROLIFIC INTER-FRANCHISE FIGHTER
Holder: *Street Fighter* (Capcom, 1995 to present)
Street Fighter has spawned the most inter-franchise fighting games, with 13 separate titles pitting its warriors against those of other franchises. The first of these was the Marvel-licensed *X-Men: Children of the Atom* (Capcom, 1995).

TOP 10 BEST-SELLING GAMES IN THE *STREET FIGHTER* SERIES

	Game	Platforms	Sales
1	Street Fighter II: The World Warrior (1991)	SNES	6.30 million
2	Super Street Fighter II Turbo (1994)	SNES	4.10 million
3	Street Fighter IV (2008)	Xbox 360, PS3	3.11 million
4	Super Street Fighter II (1993)	SNES	2.00 million
5	Street Fighter II: Special Champion Edition (1992)	Mega Drive	1.66 million
6	Street Fighter Alpha 3 (1998)	PlayStation	1.03 million
7	Super Street Fighter IV (2009)	Xbox, PS3	0.80 million
8	Street Fighter Alpha 2 (1996)	PlayStation	0.57 million
9	Street Fighter Alpha: Warrior's Dreams (1996)	PlayStation/ Saturn	0.43 million
10	Street Fighter Alpha 3 MAX (2006)	Sony, PSP	0.28 million

Source: VGChartz

»MOST VIEWED FIGHT
Holder: *Street Fighter III: Third Strike* Loser's Final, EVO 2004
The most viewed fighting game bout is that of Daigo Umehara (Japan) versus Justin Wong (USA) in the loser's bracket final of the Evolution (EVO) Championship Series 2004's *Street Fighter III: 3rd Strike* (1999) competition. While there are many videos of the fight online, the most popular has been viewed by at least 2,068,960 YouTube users as of June 2010. The match has so many hits because it features Umehara's dramatic comeback in the final stages of the fight. You can see the crowd becoming excited and getting to their feet as Umehara uses Ken to full-parry Chun-Li's Houyoku-Sen Super Art before executing his 12-hit Super Art Finish special move for the win.

» NEW RECORD » UPDATED RECORD

2D FIGHTERS

YOU CAN MOVE FORWARD OR BACK, BLOCK OR ATTACK, BUT THERE'S NOWHERE TO HIDE IN 2D FIGHTING.

NIGHTMARE GEESE   56   TERRY BOGA

03 HITS

»LARGEST NEO-GEO GAME

Holder: *The King of Fighters 2003* **(SNK Playmore, 2003)**
With a cartridge that weighed in at 716 MB, *The King of Fighters 2003* is the largest game made for the Neo-Geo system. Neo-Geo games and much of their processing power were contained on cartridges, which offered an arcade-like experience. As such, cart size was used to indicate to buyers how much memory the game used – the higher the MB of the cart, the more graphically complex the game.

» NEW RECORD
» UPDATED RECORD

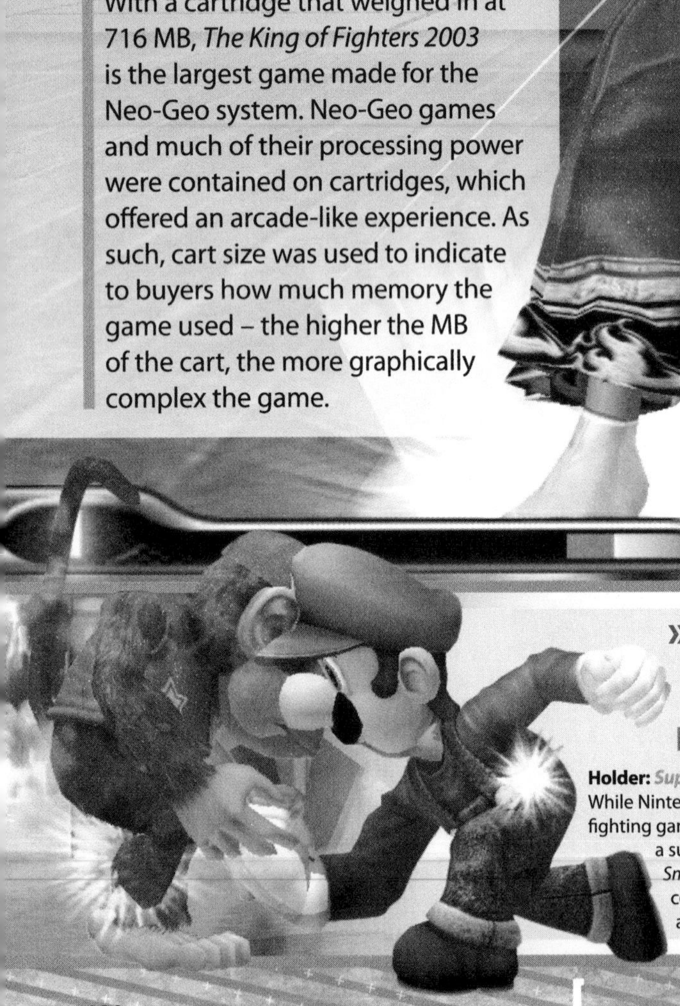

»BEST-SELLING FIGHTING SERIES ON NINTENDO HARDWARE

Holder: *Super Smash Bros.* **(Nintendo, 1999 to present)**
While Nintendo's consoles have never been known for fighting games, the *Super Smash Bros.* series has been a surprising hit, with 9.46 million units of *Super Smash Bros. Brawl* (2008) sold worldwide and combined global sales of 22.09 million units across the three games in the series.

»MOST KOs ON SUPER SMASH BROS. MELEE

Holder: James Bouchier (Canada)
James "TwIsTeD_EnEmY" Bouchier super smashed, mêléed and brawled his way to 23 KOs in a single match on *Super Smash Bros. Melee* (Nintendo, 2001) in Aberystwyth, UK, on 16 June 2010.

"WRITHE IN MY CAGE OF TORMENT, MY FRIEND."

»LONGEST-SERVING VIDEOGAME VOICE ACTOR

Holder: Ed Boon (USA) **(1993 to present)**

Aside from creating the *Mortal Kombat* fighting franchise with fellow Chicagoan John Tobias, videogame programmer Ed Boon also has the distinction of having the longest career voicing the same videogame character. Boon (above left) has provided the voice for Scorpion in the *Mortal Kombat* series since the game's initial release in October 1993.

> "FOR ME, GRAPHICS IN A 2D FIGHTER HAVE TO RETAIN A HAND-DRAWN FEEL, NO MATTER WHAT TECHNOLOGY IS USED."
> /TOSHIMICHI MORI, DESIGNER ON *BLAZBLUE: CALAMITY TRIGGER*.

DID YOU KNOW?

The King of Fighters 2003 was the last in the series to be developed for the Neo-Geo and, like previous entries in the franchise, featured fighting teams from a variety of other SNK games, such as *Fatal Fury* and *Ikari Warriors*.

»LONGEST TITLE FOR A FIGHTING GAME

Holder: *Last Blade 2: Heart of the Samurai* **(SNK, 1998)**

The full Japanese title for the critically acclaimed Neo-Geo sword-based fighter is the 67-character *Bakumatsu Roman Dai Ni Maku: Gekka no Kenshi – Tsuki ni Saku Hana, Chiri Yuku Hana*. In English this roughly translates as "The Last Blade 2 – Romance of the Bakumatsu Act II: Swordsman of the Moonlight – On the Moon a Flower Blooming, a Petal Falling". Thankfully, the game's maker, SNK, chose a more concise title for the English-language-market version.

TRIVIA TRAIL

Arc System Works' 2008 hand-drawn arcade fighter *Blazblue: Calamity Trigger* saw a number of additional features when it was ported to the Xbox 360 and PS3 in 2009, including various unlockable "Astral Heats" – difficult-to-achieve instant kill moves.

»LONGEST FIGHTING GAME MARATHON

N64 die-hards Wes Marziano, Andy Wilpizeski, Dave SanFelice and Brian Kothe (left to right, all USA) played *Super Smash Bros.* (Nintendo, 1999) on the N64 for 26 hr 27 min 40 sec at Pennsylvania State University, USA, on 21 March 2010.

»MOST OFFICIAL SEQUELS IN A FIGHTING GAME

Holder: *The King of Fighters* **(SNK Playmore, 1994 to present)**

Since the series' inception in 1994, the popular *King of Fighters* games have enjoyed 12 main title entries. A 13th instalment is due to be released by publisher SNK Playmore in 2010.

TOP 10 SURVIVAL MODE CLEAR TIMES FOR *GAROU: MARK OF THE WOLVES* ON XBOX LIVE

	Player	Time
1	MagnusLux	1 hr 46 min 2 sec
2	Regular MOW	1 hr 58 min 55 sec
3	Azutou	2 hr 3 min 39 sec
4	monkey lUffY	2 hr 3 min 55 sec
5	x yuitamu x	2 hr 7 min 23 sec
6	Babel Lafin	2 hr 8 min 45 sec
7	Hook sensei	2 hr 10 min 25 sec
8	Vandermonde	2 hr 11 min 13 sec
9	Playar h	2 hr 15 min 34 sec
10	X2000Gignited	2 hr 17 min 41 sec

Source: In-game leaderboard

3D FIGHTERS

IN A 3D FIGHTER YOU CAN DODGE AND WEAVE, BUT YOU STILL NEED TO LAND BLOWS TO WIN BOUTS.

»» NEW RECORD
»» UPDATED RECORD

»LARGEST CHARACTER ROSTER IN A FIGHTING GAME

Holder: *Tobal 2* **(Square Enix, 1997)**
Square Enix's Japan-only 3D fighting game *Tobal 2* features a grand total of 200 playable characters. Of this figure, 15 are the core characters, who are playable at the start of the game, while the 185 additional characters (including dogs, lizards and even variants of the company's iconic mascot, the Chocobo) must be unlocked via the game's extensive quest mode. *Tobal 2* also boasts the talents of Japanese videogames soundtrack composer Takayuki Nakamura, whose credits include *Virtua Fighter* and *Ehrgeiz: God Bless the Ring*.

»MOST CONSECUTIVE WINS IN TEKKEN 6

Holder: Eliot Smith-Walters (UK)
Seasoned gamer Eliot Smith-Walters (aka "Shadowforce") took down the then UK *Tekken* champion Phil McKenzie (aka "Dinosaur") and 67 other wannabes to rack up an impressive 68-win streak on *Tekken 6* at the Movie, Comics and Media (MCM) Expo in London, UK, on 24 October 2009.

"YOU HAVE ENERGY LIKE A LITTLE ANGRY BATTERY WITH NO FRIENDS."

»MOST SUCCESSFUL WEAPONS-BASED 3D FIGHTER

Holder: *Soul* series **(Namco Bandai, 1998 to 2009)**
The sword-heavy *Soul Edge/Soul Calibur* games have amassed combined sales of 8.03 million copies across all six titles in the series. These sales can be sliced into a 4.23-million prime cut for the US market, a 2.09-million stake for Europe and a 1.71-million chop for Japan.

1512   1617/2100   81/2005

»FIRST RPG SPIN-OFF FIGHTING GAME

Holder: *Dissidia: Final Fantasy* (Square Enix, 2008)
Square Enix's *Dissidia: Final Fantasy*, released for the Sony PSP in 2008, is the first fighting game to result from an RPG series. The game features 24 characters pulled from various titles in the *Final Fantasy* series. While 1998's *Ehrgeiz* featured characters from *Final Fantasy VII*, these were guest characters.

DID YOU KNOW?

The highly regarded European Dreamcast version of *Soul Calibur* lives on thanks to Namco Bandai's decision to port it to the Xbox 360 via the Xbox Live Arcade service.

»FIRST FIGHTING GAME TO USE A TWIN-STICK CONTROL SCHEME

Holder: *Virtual-On* (Sega, 1995)
Sega's arcade robot fighting game, *Cyber Troopers Virtual-On*, employed a twin-stick control scheme to simulate the controls of giant walking robots. Using combinations of stick movements, it's possible to make your "mecha" dash from side to side, leap into the air and even strafe your opponent. Fighter-jet-like stick-mounted triggers allow players to launch missile attacks while moving around.

»MOST PROLIFIC FIGHTING GAME DESIGNER

Holder: Seiichi Ishii (Japan)
Japanese game designer Seiichi Ishii has worked on a total of seven fighters – he was lead designer on *Virtua Fighter*, *Tekken*, *Tekken 2*, *Tobal No. 1*, *Tobal 2*, *Ehrgeiz* and *Kakuto Chojin: Back Alley Brutal*.

»HIGHEST SCORE ON EHRGEIZ

Holder: Tom Triffon (USA)
On 12 September 1999, Tom Triffon from Stanton, California, USA, scored 82,190 points playing the arcade version of *Ehrgeiz* (Namco, 1998). The game was played under the stringent Twin Galaxies tournament settings.

TRIVIA TRAIL

Following in the path of *Dead or Alive*, which made it to the silver screen in *DOA: Dead or Alive* (USA/Germany/UK, 2006), the next 3D fighter franchise to make its big screen debut is *Tekken* (Japan/USA, 2010), starring Luke Goss (UK), one half of British pop duo Bros.

The film's sets were built at the Louisiana State Fair Grounds in Shreveport, Louisiana, USA. The architecturally striking Hirsch Memorial Coliseum, where many of the film's key fight scenes take place, is also located at the State Fair Grounds.

TOP 10 BEST-SELLING 3D FIGHTING GAMES

	Game	Sales
1	*Tekken 3 (1998)*	*6.91 million*
2	*Tekken 2 (1996)*	*5.45 million*
3	*Tekken Tag Tournament (2000)*	*3.94 million*
4	*Tekken 5 (2005)*	*3.66 million*
5	*Tekken 4 (2002)*	*3.31 million*
6	*Soul Calibur II (2003)*	*3.28 million*
7	*Tekken (1995)*	*3.18 million*
8	*Mortal Kombat: Deadly Alliance (2002)*	*2.17 million*
9	*Virtua Fighter 3 (1998)*	*1.93 million*
10	*Dissidia: Final Fantasy (2008)*	*1.76 million*

Source: VGChartz

HACK AND SLASH

CUTTING ENEMIES DOWN TO SIZE WITH BLADES OR OTHER WEAPONS – THESE GAMES ARE ALL ABOUT VISCERAL ACTION.

»MOST SUCCESSFUL HACK AND SLASH DESIGNER

Holder: Hideki Kamiya (Japan)
Turned down as a games designer when he applied to Sega upon leaving university, Hideki Kamiya went on to become the design director behind hack and slashers *Bayonetta* (pictured) and the *Devil May Cry* series. Altogether, his hack and slash titles have sold more than 10 million copies worldwide.

DID YOU KNOW?

Bayonetta has several skills at her disposal, chief among them her magical abilities. Not only can she hurl fireballs, this wicked witch can also conjour elaborate mechanisms of death, such as a giant guillotine, to dispatch her foes – well, these games are described as "hack and slash" for good reason…

"AN EXTRA LIFE, I DO NOT CARE, IT WILL NOT HELP YOU SCRUFFY BEAR!"

TOP 10 SPEED RUNS IN *NINJA GAIDEN II*

	Player	Time
1	takemaro	1 hr 24 min 52 sec
2	CHINA NDR	1 hr 31 min 26 sec
3	platinumpwnzor	1 hr 32 min 05 sec
4	Khaled 23	1 hr 42 min 08 sec
5	Scar Leone	1 hr 48 min 28 sec
6	tkiu umberger	1 hr 48 min 34 sec
7	Death Mental	1 hr 50 min 11 sec
8	Palavikyubi	1 hr 50 min 57 sec
9	PikachuJorge	1 hr 54 min 23 sec
10	TamanegiKensi	1 hr 54 min 44 sec

Source: Xbox 360 leaderboard

»MOST CRITICALLY ACCLAIMED HACK AND SLASH GAME
Holder: *Ninja Gaiden Black* (Tecmo, 2005)
Both Capcom's *Devil May Cry* and *Ninja Gaiden Black* share a score of 94% on the game reviews aggregator Metacritic, but on Gamerankings.com *Ninja Gaiden Black* hacks in ahead with a score of 94.76% over *Devil May Cry*'s 92.6%.

»HIGHEST SCORE IN NINJA GAIDEN
Holder: Jason Wilson (USA)
Hailing from Anaheim, California, USA, Jason Wilson scored 19,100 points on the original arcade version of *Ninja Gaiden* (Tecmo 1988).

FIRST CONSOLE GAME TO USE NARRATIVE CUTSCENES
Holder: *Ninja Gaiden* (Tecmo, 1988)
When it was first ported from the arcade to the Famicom/NES in 1988, *Ninja Gaiden* employed a short animated sequence, or "cutscene", to advance the story. Although some earlier games had included animated interludes, *Ninja Gaiden* was the first major instance of this method of advancing the plot.

»MOST DIVERSE RANGE OF PRODUCTS PROMOTED BY A VIDEOGAME
Holder: *Sengoku Basara* (Capcom, 2005)
Popular hack and slash title *Sengoku Basara* has been licensed to promote at least 10 different consumer products in its native Japan, including takeaway pizza, rice, cider and a chain of karaoke bars. Characters from the game were even used in adverts designed to encourage citizens to vote.

BEST-SELLING HACK AND SLASH SERIES
Holder: *Devil May Cry* (Capcom, 2001 to present)
Hideki Kamiya's (Japan) *Devil May Cry* defined the guts and gore of the hack and slash genre. To this day, the series remains a cut above the rest of its rivals, with sales of 9.15 million units as of October 2010. The best-selling entry in the franchise is still the original *Devil May Cry*, which has sold 2.78 million copies worldwide. But the most recent adventure for Dante and his friends, 2008's *Devil May Cry 4*, is right on its pointed tail having enjoyed global sales of 2.57 million units to the same date.

»FIRST HIGH-DEFINITION REMASTERING OF A PS2 GAME
Holder: *God of War Collection* (Sony, 2010)
On 17 November 2010, the first two *God of War* games were given a high-definition makeover and released on Blu-ray as a PS3 exclusive. The titles, formerly only available on the PS2, are the first games to be rereleased in a remastered format, with narrative adventures *Ico* and *Shadow of the Colossus* due to follow (check out pp.104–105 for more on these titles).

TRIVIA TRAIL
Religious protesters caused a stir during E3 2009, when they labelled EA's game *Dante's Inferno*, which is set during the the Third Crusade, as sacrilegious and insensitive to people's beliefs. A few days after the event, EA spokesperson Tammy Schacter admitted the publisher had hired actors and that there was no actual protest.

» NEW RECORD
» UPDATED RECORD

"DON'T THINK THE DYNASTY WARRIORS SERIES HAS REACHED ITS APEX YET… THERE IS STILL MUCH SPACE FOR THE SERIES TO EVOLVE."
/DYNASTY WARRIORS' CREATIVE FORCE KOU SHIBUSAWA ON THE SCOPE OF HIS GAMES.

»MOST PLAYABLE CHARACTERS IN A HACK AND SLASH SERIES
Holder: *Dynasty Warriors* (Tecmo Koei, 1997 to present)
Since its initial release on the PlayStation in 1997, *Dynasty Warriors* (or *Sangokumusou* as it was known in Japan) has seen a total of 52 playable characters grace its roster. The vast majority of these are based on historical Chinese figures, such as the military leaders Zhang He and Wei Yan. The games themselves feature a mixture of historical battles and entirely fictional fights.

COMBAT SPORTS

BRINGING A SPORTING ELEMENT TO THE FIGHTING GENRE, COMBAT SPORTS GAMES LET YOU FIGHT AS A PRO.

»MOST PLAYABLE CHARACTERS IN A MIXED MARTIAL ARTS GAME

Holder: *UFC Undisputed 2010* **(THQ, 2010)**
In addition to 84 playable UFC characters, THQ's *UFC Undisputed 2010* also features basketball star Shaquille O'Neal and mixed martial artists the Tapout Crew, who can be unlocked via a code, making for a total of 88 playable characters.

"A MAN CHOOSES. A SLAVE OBEYS."

TOP 10 BEST-SELLING AMERICAN WRESTLING GAMES

	Game	Platform	Sales
1	WWE SmackDown! vs. RAW 2008	Various	6.81 million
2	WWF Warzone	Various	4.69 million
3	WWE SmackDown! vs. RAW 2009	Various	4.29 million
4	WWE SmackDown! vs. RAW 2010	Various	3.95 million
5	WWE SmackDown! vs. RAW 2007	Various	3.47 million
6	WWE SmackDown! vs. RAW 2006	Various	3.45 million
7	WWF SmackDown! 2: Know Your Role	PlayStation	3.20 million
8	WWF SmackDown!	PlayStation	3.11 million
9	WWE SmackDown! Shut Your Mouth	PS2	2.80 million
10	WWE SmackDown! vs. Raw	PS2	2.70 million

Source: VGChartz

»MOST VENUES IN A BOXING GAME

Holder: *Don King Presents: Prizefighter* (**2K Sports, 2008**)
With a grand total of 22 gyms and arenas, *Don King Presents: Prizefighter* has more venues than any other boxing game. Fight locations include classic US arenas such as Madison Square Garden in New York City, and Atlantic City's Trump's Taj Mahal and Boardwalk Hall.

TRIVIA TRAIL

UFC president Dana White was so unhappy at the news that EA Sports were planning their own Mixed Martial Arts (MMA) game that he banned all contracted UFC fighters from participating in the project on pain of expulsion from the UFC. White claims that prior to developing the successful *UFC* series with rival games publisher THQ, he approached EA Sports with a proposal to make a UFC game, but his idea was rebuffed.

»FASTEST VICTORY IN UFC UNDISPUTED 2009 (XBOX 360)

Holder: Patrick Scott Patterson (USA)
A denizen of Denton, Texas, USA, Patrick Scott Patterson showed his mastery of THQ's *UFC Undisputed 2009* by securing a win in 2 min 2 sec in "Expert" mode. If you want to try to beat him, remember that no custom characters are allowed for this record.

»FASTEST VICTORY IN WWE WRESTLEMANIA XIX

Holder: James Bouchier (Canada)
On 3 May 2010, James Bouchier, who is based in Aberystwyth, UK, scored a 21-second victory on *WWE Wrestlemania XIX* for GameCube. The game was played in the tournament setting of "Expert" difficulty with "Pin" and "Submit" options on.

»MOST PROLIFIC DEVELOPER OF COMBAT SPORTS GAMES

Holder: Yuke's Co. Ltd
With 71 commercially released combat sports games, including the extensive *WWE* series, female boxing game *Rumble Roses*, and *UFC Undisputed*, Yuke's Co. Ltd of Osaka, Japan, is the most prolific developer of combat sports games. Perhaps unsurprisingly, Yuke's also owns a majority stake in New Japan Pro Wrestling, a Japanese version of WWE.

»BEST-SELLING PURE BOXING GAME

Holder: *Mike Tyson's Punch-Out!!* (Nintendo, 1987)
Gaming's super-heavyweight champ *Wii Sports* includes boxing as one of its challenges and has sold 62.93 million copies worldwide, which is more than any other videogame in history. However, in terms of titles where boxing is the main attraction, *Mike Tyson's Punch-Out!!* for the NES holds the record, with over 3 million units sold.

» NEW RECORD » UPDATED RECORD

"WE'VE DONE A LOT OF WORK WITH OUR PHYSICS."
/ THQ GAME DESIGNER JONATHAN DURR, ON WHAT'S NEW IN *WWE SMACKDOWN VS. RAW 2010*.

»FASTEST VICTORY IN WWE LEGENDS OF WRESTLEMANIA

Holder: Carmelo Consiglio (USA)
One for hardcore wrestling fans: Carmelo Consiglio from Encino, California, USA, claimed victory on the "Legendary" difficulty setting in *WWE Legends of Wrestlemania* in a time of 55 seconds. Carmelo was playing the NTSC PS3 version of the game with the "Disqualification", "Give Up" and "Pin" options all switched on.

"TO BUILD A CASTLE OF APPROPRIATE SIZE HE WILL NEED A GREAT MANY STONES. BUT WHAT HE'S GOT NOW FEELS LIKE AN ACCEPTABLE START."

WWW.GUINNESSWORLDRECORDS.COM/GAMERS   **127**

PUZZLE GAMES

WHERE THERE IS A PROBLEM THERE MUST BE A SOLUTION, AND WITH PUZZLE GAMES THAT'S WHERE THE FUN IS.

»TOP PAID-FOR APP STORE GAME IN MOST COUNTRIES

Holder: *Angry Birds* **(Chillingo, 2009)**

Physics puzzler *Angry Birds* has been recognized as the top paid-for game in Apple's App Store in a record 67 territories worldwide, including the US and UK, as of October 2010. Released by publisher Chillingo on 10 December 2009, sales of *Angry Birds* are now in excess of 6.5 million copies.

"IT IS PITCH BLACK. YOU ARE LIKELY TO BE EATEN BY A GRUE."

WHAT ARE THEY?

The puzzle genre spans many types of games, including logic, spatial, physics, word and, most famously, block puzzles. All of these game types require players to engage their brain and solve a range of logical and conceptual challenges, often with a limited set of tools at their disposal. There may also be time challenges or other action elements involved, which test reflex speed and co-ordination as well as brainpower. Although puzzle games have their own place in the videogame canon, their influence can be seen reaching into every genre, whether it's pushing the correct combination of switches in *Duke Nukem,* finding out how to acquire a gold chocobo in *Final Fantasy* or figuring out which block to push in *Tomb Raider.*

WHO SAYS SO?

Mark Walton (UK) got his first taste of videogames jumping snakes in *Pitfall!* on the Atari 2600 in the '80s. He now writes for GameSpot UK, reviewing and previewing the latest games as well as hosting the GameSpot UK podcast. A self-proclaimed puzzle-game fiend, Mark loves nothing better than reminding people of his "Extreme Grand Master of *Peggle*" status, and spending his weekends trawling the internet for the latest developments and innovations in puzzle games from indie developers.

CONTENTS

TETRIS

CRITICAL HIT!

FIT BLOCKS TOGETHER TO MAKE COMPLETE LINES, WHICH THEN DISAPPEAR BEFORE YOUR EYES. THAT'S TETRIS.

DID YOU KNOW?

Tetris is the inspiration behind a challenge on the Japanese gameshow *Tonneruzu no Minasan no Okage deshita*. The task, known as *Hole in the Wall* in English-speaking territories, involves a foam wall with a hole the shape of a *Tetris* block that moves towards the contestants. The task for the contestants is simple – they must twist and contort themselves to fit through the hole. If they fail to do so, the wall pushes them into a pool of water.

»LARGEST OFFICIAL TETRIS ARCADE GAME

Holder: *Tetris Giant* **(Sega, 2009)**
Debuting in Japanese arcades in December 2009, Sega's *Tetris Giant* is the largest officially licensed version of Alexey Pajitnov's classic game. The massive cabinet, which measures 1.6 m wide, 1.7 m deep and 2.2 m high (5 ft 2 in by 5 ft 6 in by 7 ft 2 in), features two oversized controller sticks and a huge 177 cm (70 in) display. One thing is certain, you won't miss it at your local arcade!

"THEY'RE SINKING CITIES WITH A GIANT WORM!"

"I THINK THAT TETRIS INSPIRED THIS KIND OF MOTTO: 'EASY TO LEARN, HARD TO MASTER.'"

/ALEXEY PAJITNOV.

»MOST PORTED VIDEOGAME

Holder: *Tetris* **(Alexey Pajitnov, 1985)**
Originally created on a Soviet Elektronika 60 computer in 1985, *Tetris* has since been ported to over 65 different gaming platforms. The most successful of these ports is Nintendo's version that came bundled with the Game Boy – it has sold 35 million copies worldwide.

MOST EXPENSIVE VERSION OF TETRIS

Holder: *Nintendo World Championships Gold Edition* **(Nintendo, 1990)**
The special edition of *Tetris* included on the *Nintendo World Championships Gold Edition* cartridge ranks as the most expensive version of the game. A total of 26 such cartridges were given away as competition prizes by *Nintendo Power* magazine in 1990. One gold cartridge was bought in 2008 by James Baker of New York, USA, for an astonishing $15,000 (£7,600). Grey versions of the cartridge that were given away as part of an official Nintendo videogame competition are less rare, though there are still only 90 copies of these in circulation.

MOST LINES ON TETRIS DX (GAME BOY COLOR)

Holder: Harry Hong (USA)
On 13 September 2007, Harry Hong stacked up a total of 4,988 lines in a game of *Tetris DX* on the Game Boy Color at his home in Los Angeles, California, USA. Harry also reached the highest possible score, hitting the 999,999-point limit for the GBC game. A true *Tetris* junkie, Harry has also achieved the highest possible score for the NES version of the game, again with 999,999 points.

»MOST DOWNLOADED MOBILE GAME

Holder: *Tetris* **(Alexey Pajitnov, 1985)**
With over 100 million downloads to its name, *Tetris* is the most popular game for mobile phones. Perhaps surprisingly, only 25% of these are for Smartphones, with the remaining 75% being for other mobile devices. Despite this, *Tetris* still features on Apple's all-time top 20 paid App Store downloads list – a testament to its massive re-playability.

» NEW RECORD
» UPDATED RECORD

TRIVIA TRAIL

Despite having the fourth-highest score for *Tetris* on the Game Boy (see the table below), computer engineering genius and Apple co-founder Steve Wozniak's favourite version of the game is not the one for Nintendo's first multi-game handheld. Instead, "The Woz" prefers playing Alexey Pajitnov's puzzler on the Game Boy Light, a rare piece of hardware that was only released for the Japanese market and featured Nintendo's first backlit screen. Apparently the backlighting makes it ideal for playing *Tetris* on long trans-continental flights.

»BEST-SELLING PUZZLE GAME FRANCHISE

Holder: *Tetris* **(Alexey Pajitnov, 1985)**
As of June 2010, *Tetris* had sold over 170 million copies worldwide, of which 70 million were via physical media, cartridges and discs, and the rest through downloads. This might seem an amazingly unbeatable total, but *Tetris* is only the third best-selling videogame franchise of all time behind *Pokémon* and *Mario*, both of which are published by Nintendo. *Pokémon* has sold an incredible 200 million copies to date, while *Mario* tops the all-time chart with an eye-watering 222 million sales.

TOP 10 *TETRIS* HIGH SCORES (GAME BOY)

	Player	Score
1	Uli Horner (Germany)	593,286
2	Rob Cheung (UK)	589,694
3	Harry J Hong (USA)	523,746
4	Steve Wozniak (USA)	507,110
5	Phil S Strahl (Austria)	449,076
6	Brenda S Peavler (USA)	441,790
7	Chris Scullion (UK)	283,706
8	Robin J Smith (UK)	283,408
9	Scott Kimberling (USA)	212,835
10	Lance M Eustache (USA)	196,130

Source: Twin Galaxies

BLOCK PUZZLES

ARRANGE SHAPES OR COLOURS SO THEY MATCH AND DISAPPEAR FROM THE PLAYING FIELD – SIMPLE BUT ADDICTIVE.

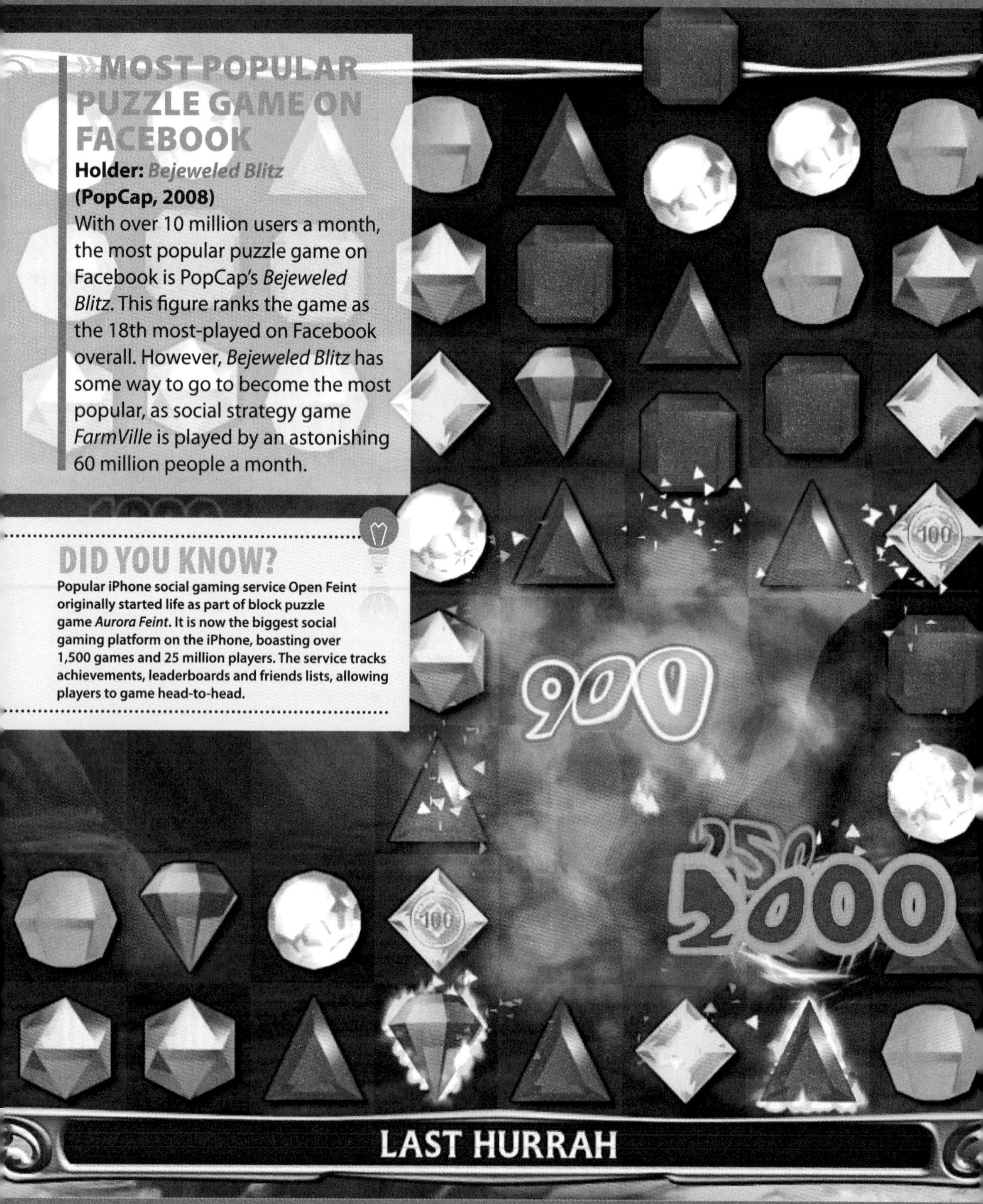

MOST POPULAR PUZZLE GAME ON FACEBOOK

Holder: *Bejeweled Blitz* **(PopCap, 2008)**

With over 10 million users a month, the most popular puzzle game on Facebook is PopCap's *Bejeweled Blitz*. This figure ranks the game as the 18th most-played on Facebook overall. However, *Bejeweled Blitz* has some way to go to become the most popular, as social strategy game *FarmVille* is played by an astonishing 60 million people a month.

DID YOU KNOW?

Popular iPhone social gaming service Open Feint originally started life as part of block puzzle game *Aurora Feint*. It is now the biggest social gaming platform on the iPhone, boasting over 1,500 games and 25 million players. The service tracks achievements, leaderboards and friends lists, allowing players to game head-to-head.

LAST HURRAH

"BEAT ME AT THE GAME AND I'LL GIVE YOU A GIFT!"

999,999: THE SCORE FOR A PERFECT GAME ON *POKÉMON PUZZLE LEAGUE*. THE FIRST PERSON TO ATTAIN THE PERFECT SCORE WAS LAWRENCE "TUSM" BROWN (USA) IN 2006.

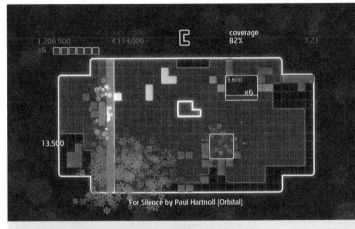

1,206,900
x6
4,114,000
coverage 82%
3,21
3,600 x6
13,500

For Silence by Paul Hartnoll (Orbital)

»FIRST XBOX 360 GAME RELEASED FOR CHARITY

Holder: *Chime* **(Zoe Mode, 2010)**
On its release in February 2010, Zoe Mode's *Chime* became the first game on the Xbox 360 released for charity. *Chime* costs 400 Microsoft Points, with 60% of proceeds going directly to OneBigGame, the videogame industry charity initiative. Though no official figures have been released, OneBigGame described sales of *Chime* as "tremendous".

TOP 10 BEST-SELLING BLOCK PUZZLE GAMES

	Game	Sales
1	Tetris (Game Boy)	30.26 million
2	Tetris (NES)	5.58 million
3	Dr. Mario (Game Boy)	5.34 million
4	Dr. Mario (NES)	4.85 million
5	Yoshi (Game Boy)	3.12 million
6	Tetris DS (Nintendo DS)	2.37 million
7	Tetris Plus (PlayStation)	2.03 million
8	Yoshi (NES)	1.98 million
9	Tetris DX (Game Boy Color)	1.93 million
10	Super Puyo Puyo (SNES)	1.70 million

Source: VGChartz

» NEW RECORD   » UPDATED RECORD

"WE GOT INSPIRATION FROM THE OPENING OF THE MATRIX WITH THE GREEN COMPUTER CODE THAT DRIPS DOWN ON THE SCREEN, EXCEPT IN THE WORLD OF METEOS, EVERYTHING IS DRIPPING UP."

/ TETSUYA MIZUGUCHI, CREATOR OF *METEOS*.

TRIVIA TRAIL

Dr. Robotnik's Mean Bean Machine is actually a re-skinned version of Japanese game *Puyo Puyo*. Sega did not own the rights to the characters in *Puyo Puyo* outside of Japan, so decided to release the game with characters from the universe of their mascot character, Sonic, instead.

»FASTEST COMPLETION OF DR. ROBOTNIK'S MEAN BEAN MACHINE (GAMECUBE VERSION)

Holder: David Greiner (USA)
David Greiner of Oswego, Illinois, USA, completed the GameCube version of *Dr. Robotnik's Mean Bean Machine* (Sega, 1994) in 305 seconds on

7 January 2010. David's record-breaking score is made all the more impressive by the fact that he played through the game on the hardest difficulty! After months of practice, he spent six consecutive hours attempting speed runs until he had a solid 13-round no-loss clear.

»FIRST PERFECT SCORE ON BEJEWELED 2 (PC VERSION)

Holder: Mike Leyde (USA)
On 23 March 2009, Mike Leyde of Riverside, California, USA, became the first person to

earn the maximum score of 2,147,483,647 on the PC version of *Bejeweled 2*. The record was achieved in 2,200 hours, in which time Mike collected 4,872,229 gems, created 48,519 power gems and 18,190 hyper cubes, and hit level 439.

»MOST CRITICALLY ACCLAIMED DS PUZZLE GAME

Holder: *Meteos* (Nintendo, 2005)
With a Metacritic score of 88%, *Meteos* is the most critically acclaimed Nintendo DS puzzle game ever. *Meteos* was one of the first puzzle games to take full advantage of the DS's touch screen, and was released just one year after the handheld's introduction in 2004. The next most acclaimed puzzle game is *Planet Puzzle League* (Nintendo, 2007), which scored 86.

»HIGHEST SCORE ON DR. MARIO (NES VERSION)

Holder: Steve Germershausen (Canada)
The highest score in the high-speed mode of the NES version of *Dr. Mario* (Nintendo, 1990) is 1,599,900, set by Steve Germershausen of Calgary, Canada, on 12 February 2010. A higher score of 4,000,000 has been reached, but only in the easier low- and medium-speed modes, where Steve currently holds second place.

SPATIAL PUZZLES

WHEN IT COMES TO SPATIAL PUZZLES, MOVING OBJECTS FROM HERE TO THERE IS RARELY AS SIMPLE AS IT SOUNDS.

»FASTEST COMPLETION OF LOSTWINDS

Holder: Justin Salamon (USA)

On 17 March 2009, Justin Salamon demonstrated his mastery of elemental puzzler *LostWinds* (Square Enix, 2008), in which players use the power of the wind to guide their character through multiple puzzles, by completing a single-segment speed run of the full game in 21 min 53 sec. A resident of Midland, Michigan, USA, Justin managed to shave the time down further to 18 min 31 sec, but only by breaking the game into 18 segments that he played individually.

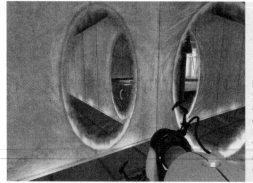

»FIRST WESTERN PIECE OF MUSIC PERFORMED AT THE "PRESS START SYMPHONY OF GAMES" CONCERT

Holder: "Still Alive" from *Portal* **(Valve, 2007)**

Since its inception in 2006, Japan's "Press Start Symphony of Games" has established itself as one of the foremost celebrations of videogame music in the world. However, Press Start focuses on the Japanese games industry, so the inclusion of the first Western theme – "Still Alive" from *Portal*, performed in Japanese by vocalist Mariko Otsuka – at the 2009 celebration was a landmark event.

»HIGHEST SCORE ON INTELLIGENT QUBE

Holder: Phil Tesseneer (USA)

Known as *Kurushi* in Europe and Australia, *Intelligent Qube* tasks players with deactivating moving cubes in a series of mazes. The game won the Excellence Award for interactive art at the 1997 Japan Media Arts Festival, so it probably comes as little surprise that just over 1 million

"THAT WASN'T A BATTLE, IT WAS ASSISTED SUICIDE."

»MOST CRITICALLY ACCLAIMED CURRENT GENERATION CONSOLE PUZZLE GAME

Holder: *Braid* **(Jonathan Blow, 2008)**

US Computer Science graduate Jonathan Blow's independently developed puzzle game *Braid* took the indie games world by storm upon its release in 2008. The game is an imaginative reinvention of the conventions of 2D platform games – instead of having three lives, the player has to manipulate time to complete each level. Critics and gamers alike were wowed by the game's originality, with the Xbox 360 and PS3 versions each achieving an aggregate review score of 93% on on Metacritic.

»MOST LEMMINGS SAVED

Holder: **Martijn Cobussen (Netherlands)**

Japanese publisher Data East once attempted to convert PC puzzle game *Lemmings* (Psygnosis, 1991) into an arcade game. Although the prototype cabinet was never released commercially, it reached the playing public via the Multiple Arcade Machine Emulator (MAME). The record for most lemmings saved on the MAME version is held by Martijn Cobussen, who rescued 366 of the pixelated rodents in a campaign on 2 August 2010.

"WE WERE ALWAYS VERY DELIBERATELY WATCHING OUR PLAYERS TO SEE HOW WE COULD MAKE THE [GAMEPLAY] EXPERIENCE BETTER FOR THEM."
/KIM SWIFT, LEAD DESIGNER ON *PORTAL*.

»FASTEST COMPLETION OF ADVENTURES OF LOLO

Holder: **Jeff Feasel (USA)**

Released in 1988 by HAL America, *Adventures of Lolo* was one of the first spatial puzzle games for the Famicom/NES. Its fastest completion time occurred on 11 June 2009 when Jeff Feasel raced through the game's 50 levels in just 23 min 17 sec.

» **NEW RECORD** » **UPDATED RECORD**

TOP 10 LARGEST STARS (AND A MOON) IN *KATAMARI DAMACY*

	Level	Diameter
1	Make the Moon	883.77 metres
2	Make a Star 9	58.68 metres
3	Make a Star 8	25.86 metres
4	Make a Star 7	11.37 metres
5	Make a Star 6	7.86 metres
6	Make a Star 5	2.93 metres
7	Make a Star 4	1.34 metres
8	Make a Star 3	1.20 metres
9	Make a Star 2	0.38 metres
10	Make a Star 1	0.19 metres

Source: Twin Galaxies

FASTEST COMPLETION OF KATAMARI DAMACY

Holder: **Tom Batchelor (USA)**

Not only has Katamari king Tom Batchelor completed Namco's 2004 *Katamari Damacy* in a record 30 min 26 sec, but he also holds all the "Make a Star" size records (see table, left).

TRIVIA TRAIL

Colourful "jigsaw of light" puzzler *Chromixa* (Simon Watson, 2010), for the iPhone, originally started life as a digital art project. Designer Simon Watson built it as a real-life art installation using hundreds of red, green and blue LEDs. Described by Watson as a "wonderfully interactive and relaxing experience", it has been well-received by critics and gamers alike.

of its global sales total of 1.21 million units came from the Japanese market. The top "Qubist" is Phil Tesseneer of Indianapolis, Indiana, USA, who racked up a score of 1,244,800 points on 10 December 2008. Phil's record looks pretty safe for the moment – his closest rival for the title is fellow American Brandan Lumzy, who has managed a score of "just" 759,700 points.

"WE'RE NOT DATING, JONES; THIS IS NOT A DATE. IF IT WAS A DATE, I WOULD'VE STOOD YOU UP!"

WWW.GUINNESSWORLDRECORDS.COM/GAMERS **135**

PHYSICS-BASED PUZZLES

YOU DON'T NEED TO BE NEWTON TO PLAY THESE GAMES BUT IT HELPS TO KNOW WHICH WAY THINGS ARE GOING TO FALL.

» **NEW RECORD**
» **UPDATED RECORD**

»MOST BOOM BLOX MASTER CHALLENGE RECORDS

Holder: Marc Cohen (USA)
When it comes to the Master Challenge levels of tower tumbler *Boom Blox*, Marc Cohen of Henderson, Nevada, USA, is sitting pretty with the highest score on 12 of the 24 challenges. His nearest rival for dominance is fellow American Ryan Fenton of Jackson, Wisconsin, USA, who holds nine challenge high scores.

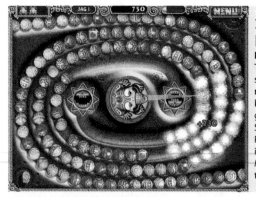

»BEST-SELLING PHYSICS-BASED PUZZLE

Holder: *Zuma* (PopCap, 2003)
The Aztec-themed ball elimination puzzler *Zuma* has sold 17 million units across multiple platforms since its release in 2003. Aside from being fiendishly playable, a key reason for *Zuma*'s success, as with many of PopCap's games, is the diversity of platforms it is available on. Supported systems include PC, Mac, Xbox 360 and PlayStation 3, as well as mobile phones, such as the iPhone. PopCap's other physics-based puzzle game, *Peggle*, has been downloaded over 50 million times, but that figure includes free trial versions of the game.

»HIGHEST-SCORING SINGLE SHOT IN PEGGLE (PC VERSION)

Holder: Steve Day (UK)
On 25 April 2008, Steve Day of Portsmouth, UK, racked up a mind-boggling score of 18,061,920 points from a single shot on the pachinko puzzler *Peggle*. Steve achieved his incredible score on the "Beyond Reason" level. His huge score was largely thanks to a lucky triple-score power-up.

"I HAVE BESTED FRUIT, SPIKE AND MOON! NOW I SHALL BEST YOU, THE GUY!"

»HIGHEST SCORE ON BUST-A-MOVE (NEO-GEO ARCADE VERSION)

Holder: Kim Korpilahti (Sweden)

The highest score on the definitive Neo-Geo arcade version of *Bust-A-Move* is the 16,013,660 points popped by Kim Korpilahti of Varberg, Sweden, on 21 May 2008. Kim beat the previous high score of 13,874,390 points, held for over 10 years by American Steven Krogman. Krogman still holds the record for the game's sequel, *Bust-A-Move II*, with a score of 75,275,450 points.

TOP 10 TALLEST TOWERS BUILT IN *WORLD OF GOO*

	Name	Height	Goo Balls
1	Peter	51.10 metres	300
2	.Kamal	50.82 metres	300
3	kamal	48.61 metres	299
4	OMON	48.25 metres	300
5	Cycl4mate	47.54 metres	300
6	skiz0r	45.45 metres	297
7	Palistinian	44.56 metres	299
8	V	44.39 metres	300
9	Richard	44.12 metres	300
9	Bruno	44.12 metres	295

Source: http://goofans.com/leaderboard

»TALLEST TOWER BUILT IN WORLD OF GOO

Holder: "Peter"

A gamer known only as "Peter" created a colossal goo structure measuring 51.10 m (167 ft 7 in) playing *World of Goo* (2D Boy, 2008) on 6 June 2010, breaking the record of 50.82 m (166 ft 8in) set by Kamal Hassiba. Peter used 300 goo balls to make the tower, and based his design on Kamal's structure. See the table above for the Top 10 goo towers.

»FASTEST SINGLE-SEGMENT COMPLETION OF WORLD OF GOO

Holder: Nigel "ridd3r" Martin (UK)

Speed demon Nigel "ridd3r" Martin zoomed through 2D Boy's gooey construction puzzler *World of Goo* in 53 min 41 sec on 7 September 2009. Through months of practice he found the fastest ways to complete levels and insists a time of under 50 minutes is a possibility.

"I CAN'T TELL YOU HOW GOOD IT FEELS TO WATCH SOMEONE PLAY THE GAME AND LAUGH OUT LOUD."
/RON CARMEL OF *WORLD OF GOO* CREATOR 2D BOY.

»FIRST PHYSICS-BASED VIDEOGAME

Holder: *Tennis for Two* (William Higinbotham)

Pioneering videogame *Tennis for Two*, created by American physicist William Higinbotham, is reckoned to be the third videogame ever created, and was the first game to attempt to simulate physics. It was unveiled at the Brookhaven National Laboratory in New York City, USA, on 18 October 1958. Instead of displaying on a monitor, the game was viewed on an oscilloscope, which is a type of electronic test instrument that displays varying signal voltages as a 2D graph. The game's "graphics" were representations of changes in voltage across the computer on which it was played.

DID YOU KNOW?

William Higinbotham, who helped design the timing circuits for the first atomic bomb during World War II, created *Tennis for Two* on primitive analog computers that had originally been designed to accurately simulate ballistic missile trajectories. Although the computers had to be reprogrammed for gaming, it explains why the game's physics were so advanced for the time.

»FIRST PHYSICS-BASED PUZZLE GAME ON IPHONE/IPOD TOUCH

Holder: *Enigmo* (Pangea Software, 2008)

Announced alongside the App Store at Apple's World Wide Developers Conference in 2008, the liquid storage game *Enigmo* was used to demonstrate how games developers could exploit the iPhone and iPod Touch's multitouch screens.

Since the launch of the App Store on 10 July 2008, hundreds of physics-based puzzle games have been distributed through Apple's service, including the popular titles *Crayon Physics Deluxe*, *Ragdoll Blaster* and *Topple*.

TRIVIA TRAIL

Construction puzzler *World of Goo* racked up average review scores of 90% and 94% for the PC and Wii versions respectively on review aggregator site Metacritic. It has also won a string of awards including Best Independent Game from the Spike TV Video Game Awards, the Design Innovation Award from the Independent Games Festival, and GameSpot's Best Game No One Played award.

LOGIC PUZZLES

IT'S NOT ABOUT WINNING, IT'S ABOUT WORKING OUT THE ANSWERS... AND FOR THESE GAMES IT'S ALL LOGICAL.

DID YOU KNOW?

While *Curious Village* and its sequels follow the adventures of Professor Layton, this series of logic puzzle games actually owe their existence to Professor Akira Tago, a real-life academic from Chiba University, Japan. Tago penned a series of puzzle books for children entitled *Head Gymnastics* and was later hired by game developer Level-5 to craft puzzles for a videogame – the *Professor Layton* titles were the result.

»FIRST MOVIE BASED ON A PUZZLE GAME

Holder: *Professor Layton and the Eternal Diva* **(Japan, 2009)**
Although many action-adventure videogames have made the move to the silver screen, *Professor Layton and the Eternal Diva* is the first movie to be based on a puzzle game. The film retains many elements of the original videogames, including puzzle sections, during which audience members are given time to form their own solutions before the answer is revealed.

»FIRST LOGIC PUZZLE GAME
Holder: *Rocky's Boots* **(The Learning Company, 1982)**
Rocky's Boots is a puzzle game that pioneered the use of computers in education. The game challenged players to kick some objects and avoid others to score points. The educational element came in the form of logic gates that players had to construct in order to activate the boots.

»FASTEST COMPLETION OF MINESWEEPER
Holder: Fritz Löhr (Germany)
Fritz Löhr of Munich, Germany, set the fastest completion time on *Minesweeper* (Microsoft, 1990) set to "Expert Plus" with a 74.406-second game on 13 February 2010 (beating the previous best of 75.177 seconds). Fritz also beat the previous "Expert" best time of 53.445 seconds with a 47.828-second effort, but he's yet to beat the record "Intermediate" score of 11.738 seconds set by the UK's D Jockser.

»BEST-SELLING LOGIC PUZZLE GAME
Holder: *Dr. Kawashima's Brain Training* **(Nintendo, 2005)**
Dr. Kawashima's Brain Training (aka *Brain Age* in the USA) has sold over 19 million copies since its launch. Those sales also make it the 13th best-selling game of all time. By contrast, the Game Boy version of *Tetris* is the **»best-selling puzzle game** and the fourth best-selling game ever (see pp.132–133 for more *Tetris* records). The sequel to *Dr. Kawashima's Brain Training* (2005), *More Brain Training* (2005), has also been a big hit, selling over 14 million units worldwide.

"BRING IT ON, YA ALIENS!"

TOP 10 FASTEST TIMES TO COMPLETE 100 CALCULATIONS IN *BRAIN TRAINING*

	Name	Time	Date
1	Viktor "Vikke" Strauss	42 seconds	26 October 2008
2	Melinha "SuperBab"	44 seconds	19 April 2008
3	Franclu "bankai001" Chua	47 seconds	27 September 2006
4=	Alexandre "Doraki" Viel	48 seconds	28 June 2007
4=	Alexandre "Starkiller"	48 seconds	27 April 2008
4=	Diego Arturo "DiegoAvp11"	48 seconds	21 April 2009
7	Vic "bubbaabdul" Lam	49 seconds	25 July 2006
8	Chris "Chanmania" Chan	51 seconds	23 July 2006
8	Barron "tetriseffect" Ng	51 seconds	27 July 2006
10	Phil "PhilDuro" Phil	53 seconds	24 July 2006

Source: http://www.cyberscore.me.uk/chart-26779.php

"[I WANT] TO PUT MY BRAIN IN A COMPUTER SO IT [WILL] BE AROUND TO SEE THE LAST DAY OF HUMANITY." /DR KAWASHIMA.

»DS GAME WITH THE MOST VARIANTS
Holder: Sudoku
Sudoku number games, which are thought to originate from puzzles published in French newspapers in the 1890s, have become a global phenomenon. To date, there have been 20 different sudoku titles on the DS alone. In addition to titles that have the word in their name, sudokus are also a staple feature of many DS puzzle game compilations, including *Dr. Kawashima's Brain Training*.

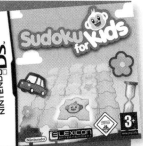

TRIVIA TRAIL

An experiment undertaken by the BBC and published by scientific journal *Nature* found that brain training games had no effect on improving memory or other mental skills. A sample of 11,000 people played the game for six weeks, but it was found that the volunteers did no better than a control group who had spent a similar amount of time simply surfing the internet.

»FIRST DSiWARE PUZZLE GAMES
Holders: *Art Style* series and *Brain Training Express* **(Nintendo, 2008 to present)**
The first puzzle games available for download on the Nintendo DSi were *Art Style: AQUIA*, *Art Style: Code* and *Brain Training Express*. Launching alongside the DSi in 2008, they paved the way for future puzzle games that followed for the platform, including *Mighty Flip Champs!* and *PiCTOBiTS*.

»MOST PICROSS DS FASTEST TIMES
Holders: Eduardo Nakagawa (Brazil)
In DS picture puzzler *Picross DS* (Nintendo, 2007), each level sees the player use logic to mark each square on a grid as either full or empty, which leads to a picture being revealed in the grid. As of 30 July 2010, Brazilian Eduardo Nakagawa had recorded the fastest times on 284 out of 345 levels of the game.

»FIRST EPISODIC PUZZLE GAME
Holder: *Blue Toad Murder Files* **(Relentless Software, 2009)**
While logic puzzles are a key element in the episodic point-and-click adventure series *Sam & Max*, the first true downloadable episodic puzzle game was *Blue Toad Murder Files*. *Blue Toad* was released in six separate episodes, individually and as part of a bundle, over the course of five months. As the title suggests, the game tasks players with solving various murders, forcing them to solve puzzles along the way.

» NEW RECORD
» UPDATED RECORD

WORD PUZZLES

TEST YOUR VOCABULARY WITH PUZZLES THAT INVOLVE IDENTIFYING, CREATING OR RE-ASSEMBLING WORDS.

Welcome,
Lex
(Click here to change users)

ADVENTURE REPLAY

MINI GAMES

OPTIONS

PopCap

» FIRST GAME TO COMBINE PUZZLE AND RPG GENRES

Holder: *Bookworm Adventures* **(PopCap, 2006)**
Released exclusively for the PC in 2006, PopCap's *Bookworm Adventures* was the first game to mix puzzle and RPG genres. In the game, bookworm Lex, "the world's greatest literate invertebrate", needs help to form words from random letters to rescue his kidnapped friend, Cassandra. As a result of this innovative gameplay, *Bookworm Adventures* has won many awards including Downloadable Game of the Year at the 2007 Interactive Achievement awards.

It's Tetris Made Letter Perfect!

Spectrum HoloByte

SUPER NINTENDO

» HIGHEST WORD TOTAL ON WORDTRIS
Holder: Brenda Peavler (USA)
Wordtris fanatic Brenda Peavler of New Castle, Indiana, USA, achieved a 184-word score in a *Wordtris* game on 20 November 2006. In the same session, she also set the record for the **highest *Wordtris* score** with an impressive points total of 22,685.

TRIVIA TRAIL

Wordtris was developed by famed *Tetris* creator Alexey Pajitnov (Russia) and originally released for the PC in 1991. It was the sixth game designed by Pajitnov, following the less than enthusiastically received *Welltris* (1989), a top-down pseudo 3D version of *Tetris*; and *Hatris* (1990), another game with an obvious *Tetris* influence that requires players to match different styles of hat as they tumble down the screen.

» **NEW RECORD**
» **UPDATED RECORD**

["YOU ARE ABOUT TO ENTER THE ROOM THAT HOUSES THE NEXUS, CORPORAL KANE. WATCH YOURSELF, NO DOUBT IT WILL BE HEAVILY GUARDED."]

»MOST POPULAR MOBILE WORD PUZZLE GAME

Holder: *Words with Friends* **(Newtoy Inc, 2009)**
A viral hit, the multiplayer *Scrabble*-esque word puzzle game *Words with Friends* has amassed 1.6 million daily active users as of June 2010. The brainchild of former Ensemble Studios employees Paul and David Bettner, the game amassed its impressive userbase in under 11 months. A key reason for its success is that *Words with Friends* is only playable as a multiplayer game – you need to get your friends to download it so they can play with you. With over 1 billion words played in matches over the game's first year, its already impressive userbase looks set to grow and grow.

»HIGHEST SCORE ON SCRABBLE BLAST!

Holder: Kelly R Flewin (Canada)
On 8 February 2009, Kelly Flewin of Winnipeg, Manitoba, Canada, scored a record 3,451 points playing the original Game Boy Advance version of *Scrabble Blast!* (EA, 2005). Since its initial GBA release, *Scrabble Blast!* has been made available by publisher EA on all mobile phones except the iPhone, where only the traditional version of *Scrabble* is available.

DID YOU KNOW?

In December 2009, an internet user claimed to have hacked the ROM for *Scribblenauts*, showing the game to have 22,802 words in its vocabulary. This total was disputed by creative director Jeremiah Slaczka (USA), who commented that the hacker "did not know anything".

"IT'S THE BEST KIND OF MARKETING: NO CELEBRITIES, NO BUCKETS OF CASH, JUST PEOPLE GENUINELY HAVING A BLAST."
/JEREMIAH SLACZKA, CREATIVE DIRECTOR OF *SCRIBBLENAUTS* TALKING TO JOYSTIQ.COM.

»MOST DOWNLOADED WORD PUZZLE GAME

Holder: *Bookworm* **(PopCap, 2003)**
With over 100 million downloads recorded, PopCap's *Bookworm* is the most downloaded word puzzle game of all time. First appearing as a PC title in 2003, *Bookworm* has since been released on a variety of platforms including Nintendo DS, Wii and iPhone. The game's appeal shows no signs of slowing, as its regular showing in the top 10 list of word games on Apple's App Store proves. As with most of PopCap's titles, *Bookworm*'s success comes from its simple yet compelling gameplay, which challenges players' spelling ability, reaction times and decision making.

»FIRST FACEBOOK GAME TO CAUSE A LAWSUIT

Holder: *Scrabulous* **(Rajat Agarwalla, Jayant Agarwalla, 2007)**
Scrabulous was one of the most popular games on Facebook, at its peak attracting 2.4 million users and making its creators a healthy $25,000 (£13,000) a month from advertising revenue. However, toy manufacturing giants Mattel and Hasbro, who own the rights to the classic word game *Scrabble*, recognized the similarities between *Scrabulous* and their own game and weren't amused by the copycat's success. The result was a lawsuit from the toy-making duo claiming breach of copyright. A subsequent cease and desist order ended the life of *Scrabulous*, which was later relaunched as *Wordscraper* with substantial changes to the gameplay.

TOP 10 HIGHEST-GROSSING iPHONE WORD GAMES

	Name
1	Scrabble (EA, 2008)
2	Boggle (EA, 2009)
3	Words with Friends (Newtoy Inc, 2009)
4	Bookworm (PopCap, 2009)
5	Moxie 2 (Blue Ox Technologies, 2010)
6	Dingbats (Starberry, 2009)
7	Whirly Word (Mighty Mighty Good Games, 2009)
8	Wordsearch Unlimited (Virtuesoft.com, 2009)
9	MASH (Magnate Interactive, 2010)
10	iAssociate (Fredrik Wahrman, 2009)

Source: iTunes

FIRST PORTABLE TITLE TO WIN BEST ORIGINAL GAME IN THE BEST OF E3 AWARDS

Holder: *Scribblenauts* **(Warner Bros., 2009)**
Each year, representatives of leading games publications get together to pick out the best games at E3, the videogames industry expo. Among the most coveted "Best of E3" awards is that for Best Original Game, which until 2009 had always gone to a title on home console or PC. However, in 2009 *Scribblenauts*, a Nintendo DS-exclusive from Warner Bros., bucked the trend, becoming the first portable title to capture the prize. The puzzler with the strapline "Write Anything, Solve Everything" was celebrated by the critics for its innovative use of in-game objects to solve problems.

COLLECTORS & COSPLAYERS

THE JAPANESE HAVE A WORD FOR OBSESSIVE VIDEOGAMES FANS, IT'S *OTAKU*. NEED WE SAY MORE...?

»LARGEST COLLECTION OF SUPER MARIO MEMORABILIA

Holder: Mitsugu Kikai (Japan)

When representatives from *Gamer's Edition* visited Mitsugu Kikai in his apartment in Tokyo, Japan, to count his collection of Mario memorabilia on 15 July 2010, they found that he had an incredible 5,400 individual items! Mitsugu was born in 1985, the same year the first *Super Mario Bros.* game was released by Nintendo, and has collected Mario merchandise since he was a boy.

DID YOU KNOW?

In Nintendo's *Mario vs. Donkey Kong* series of puzzle games, Mario is the boss of a toy company that makes Mini Mario toys. Maybe the entrepreneurial plumber should get in touch with Mitsugu – he would surely be Mario's best customer!

"CONGLATURATION!!! YOU HAVE COMPLETED A GREAT GAME AND PROVED THE JUSTICE OF OUR CULTURE. NOW GO AND REST OUR HEROES!"

$41,300: THE SUM PAID (EQUIVALENT TO £27,100) IN FEBRUARY 2010 BY AN ANONYMOUS BUYER FOR AN UNOPENED COPY OF THE RARE NES GAME *STADIUM EVENTS*.

TRIVIA TRAIL

The MCM Expo is an annual event held at the ExCel exhibition centre, London, UK, that often has a strong gaming focus. MCM stands for Movie/Comic/Media.

»LARGEST GATHERING OF PEOPLE DRESSED AS MARIO CHARACTERS

On 18 August 2010, 230 school students from Chifeng City in the Inner Mongolia Autonomous Region, China, set the record for the largest gathering of people dressed as *Mario* characters. The record number could have been higher, but some people were disqualified for having the wrong colour overalls. The event was hosted by Red Star Macalline Home Furniture Shopping Mall.

LARGEST GATHERING OF PEOPLE DRESSED AS VIDEOGAME CHARACTERS

On 23 May 2009, at the MCM Expo at the ExCel centre in London, UK, 376 people, each decked out as a character from their favourite game, came together to form the largest gathering of people dressed as videogame characters. *Gamer's Edition* adjudicators were on hand to count the participants and verify their costumes.

LARGEST COLLECTION OF POKÉMON MEMORABILIA

Holder: Lisa Courtney (UK)
Lisa Courtney has a collection of Pokémon memorabilia that numbered 14,410 different items when counted in October 2010. Lisa has been collecting for over 14 years, and her favourite item is a doll of the Pokémon Absol that she bought through eBay. Her collection includes items from the UK, USA, France and, of course, Japan.

Since appearing in last year's *Gamer's Edition*, Lisa has been honoured by Hertford Museum, UK, which has run an exhibition featuring some of Lisa's amazing collection and her *Guinness World Records* certificate.

LARGEST COLLECTION OF PLAYABLE VIDEOGAMING SYSTEMS

Holder: Richard Lecce (USA)
As of September 2010, gaming enthusiast Richard Lecce has amassed an amazing collection of 517 different playable videogaming systems, including home consoles, portable games and LCD mini-systems.

Richard also has the »**most complete collection of games**, owning every game ever produced for NES (798 games including the fabled *Nintendo World Championships* gold cart), Sega Master System, Atari 5200, Fairchild Channel F, RCA Studio II, Magnavox Odyssey 2, APF MP 1000 and Sega 32X – a total of eight systems – and the »**largest collection of videogames** with 8,616 unique items.

ROLE-PLAYING GAMES

A SPACE SHIP COMMANDER, AN ELF OR A SURVIVOR OF A NUCLEAR WAR... IN RPGs YOU CAN PLAY ANY ROLE..

»MOST CRITICALLY ACCLAIMED RPG

Holder: *Mass Effect 2* **(EA, 2010)**
With a score of 96% on the review aggregator site Metacritic, *Mass Effect 2* is the most critically acclaimed RPG of all time. The game comes in just ahead of *Baldur's Gate II: Shadows of Amn* (Black Isle Studios, 2000), which scores 95%. Both games were created by BioWare, who also crafted the third highest rated RPG, *Star Wars: Knights of the Old Republic* (LucasArts, 2003), which scored 94%.

"YES... ACTIVATE HALO'S DEFENSES, AND DESTROY THE FLOOD, WHICH IS WHY WE BROUGHT THE INDEX TO THE CONTROL CENTRE."

GUINNESS
WORLD RECORDS

WHAT ARE THEY?

No keener are the differences between Japanese and Western games felt than in the role-playing game (RPG) genre. Over the last 30 years, Western developers have wowed PC owners with open-ended experiences while the Japanese have dazzled console gamers with linear story-telling. Today, despite efforts from both sides to evolve the genre and the emergence of the massively multiplayer online role-playing game (MMORPG), the digital divide shows no sign of closing up. As Western creators blur the line between shooter and RPG with the likes of *Mass Effect 2* (EA, 2010), Japanese stalwart Square Enix adds *Call of Duty*-inspired set-pieces to the gorgeous cut-scenes in *Final Fantasy XIII* (Square Enix, 2010).

WHO SAYS SO?

Wesley Yin-Poole (UK) is the news editor of Eurogamer.net, where he writes about all things videogame-related. He's a huge fan of all types of games, but RPGs are a particular favourite. He's pumped literally hundreds of hours into *Fallout 3*, the *Mass Effect* series and the *Final Fantasy* franchise over the years, but his all time favourite is *World of Warcraft*. He once took half a year off all other work just to play it!

CONTENTS

"SO! YOU'RE THE BOY WHO DEFEATED VERAN, SORCERESS OF SHADOWS! I'LL NOT FALL AS EASILY AS SHE!"

FALLOUT

CRITICAL HIT!

EXPLORING THE NUCLEAR WASTELAND THAT WAS ONCE THE USA... WATCH OUT FOR RAD SCORPIONS!

» NEW RECORD » UPDATED RECORD

»FASTEST COMPLETION OF FALLOUT 2

Holder: Larry "Id" Eggleston Jr (USA)
Larry Eggleston Jr recorded the fastest completion of *Fallout 2* (Interplay, 1998) on 21 April 2004, when he achieved the feat in 17 min 51 sec. Larry began his impressive speed run by creating a character with a high perception skill, which reduces the number of random encounters generated by the game, and a high speech skill, which allowed him to convince Non-Player Characters (NPCs) to follow his orders. Larry often steals from NPCs so that he has loot to barter with, avoiding having to engage in combat.

»FASTEST COMPLETION OF FALLOUT

Holder: Devin Herron (USA)
On 22 December 2005, Devin Herron completed *Fallout* (Interplay, 1997) in just 9 min 19 sec. To achieve his record time, Devin "lockpicked" every door he found, avoiding most of the stairs; but his most cunning trick was to leave each fight by holding down the "a" key, thereby sneaking around all of the enemies in the game.

»MOST LINES OF DIALOGUE IN A SINGLE-PLAYER ROLE-PLAYING GAME

Holder: *Fallout: New Vegas* **(Bethesda Softworks, 2010)**

According to Jason Bergman (USA), the senior producer on *Fallout: New Vegas*, the latest entry in the *Fallout* series contains around 65,000 lines of dialogue, easily beating the 40,000-line script boasted by the previous record-holder, *Fallout 3* (*Bethesda Softworks, 2008*).

> "WE HAVE A LOT OF ALTERNATE VERSIONS OF THE SAME LINES BECAUSE PLAYERS CAN ALIGN THEMSELVES WITH ANY ONE OF THREE MAIN FACTIONS."
> /JASON BERGMAN, SENIOR PRODUCER ON *FALLOUT: NEW VEGAS*.

»FASTEST COMPLETION OF FALLOUT 3

Holder: Isaac "error1" Wehmanen (USA)

For most gamers, *Fallout 3* (Bethesda Softworks, 2008) is an epic game that will take days to fully explore, but for Isaac Wehmanen it is a far faster feat – he can finish the game in a mere 30 min 9 sec, as he proved on 11 January 2009. The key to this speedy time is a number of glitches in the game: after leaving Vault 101, Isaac heads straight for the Citadel, where he exploits an item bug that gives him access to the compound and triggers a quest that shouldn't be possible until later in the game. Isaac also exploited an error in the Jefferson Memorial building that allowed him to skip part of the game.

»FASTEST-SELLING WESTERN RPG

Holder: *Fallout 3* **(Bethesda Softworks, 2008)**

Shifting 4.7 million copies since its launch, *Fallout 3* not only outsold the previous two titles in the series and its two spin-off titles, *Fallout Tactics* and *Fallout: Brotherhood of Steel*, combined, it also outsold every other Western RPG title, generating $300 million (£207 million) worldwide during its launch period. The game's staggering success beat the previous record-holder, Bethesda's own *The Elder Scrolls IV: Oblivion* (2006), which sold 2.67 million units.

»MOST CRITICALLY ACCLAIMED FALLOUT

Holder: *Fallout 3* (Xbox 360) **(Bethesda Softworks, 2008)**

The Xbox 360 version of *Fallout 3* has an average Metacritic review score of 93%, beating the scores of both the PC version, which has a review average of 91%, and the PS3 version with a 90% average.

TRIVIA TRAIL

Fallout is widely thought to be the spiritual successor to *Wasteland* (EA, 1988), a post-apocalyptic Western RPG set in the aftermath of a US-Soviet nuclear war. *Wasteland* was designed by Brian Fargo (USA), the founder of Interplay, the *Fallout* series' original publisher.

TOP 10 MOST POWERFUL WEAPONS IN *FALLOUT 3*
IN DAMAGE POINTS PER SECOND (DPS)

	Weapon	DPS
1	Experimental MIRV	2,542
2	Fat Man	443
3	Nuka Grenade	275
4	Rock-It Launcher	167
5	Bottlecap Mine	155
6	Callahan's Magnum	146.25
7	The Kneecapper	140.62
8	Alien Blaster	125
9	Blackhawk	123.75
10	The Terrible Shotgun	120

Source: http://fallout.wikia.com

DID YOU KNOW?

Some of the developers now working at Obsidian Entertainment, the studio that created *Fallout: New Vegas* (Bethesda Softworks, 2010), used to work at Black Isle Studios, the developer behind the original *Fallout* games. They were working on their own version of *Fallout 3*, codenamed "Project Van Buren", before parent company Interplay Entertainment collapsed. Their work wasn't in vain, though, as some of Van Buren's story elements, such as the post-apocalyptic Nevada setting, were used in *Fallout: New Vegas*.

JAPANESE RPGs

LINEAR STORYTELLING, TURN-BASED BATTLES AND GLORIOUS FULL-MOTION VIDEO ARE THE HALLMARKS OF JRPGs.

FASTEST SELLING CONSOLE RPG

Holder: *Final Fantasy X*
(Square, 2001)

Selling a reported 1,455,732 copies within 24 hours of its Japanese release, *Final Fantasy X* is the fastest selling console RPG. Unfortunately, despite being the first PS2 game to shift 4 million copies, its sales were not enough to offset the costs publisher Square incurred producing the computer animated film *Final Fantasy: The Spirits Within* (USA/Japan, 2001), released in the same year.

NEW RECORD
» UPDATED RECORD

{ "BOUND ONLY BY THE PAPER-THIN WRAPPER OF MORTALITY, A SOUL HERE LIES, STRUGGLING TO BE FREE. AND SO IT SHALL, THANKS TO A BOWL OF BAD GAZPACHO, AND A MAN NAMED... CALAVERA." }

»FASTEST COMPLETION OF FINAL FANTASY VII

Holder: Andrew "Farringa" Farrington (USA)
Andrew "Farringa" Farrington completed *Final Fantasy VII* (Square, 1997) in a record time of 7 hr 41 min on 4 June 2007.

»MOST POPULAR AD-HOC WIRELESS GAME FEATURE

Holder: *Dragon Quest IX* (Square Enix, 2009)
The "Chance Encounter" mode of *Dragon Quest IX* is the most popular ad-hoc wireless game feature, having been used 117,577,073 times as of March 2010. Known as "Surechigai" in Japan, Chance Encounter enables players to share game data anonymously when they bump into each other in real life, even if they're not playing the game, using the Nintendo Wi-Fi function on their DS. The stunning number of connections reflects the game's huge popularity in Japan, where it has sold 4.93 million copies to date.

LONGEST-RUNNING JAPANESE RPG SERIES

Holder: *Dragon Quest* (Square Enix, 1986 to present)
Square Enix's *Dragon Quest* franchise has been live for 24 years and has seen 10 main game releases, making it the longest-running JRPG series. Originally released for the Nintendo Famicom in 1986, *Dragon Quest* is a phenomenon in its native Japan, where it has inspired dozens of clones, including *Final Fantasy*. A February 2010 press release from Square Enix revealed that the series has shipped over 53 million units worldwide.

»BEST-SELLING FINAL FANTASY GAME

Holder: *Final Fantasy VII* (Square, 1997)
Final Fantasy VII has sold over 9.7 million copies since its initial Japanese release for PlayStation in 1997. Of that number, the game has sold 3.9 million copies in Japan and 5.8 million in North America and Europe.

»FASTEST COMPLETION OF VAGRANT STORY

Holder: Rodrigo Lopes (Brazil)
Japanese RPG fan Rodrigo Lopes, who hails from the town of Penha in the state of Santa Catarina, Brazil, completed Square's critically acclaimed PlayStation classic *Vagrant Story* (2000) in 1 hr 41 min on 22 January 2002. Lopes achieved his record fast time using experienced characters and the New Game Plus option. The game was re-released through the PlayStation Network in 2009.

»MOST CRITICALLY ACCLAIMED PS2 RPG

Holder: *Shin Megami Tensei: Persona 4* (Atlus, 2008)
Shin Megami Tensei: Persona 4 is widely regarded as the last great game released for the PlayStation 2, and its rating of 92.40% on GameRankings.com cements it as the most critically acclaimed RPG for the system.

TOP 10 BEST-SELLING JAPANESE RPG HEROES

	Hero	Game	Sales
1	Cloud Strife	*Final Fantasy VII* (PS) (1997)	9.72 million
2	Tidus	*Final Fantasy X* (PS2) (2001)	7.95 million
3	Squall Leonhart	*Final Fantasy VIII* (PS) (1999)	7.86 million
4	Vaan	*Final Fantasy XII* (PS2) (2006)	5.71 million
5	Zidane Tribal	*Final Fantasy IX* (PS) (2000)	5.30 million
6	Yuna	*Final Fantasy X-2* (PS2) (2003)	5.21 million
7	Claire "Lightning" Farron	*Final Fantasy XIII* (PS3) (2009)	4.26 million
8	Luneth	*Final Fantasy III* (SNES) (1990)	3.42 million
9	Mario	*Mario & Luigi: Bowser's Inside Story* (DS) (2009)	2.78 million
10	Bartz Klauser	*Final Fantasy V* (SNES) (1992)	2.40 million

Source: VGChartz

"I WANT MORE ON THAT VICIOUS TWO-HEADED SQUIRREL THAT'S BEEN ATTACKING CAMPERS."

WESTERN RPGs

NO, NOT COWBOYS, BUT PLAYER-DRIVEN EXPERIENCES WITH OPEN WORLDS, DIALOGUE AND DECISION-MAKING.

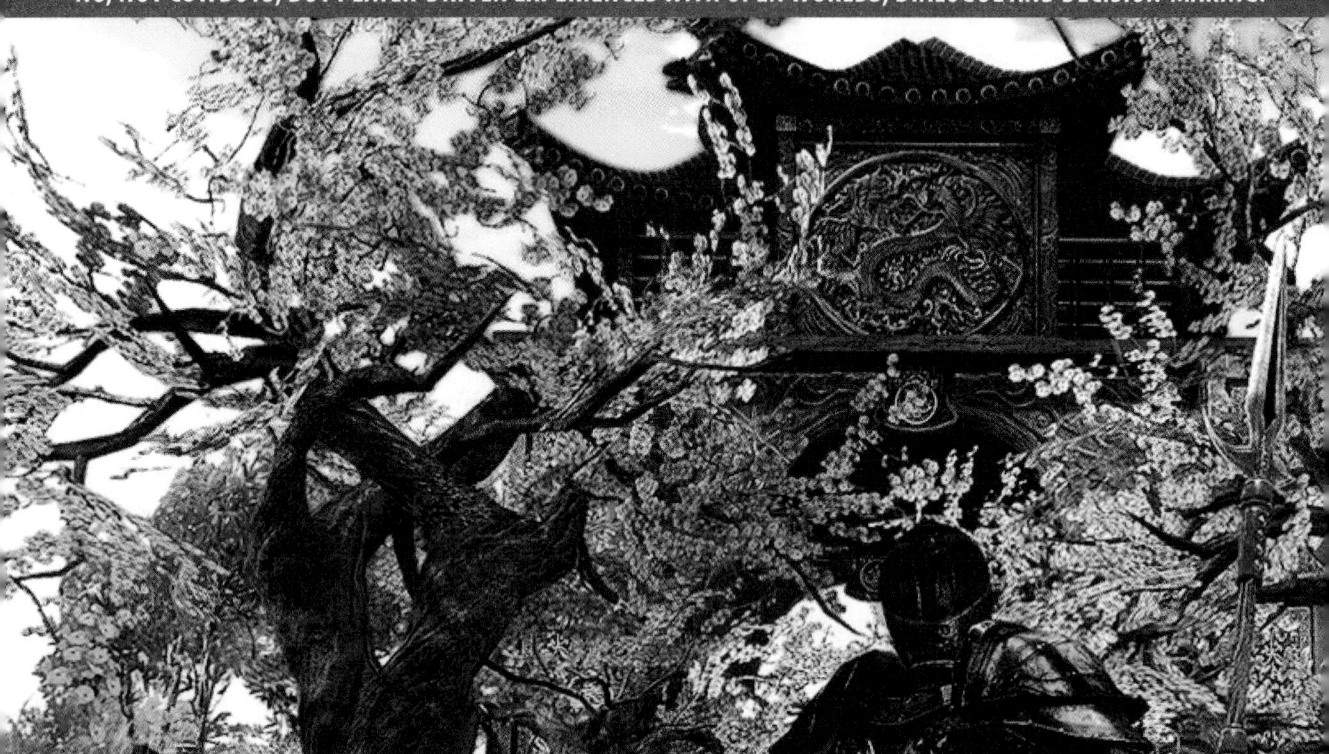

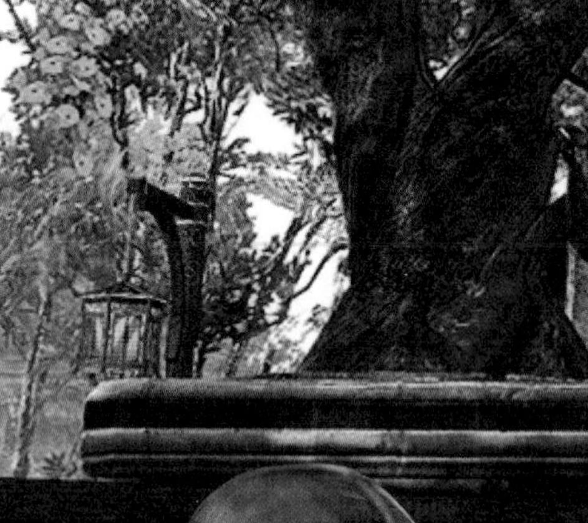

»LONGEST-RUNNING RPG FRANCHISE

Holder: *Ultima* (Origin Systems/EA, 1980 to present)

Ultima, the seminal fantasy computer role-playing game created by legendary game creator Richard Garriott (UK), aka Lord British, extended its longest-running RPG franchise world record by one year to 30 years with the release of *Lord of Ultima* (EA, pictured) in 2010. Set in the *Ultima* universe on the new world of Caledonia, the free-to-play browser-based title is more of a strategy game than a role-playing game, but *Lord of Ultima* definitely continues the heritage of the beloved *Ultima* brand and is seen as part of the series.

» NEW RECORD » UPDATED RECORD

»FIRST RPG TO FEATURE A CHARACTER IMPORT SYSTEM

Holder: *Wizardry II: The Knight of Diamonds* (Sir-Tech Software, Inc., 1982)

Wizardry II: The Knight of Diamonds is recognized as being the first role-playing game to feature a character import system, in which decisions made about a character in one game can be directly imported into

["I'VE BEEN WATCHING YOU, NARIKO. YOU FIGHT WITH STYLE. I LOVE STYLE."]

23: THE NUMBER OF GAMES IN THE LONG-RUNNING *ULTIMA* SERIES, NOT INCLUDING PORTS OR UNOFFICIAL TITLES, PUBLISHED SINCE THE ORIGINAL *ULTIMA* RELEASE IN 1980.

GUINNESS WORLD RECORDS

»MOST ADVANCED SPELL CREATION SYSTEM IN A VIDEOGAME

Holder: *Two Worlds II* **(Southpeak Interactive, 2011)**
Southpeak Interactive's *Two Worlds II* has the most advanced spell creation system of any videogame, allowing magic users access to 993,654 spells with unique effects. The game also boasts a sophisticated alchemy system, whereby players can create special potions to strengthen one or more of the hero's skills. Ingredients include plants, minerals and animals, which can be collected in the vast fantasy game world, bought in merchants' stores or taken from the corpses of defeated opponents.

»FIRST CONSOLE GAME TO CHARGE TO ACCESS ONLINE CONTENT

Holder: *Dragon Age: Origins* **(EA, 2009)**
As the first game released under publisher EA's "Project Ten Dollar" scheme, *Dragon Age: Origins* was the first console game to charge players to access online content. Project Ten Dollar forces those who purchase a second-hand copy of the bloody fantasy RPG to pay for access to what would otherwise be free content via Xbox LIVE and PSN.

continuing their progress. Players who do so receive in-game bonuses, such as credits, mineral resources and experience points. The game world is also affected by decisions made in the first game, with key characters and organizations returning if they survived. Even romances are taken into consideration.

TRIVIA TRAIL

BioWare describes *Dragon Age: Origins* (EA, 2009) as the spiritual successor to *Baldur's Gate* (Black Isle Studios, 1998), one of the most influential WRPGs of all time, even though BioWare created a sequel, *Baldur's Gate II: Shadows of Amn* (Interplay, 2000) and an associated expansion pack, *Baldur's Gate II: Throne of Bhaal* (Interplay, 2001).

the next game in a series, thus affecting gameplay. In order to play *Wizardry II*, players had to import their party from the game's predecessor, *Wizardry: Proving Grounds of the Mad Overlord* (Sir-Tech Software, Inc., 1981). This enforced-party-transfer system laid the groundwork for more relaxed character import systems seen in subsequent Western RPGs.

»MOST ADVANCED CHARACTER IMPORT SYSTEM
Holder: *Mass Effect 2* **(EA, 2010)**
Mass Effect 2 has a more advanced character import system than any other videogame. If *Mass Effect 2* detects a *Mass Effect* (EA, 2007) game save, players have the option of importing over 400 character details from the first game and

TOP 10 BEST-SELLING WESTERN RPG VILLAINS

	Villain	Game	Sales
1	John Henry Eden	*Fallout 3* (2008)	5.52 million
2	Lord Lucien	*Fable II* (2008)	3.72 million
3	Mehrunes Dagon	*The Elder Scrolls IV: Oblivion* (2006)	4.39 million
4	Archdemon	*Dragon Age: Origins* (2009)	2.92 million
5	Jack of Blades	*Fable* (2003)	2.59 million
6	Sovereign	*Mass Effect* (2004)	2.27 million
7	Darth Revan	*Star Wars: Knights of the Old Republic* (2003)	2.01 million
8	Harbinger	*Mass Effect 2* (2010)	1.95 million
9	Dagoth Ur	*The Elder Scrolls III: Morrowind* (2002)	1.84 million
10	Darth Traya	*Star Wars: Knights of the Old Republic II* (2004)	1.33 million

Source: VGChartz

"SEE, LAZLOW, YOU SEE? I REMEMBER JERRY SO WELL. HE COME IN, HE IS LIKE A BROKEN MAN. BUT A HALF A MAN... A 'MA', IF YOU WILL. HE HAS NO 'N' ANYMORE."

WWW.GUINNESSWORLDRECORDS.COM/GAMERS **151**

ACTION RPGs

EXPLORE A FANTASY WORLD, BUT BEWARE — MULTIPLE MONSTER FIGHTS AWAIT YOU IN ACTION RPGs.

»FASTEST COMPLETION OF DEMON'S SOULS LEVEL 1

Holder: Fred Vasquez (Canada)
Fred "Thanatos" Vasquez recorded a 4-min 44-sec completion of the first level of *Demon's Souls* (Sony, 2009) at his home in British Columbia, Canada, on 9 August 2010. The secret of Fred's speed was his ability to dodge and tumble out of the way of most enemies, a tactic enhanced by finding and using the Thief's Ring, and detouring only to collect fire weapons to make the end-of-level boss fight easier. Adding turpentine to his sword before the final fight gave him a further flaming edge.

»OLDEST VOICE ACTOR IN A VIDEOGAME

Holder: Christopher Lee (UK)
A veteran of stage and screen, Christopher Lee (b. 27 May 1922) also has an impressive body of work providing voices for videogames, dating back to *Ghosts* (Sony, 1994), in which he voiced the ghost hunter Dr Marcus Grimalkin. His latest videogames turn is in the twin roles of Diz and Ansem the Wise in the English-language version of *Kingdom Hearts 358/2 Days* (Square Enix, 2009). Lee was aged 87 years 124 days on the date of the game's North American release, 29 September 2009.

»BEST-SELLING ACTION RPG SERIES

Holder: *Monster Hunter* (Capcom, 2004 to present)
Capcom's *Monster Hunter* series, an action RPG with a co-operative multiplayer mode, is relatively unknown in the West. However, the games are massively popular in Japan, which is where the vast majority of the series' 11 million sales, spread across 13 titles, have been made.

"WAR. WAR NEVER CHANGES."

DID YOU KNOW?

A special edition of *Demon's Souls*, dubbed the Black Phantom Edition, was released for the European market. It contained an art book, soundtrack CD and strategy guide.

»FIRST THIRD-PARTY Wii EXCLUSIVE TO SELL ONE MILLION UNITS

Holder: *Monster Hunter Tri* **(Capcom, 2009)**
The first game in the *Monster Hunter* series to be released on the Wii, Capcom's *Monster Hunter Tri* has sold 1.58 million units since its launch, making it the first third-party Wii exclusive to pass the 1 million mark. A key innovation for the title's home console debut is support for the Wii's little-used Wii Speak microphone peripheral, which allows up to four players to communicate simultaneously online. This is an extremely useful bonus feature for a game that requires close co-operative online team play to defeat some of the game's bigger monsters.

»FASTEST 100% COMPLETION OF DIABLO II

Holder: Alan Burnett (USA)
The fastest full completion of *Diablo II: Lord of Destruction* (Blizzard, 2001), a gruelling action RPG with a hack and slash flavour, is 4 hr 22 min, set by Alan Burnett on 14 November 2008. In this game a complete speed run involves going through all three of the game's difficulties ("Normal", "Nightmare" and "Hell") sequentially and completing all the quests. Opting to use a Sorceress-class character, Alan's strategy was to find the most efficient way to level-up his character through gaining experience points. Using an "EXP Shrine", he was able to double the number of experience points gained for a short time.

> "[IF] YOU KEEP COMBINING ATTACKS... YOU MIGHT HAVE A MONSTER ATTACKING PEOPLE FROM DIFFERENT DIRECTIONS."
> /RYOZO TSUJIMOTO, LEAD PRODUCER ON MONSTER HUNTER TRI, DISCUSSES FIGHTING TACTICS.

» NEW RECORD
» UPDATED RECORD

TRIVIA TRAIL

In Japan, the action RPG *Nier* (Square Enix, 2010) was released in two versions: *Nier* "Gestalt" on Xbox 360 and *Nier* "Replicant" on PS3. The two versions of the game are identical except for the appearance of protagonist Nier and his relationship with the female character Yonah. The "Replicant" Nier is a young man of slight build and Yonah is his sister. The "Gestalt" Nier is a muscular older man and Yonah is his daughter. Outside Japan, only the "Gestalt" version is available.

TOP 10 BEST-SELLING *MONSTER HUNTER* GAMES* (CONSOLE AND HANDHELD)

	Game	Sales
1	Monster Hunter Portable 2G (Capcom, 2008)	4.75 million
2	Monster Hunter Portable 2 (Capcom, 2007)	2.42 million
3	Monster Hunter 3 (Capcom, 2009)	1.58 million
4	Monster Hunter Portable (Capcom, 2005)	1.43 million
5	Monster Hunter 2 (Capcom, 2007)	0.63 million
6	Monster Hunter (Capcom, 2004)	0.28 million
7	Monster Hunter G** (Capcom, 2005)	0.25 million
8	Monster Hunter G*** (Capcom, 2005)	0.23 million
9	Monster Hunter Online**** (Capcom, 2006)	0.12 million
10	Monster Hunter i (Capcom, 2006)	(unknown)

Source: VGChartz   *Japanese titles used **Wii ***PS2 ****Xbox 360

MMORPG: FANTASY & SCI-FI

MASSIVELY MULTIPLAYER ONLINE ROLE-PLAYING GAMES THAT TRULY TAKE YOU OUT OF THIS WORLD.

DID YOU KNOW?

A survey of nearly 19,000 gamers, carried out by the market research company NPD in May 2010, found that 68% of MMORPG gamers are male and 32% are female. The survey also found that these games are most popular among gamers who are between 25 and 34 years old, and that the majority of MMORPGers spend over 20 hours a week playing the online games.

»LARGEST GATHERING OF PEOPLE DRESSED AS STAR TREK CHARACTERS

To celebrate the launch of *Star Trek Online* (Atari, 2010) Namco Bandai Partners in association with Atari gathered an intergallactic crew of 99 "Trekkers", lead by professional Captain Jean-Luc Picard impersonator Giles Aston (UK, pictured far right), who boldly gathered on the Millennium Bridge, London, UK, on 14 February 2010. Like Picard before him, Giles also took on the role of arbitor to ensure only those properly attired in starfleet uniforms or as members of various alien races from around the *Star Trek* universe counted towards the final tally.

"WHAT DO YOU WANT?! DO YOU HAVE SOMETHING TO SAY TO ME, SILLY RABBIT?!"

250,000: THE NUMBER OF ACTIVE *ULTIMA ONLINE* PLAYERS AT THE PEAK OF THE FANTASY MMORPG's POPULARITY IN THE MIDDLE OF 2003.

»MOST CRITICALLY ACCLAIMED SCI-FI MMORPG

Holder: *Phantasy Star Online* (Sega, 2000)
A Dreamcast-exclusive title, *Phantasy Star Online* claims an average review score of 89% according to the games review aggregator Metacritic. The title was also the **first console MMORPG** and at launch it was particularly praised for the quality of its online functionality, a real feat in the days of dial-up internet connections.

»LONGEST-RUNNING ONLINE GAMING GUILD

Holder: The Syndicate
Set up in February 1996, The Syndicate (*www.LLTS. org*) is the longest-running online guild, with 14 years, 5 months and 22 days of continuous operation as of 7 July 2010. The Syndicate exists in multiple games, including both *Ultima Online* and *World of Warcraft*, and also beta tests for various MMORPG developers.

»LONGEST-RUNNING SCI-FI MMORPG

Holder: *Anarchy Online* (Funcom, 2001 to present)
The science fiction MMORPG *Anarchy Online*, which first saw life as a small research project in 1995, has run live on servers since 27 June 2001, a period spanning more than nine years.

TOP 10 LONGEST-RUNNING CURRENT MMORPGs

	Game	Established
1	The Realm Online	1996
2	Nexus: Kingdom of the Wind*	1996
3	Tibia	1997
4	Hostile Space	1997
5	Continuum**	1997
6	Ultima Online	1997
7	Lineage	1998
8	Everquest	1999
9	The 4th Coming	1999
10	Dark Ages	1999

All games still active at time of press.
*South Korean release date ** aka Subspace.

TRIVIA TRAIL

Zachary Quinto, the actor who played the young Spock in JJ Abrams' *Star Trek* (USA/Germany, 2009), also served as a voice actor on *Star Trek Online* (Atari, 2010) playing the role of an emergency medical hologram/tutor.

» NEW RECORD
» UPDATED RECORD

»MOST PROLIFIC MMORPG PUBLISHER

Holder: NCsoft (Korea) (1998 to date)
With 24 MMORPG titles published since 1998, including the divinity-themed *Aion: Tower of Eternity* (pictured), South Korea's NCsoft has crafted more hit MMORPGs than any other videogame publisher.

"AT LEVEL TEN, YOU WILL 'ASCEND TO DIVINITY' AND EARN YOUR WINGS."
/LANI BLAZIER, COMMUNITY MANAGER FOR *AION: TOWER OF ETERNITY* ON GETTING YOUR CHARACTER OFF THE GROUND.

»FIRST FULLY VOICE-ACTED MMORPG

Holder: *Star Wars: The Old Republic* (LucasArts, 2011)
While full voice acting (where every piece of text dialogue is accompanied by a voice-acted soundtrack) has long been a feature of RPGs such as Lucas Arts' *Knights of the Old Republic* (2003) that game's MMORPG sequel *Star Wars: The Old Republic* marks the advent of full voice acting for all the non-player-characters in an MMO. In crafting their game, developer BioWare created and recorded hundreds of thousands of lines of dialogue, covering all possible gameplay scenarios, a feat that they claim is the largest voice-over project in videogame history.

"A DOZEN COVENANT SUPERIOR BATTLESHIPS AGAINST A SINGLE HALCYON-CLASS CRUISER. GIVEN THOSE ODDS, I'M CONTENT WITH THREE... MAKE THAT FOUR KILLS."

MMORPG: SOCIAL

WITH SOCIAL MMORPGs, THE FOCUS IS ON PEOPLE PLAYING TOGETHER, AND OFTEN IT'S ENTIRELY FREE!

»MOST EXPENSIVE VIRTUAL PROPERTY

Holder: Crystal Palace Space Station
Value is often in the eye, and the wallet, of the purchaser – and that is certainly true of the USA's Erik Novak (aka Buzz "Erik" Lightyear). In January 2010, Erik paid 3.3 million Project Entropia Dollars ($330,000 or £228,263) at a public auction for the luxurious Crystal Palace Space Station (pictured) in the social MMORPG *Planet Calypso* (formerly *Entropia Universe*, MindArk, 2003). This purchase beat the previous record held by Club Neverdie, an asteroid space station resort in the same game, which fetched $100,000 (£59,000) in September 2005.

»NEW RECORD » UPDATED RECORD

»LARGEST VIRTUAL COMMUNITY FOR TEENS

Holder: *Habbo* (Sulake, 2000)
Finnish publisher Sulake's online *Habbo* community has over 15 million unique users per month, over 90% of whom are under the age of 18, according to Sulake. Since the community launched in 2000, over 178 million *Habbo* characters have been created by users.

»LONGEST-RUNNING SOCIAL MMORPG

Holder: *Furcadia* (Dragon's Eye Productions, Inc., 1996 to present)
With a background in the "Furry" subculture of anthropomorphic animals, *Furcadia* predated the term MMORPG, and with its online multi-user graphic interface and prominent social aspect, it also prefigured many of the social MMORPGs that were to follow.

Furcadia has developed and survived since 1996, thanks to its passionate and active users, who have created much of the game's continued content and its free-form role-playing.

»LARGEST USER-GENERATED VIRTUAL ECONOMY

Holder: *Second Life* (Linden Lab, 2003)
With in-game transactions worth $567 million (£355 million) carried out in 2009, *Second Life* continues to boast the largest virtual economy. In the first quarter of 2009, *Second Life*rs earned $55 million (£38 million); in the first quarter of 2010, user transactions totalled $160 million (£106 million), a 30% increase on the previous year and an all-time high for the game. The number of residents

TRIVIA TRAIL

Although officially called Agni after the Hindu god, the virtual space of *Second Life* is nicknamed "The Grid". Despite encompassing the whole of the *Second Life* world, The Grid is effectively split into two separate playing areas, the main *Second Life* zone and one reserved solely for gamers aged between 13 and 17, which is dubbed "Teen *Second Life*".

"EVER SEEN A SIREN IN ACTION? HERE'S YOUR CHANCE."

TOP 10 PLAYERS IN *FREE REALMS* RANKED BY ENEMIES DEFEATED

	Player	Enemies
1	Dan Crosschecker	1,534,863
2	Danielle Honeyface	1,524,653
3	Victoria Fieryspring	1,229,799
4	Maddison1	1,099,252
5	Owen Wolfgate	672,407
6	Zhouz	608,336
7	Leonardo Rabbitfoot	535,371
8	Noble Stormcastle	429,718
9	Troy Azureshield	371,813
10	Numberoneson	362,398

Source: In-game leaderboard

DID YOU KNOW?

In 2007, social MMORPG *Club Penguin* was accused of teaching its young players how to cheat in real life. Some were found to be downloading illicit software that helped them gain virtual gold coins instead of earning them fairly. In the same year, the *Chicago Tribune* newspaper suggested that the practice could affect the behaviour of players in the real world.

active in the game's economy reached 517,349 in March 2010. Monthly unique users with repeat logins peaked in the same month at 826,214, a 13% increase on the previous year.

»MOST POPULAR CONSOLE MMORPG
Holder: *PlayStation Home* **(Sony, 2008)**
Accessible via Sony's online PlayStation Network, the PlayStation 3's own MMORPG *PlayStation Home* boasts 14 million registered accounts. The service allows PlayStation 3 users to create a custom avatar and virtual apartments before venturing online.

»MOST MONEY RECEIVED FOR A VIRTUAL WORLD
Holder: *Club Penguin* **(New Horizon Interactive, 2005)**
When Disney bought *Club Penguin* from the game's original publisher, New Horizon Interactive, in 2007, it paid a staggering $350 million (£175 million). Even more impressive, the New Horizon team were promised a further $350 million if they hit certain targets by the end of 2009. Unfortunately for the staff involved, the game's userbase failed to grow quickly enough, so they were unable to cash in on the bonus payday.

»MOST ADVANCED VIDEO CREATION SYSTEM IN AN MMORPG
Holder: *Free Realms* **(Sony, 2009)**
The MMORPG *Free Realms* boasts its own video creation system, which enables players to capture footage of their virtual adventures and upload it directly to video-sharing website YouTube from within the game. Players can determine the resolution of their gameplay videos, save them to their computers and view or edit them using software that supports the .AVI file format. *Free Realms* is the first MMORPG to offer this system.

"I WOULD HAVE BEEN YOUR DADDY, BUT A DOG BEAT ME OVER THE FENCE."

WWW.GUINNESSWORLDRECORDS.COM/GAMERS **157**

WORLD OF WARCRAFT

CRITICAL HIT!

WHEN IT COMES TO MMORPGs, WORLD OF WARCRAFT IS STILL KING OF THE HILL.

»FASTEST-SELLING EXPANSION PACK

Holder: *Wrath of the Lich King* **(Blizzard, 2008)**

Wrath of the Lich King, the second expansion to the mega-popular online game *World of Warcraft* (Blizzard, 2004), sold 2.8 million copies in its first 24 hours on sale. This beat the previous record for the fastest-selling expansion pack of 2.4 million copies in 24 hours, set 22 months earlier by the first *World of Warcraft* expansion, *The Burning Crusade*. With *Cataclysm*, the third expansion in the series (pictured), due for release on 7 December 2010, expectation is high that this record will soon be beaten.

"CATACLYSM'S EASILY THE BIGGEST CHANGE WE'VE EVER MADE TO OUR CLASSES BY FAR." /DESIGNER CORY STOCKTON ON THE CHANGES IN THE LATEST *WORLD OF WARCRAFT* EXPANSION.

»MOST POPULAR SUBSCRIPTION MMORPG

Holder: *World of Warcraft* **(Blizzard, 2004)**

According to a 2009 report published by analyst group Screen Digest, *World of Warcraft* boasted a dominant 58% share of the subscription-based MMORPG market in the West. As of October 2010, the game had 12 million subscribers worldwide – that's more than the population of Cuba!

»FIRST PLAYER TO "COMPLETE" WORLD OF WARCRAFT

Holder: "Little Gray" (Taiwan)

Although *World of Warcraft* (Blizzard, 2004) is open-ended and therefore a game that, technically, has no end point, the first person reported to have successfully completed all of the achievements in the title, and therefore "completed" the game, is "Little Gray" (Taiwan). Playing as a Tauren Druid, he reached 986 out of 986 points listed in the Armory (the game's vast searchable database of information taken from the *WoW* servers) on 27 November 2009. According to his stats in the Armory, Little Gray killed 390,895 creatures, died 8,543 times, inflicted 7,255,538,878 damage points and did 5,906 quests (an average of 14.6 quests per day).

"CHILI CON CARNE!"

»FIRST PLAYER TO REACH LEVEL 70 IN WORLD OF WARCRAFT

Holder: Gabriel Wael (France)

The first expansion pack for *World of Warcraft, The Burning Crusade,* raised the level cap on the game from 60 to 70. The expansion was released on 16 January 2007, and it took Gabriel Wael less than a day to become the first to grind his way to the new upper limit on 17 January 2007. The game's latest expansion, *Cataclysm,* will raise the level cap even further to 85 and there will surely be a race to be the first to hit this new limit.

» **NEW RECORD**
» **UPDATED RECORD**

TOP 10 MMORPGs FORMER *WORLD OF WARCRAFT* PLAYERS ARE NOW PLAYING

	Game	Developer
1	Runescape	Jagex, 2001
2	Dungeons and Dragons Online	Atari, 2006
3	Guild Wars	NCsoft, 2005
4	Final Fantasy XI	Square Enix, 2002
5	Age of Conan	Funcom, 2008
6	The Lord of the Rings	Codemasters, 2007
7	Aion	NCsoft, 2008
8	Warhammer Online	EA, 2008
9	Pirates of the Caribbean	Disney, 2007
10	Dark Age of Camelot	EA, 2001

Source: The NPD Group

TRIVIA TRAIL

The Chinese government has banned *World of Warcraft* (Blizzard, 2004) a number of times, most recently in April 2009. The government accused Blizzard's partner in the region of committing "gross violations" of Chinese law. China has sought to curb online gaming in recent years following a raft of deaths associated with fatigue. In November 2005, hundreds of Chinese players held a virtual funeral for a girl known only as "Snowly", who died after a marathon three-day session (left).

»FIRST GUILD TO DEFEAT ARTHAS IN WORLD OF WARCRAFT: WRATH OF THE LICH KING

Holder: Blood Legion (USA)

On 2 February 2010, a 10-man group known as the Blood Legion guild became the first guild to defeat Arthas Menethil, the final and hardest boss in the *Wrath of the Lich King* expansion. Each earned the title "Kingslayer" and the "world first" achievement for their efforts.

»BEST-SELLING VIRTUAL ITEM

Holder: Celestial Steed

The "Celestial Steed" mount in *World of Warcraft* (Blizzard, 2004), became the best-selling virtual item when 140,000 fans queued to buy it on release on 15 April 2010. Costing $25 (£16), the virtual horse travels at the speed of the purchaser's fastest existing mount and offers no in-game benefit apart from being a status symbol.

FIRST PLAYER TO REACH LEVEL 80 IN WORLD OF WARCRAFT

Holder: "Nyhm"

With the initial release of *World of Warcraft* (Blizzard, 2004), the highest rank you could reach was level 60. When the *Wrath of the Lich King* expansion came out on 13 November 2008, that bar was raised to level 80. The first person to reach this new benchmark was a gamer known only as "Nyhm", who hit the new cap just 27 hours after the pack was launched.

STRATEGY & SIMULATION GAMES

GAMING FOR THOSE WHO ARE LOOKING TO LIVE OUT THEIR DREAMS IN AN ALTERNATIVE WORLD.

["FORGET ABOUT FREEMAN, WE ARE CUTTING OUR LOSSES AND PULLING OUT! ANYONE LEFT DOWN THERE NOW IS ON HIS OWN. REPEAT, IF YOU WEREN'T ALREADY, YOU ARE NOW!"]

92%: THE METACRITIC AGGREGATE REVIEW SCORE FOR *ROME: TOTAL WAR*, RELEASED IN SEPTEMBER 2004. THE FIRST RELEASE IN THE SERIES, *SHOGUN: TOTAL WAR*, SCORED 84%.

GUINNESS WORLD RECORDS

»MOST PROLIFIC HYBRID STRATEGY SERIES

Holder: *Total War*

(Sega, 2000 to present)

With 15 entries including multiple formats and expansion packs, *Total War* is the most prolific hybrid strategy game series to date. The first title in the franchise, *Shogun: Total War,* was released in 2000, while the latest, *Shogun 2: Total War* (pictured), is due out in 2011.

Hybrid strategy combines the thrill of real-time battles with turn-based empire building, employing the "4X" gameplay (explore, expand, exploit, exterminate) that was made famous by the likes of *Civilization* (MicroProse, 1991).

WHAT ARE THEY?

Whether you're assembling an army to battle a hostile enemy or making preparations to bring a newborn into the world, strategy and simulation games are all about considered thinking and measured actions. They sit at the opposite end of the gaming spectrum to arcade and shooting titles, yet they are just as popular, with long-running franchises such as *Command & Conquer*, *Civilization* and *The Sims* selling millions of copies and attracting huge fan bases. With recent releases, such as *StarCraft II: Wings of Liberty* on PC and *The Sims 3* on console, attracting widespread acclaim, the strategy and simulation genre continues to be a dominant force on the gaming landscape.

WHO SAYS SO?

Martyn Carroll's (UK) first article on gaming was published in 1997, and since then he's contributed myriad features and reviews to many publications including *Retro Gamer*, *GamesTM*, *Micro Mart* and Eurogamer.net. Martyn has compiled records for the *Gamer's Edition* since it launched in 2008 and hopes to one-day emulate his high-score heroes with a videogame record of his own.

CONTENTS

CIVILIZATION

SID MEIER'S GAMES INTRODUCED THE WORLD TO THE UNDENIABLE ADDICTION OF "JUST ONE MORE TURN…"

DID YOU KNOW?

In *Sid Meier's Civilization Revolution* (2K, 2008), there are six artefacts distributed around the map that bestow bonuses upon those who find them first. The Lost City of Atlantis artefact rewards the finder with technology, for example, while the Seven Cities of Gold artefact boosts the finder's bank balance.

» **NEW RECORD**
» **UPDATED RECORD**

MOST PROLIFIC TURN-BASED STRATEGY SERIES

Holder: *Sid Meier's Civilization*
(MicroProse, 1991 to present)
The *Civilization* franchise has seen a total of 41 releases since its 1991 debut, just squeezing past the trading-card-based *Yu-Gi-Oh!* (Konami, 2000 to present) series of games, which has 39 turn-based strategy titles.
Although particularly well-known as a PC series, the *Civilization* games have also been released on platforms as diverse as the Amiga and Sega Saturn as well as the PS3, Nintendo DS and even iPhone.

» **MOST GAMES HEADLINED BY A DESIGNER**
Holder: Sid Meier (Canada)
A legendary games designer – he was the second person to be inducted into the Academy of Interactive Arts and Sciences' Hall of Fame, after Japan's Shigeru Miyamoto – Sid Meier's name has such pulling power that it has been in the title of 19 games and 53 total releases since 1987.

"PLANET EARTH, OR, AS THE REST OF THE OMNIVERSE CALL IT, THE ORB OF DREAMS"

CRITICAL HIT!

GUINNESS WORLD RECORDS

»FIRST GAME TO HAVE AN OFFICIALLY RECOGNIZED DAY

Holder: *Sid Meier's Civilization V* **(2K Games, 2010)**

Martin O'Malley, the Governor of the US state of Maryland, declared 21 September 2010 "*Sid Meier's Civilization V* Day" to coincide with the launch of the latest game in the *Civilization* series – the first time a game has been recognized in this way by a public official. Governor O'Malley made the declaration to help celebrate the strength of the videogame development industry in his state, which is home to *Civilization* developer Firaxis.

»MOST VICTORY CONDITIONS IN A GAME

Holder: *Sid Meier's Civilization IV* **(2K, 2005)**

While most linear games typically have one goal (reach the end of the game), *Civilization IV* has six different criteria on which a victory outcome is judged: time, domination, conquest, culture, diplomatic and space race. Each criterion offers the opportunity to win but requires a different approach to the game. For example, Domination and conquest (pictured above) both require taking down their opponents' cities, while diplomacy requires the United Nations to vote in favour of the player. A space race victory hinges on the player being the first to reach Alpha Centauri, while a time-limited game compares civilization scores in the year 2050.

»BEST-SELLING TURN-BASED STRATEGY SERIES

Holder: *Sid Meier's Civilization* **(MicroProse, 1991)** The *Civilization* series has amassed worldwide sales of more than 9 million units since it was launched in May 1991, making it the top-selling turn-based strategy series. This impressive figure is set to rise as it does not include sales of *Sid Meier's Civilization V* (2K, 2010).

»MOST CRITICALLY ACCLAIMED TURN-BASED STRATEGY GAME

Holder: *Sid Meier's Civilization IV* **(2K, 2005)** Scoring an average of 93.24% on review aggregator site GameRankings.com, *Civilization IV* ranks as the top turn-based strategy title. The game was further enhanced for its fans by the expansion packs *Warlords* and *Beyond the Sword*.

TRIVIA TRAIL

Published in 2008 by 2K, *Civilization: Colonization* was a total conversion of *Civilization IV*. The game engine and core design were repurposed to make a new game in which the aim was to set up a colony that would eventually be strong enough to win a fight for its own independence.

CIVILIZATION IV PLAYER RANKINGS AS OF SEPTEMBER 2010

	Player	Points	Games
1	veryhard	24,756,377	139
2	The-Hawk	20,097,686	210
3	billator	19,771,070	206
4	Bozso77	17,173,665	204
5	Hindi	16,585,034	513
6	Moonsinger	16,009,166	216
7	Misotu	13,979,469	396
8	babaBrian	13,383,594	495
9	Miraculix	12,504,393	415
10	WastinTime	11,554,942	185

Source: CivFanatics.com

"WHENEVER WE LOOK AT A NEW VERSION OF CIVILIZATION WE ARE FACED WITH THE QUESTION 'HOW MANY THINGS DO WE CHANGE?'" /CIVILIZATION CREATOR SID MEIER PONDERS GAMEPLAY DEVELOPMENT.

TURN-BASED STRATEGY

PLANNING AND PLOTTING YOUR NEXT MOVE, MAKE SURE YOU'RE ALWAYS ONE STEP AHEAD OF THE GAME.

DID YOU KNOW?

The original *Magic: The Gathering* videogame was the last game from MicroProse that the legendary Sid Meier (Canada) worked on before he jumped ship to found Firaxis Games. Firaxis have gone on to release a host of hit turn-based strategy games, including *Civilization IV* (2K, 2005).

»LONGEST-RUNNING VIDEOGAME TCG SERIES

Holder: *Magic: The Gathering*

(MicroProse, 1998 to present) Based on Wizards of the Coast's long-standing trading card game (TCG) of the same name, the first *Magic: The Gathering* videogame was released by MicroProse in March 1998 and the series has thrived ever since with its successful online client. The most recent addition has been *Duels of the Planeswalkers*, a simplified version of the game for Xbox Live released in 2009 – it sold over 300,000 copies in its first week of release.

"THEIR WEAPONS ARE NO MATCH FOR OUR MILITARY MIGHT. MODERATE TO LOW RESISTANCE. ENEMY MORALE AT AN ALL-TIME LOW. I GUESS SOMEBODY FORGOT TO TELL THE HELGHAST."

410,000: THE TOTAL GLOBAL SOFTWARE SALES OF *ADVANCE WARS: DAYS OF RUIN* (NINTENDO, 2008), THE LATEST IN THE PUBLISHER'S *WARS* SERIES.

»MOST PORTED TURN-BASED STRATEGY SERIES

Holder: *Worms* (Team17, 1995)

An archetypal artillery series, *Worms* tasks players with wiping out an opponent's force of heavily armed annelids. The game has appeared on 27 different platforms over the years, ranging from the Commodore Amiga to the PS3 and Xbox 360. The simple gameplay and diverse weaponry have allowed the series to cross the divide between casual and hardcore gamers in a way that few other titles have achieved.

"NEWTONIAN PHYSICS ARE A STARTING POINT, BUT WE MASSAGE THOSE TO ENSURE THE GAME FEELS AND PLAYS CORRECTLY."

/TEAM17'S MARTYN BROWN EXPLAINS HOW PLAYING WITH PHYSICS IS ALL IN A DAY'S WORK WHEN MAKING THE LATEST *WORMS* TITLE.

»FIRST TURN-BASED STRATEGY GAME

Holder: *Nim* (Ferranti, 1951)

The Nimrod computer was built by manufacturer Ferranti in 1951 to show off British technological prowess. The company's aim was to demonstrate that a machine could be made that could play the strategy board game *Nim* against human opposition. The computer was exhibited at that year's Festival of Britain, where it won plenty of games against its human opponents. As such, Nimrod's *Nim* was the first example of a digital turn-based strategy game.

»LONGEST-RUNNING CONSOLE STRATEGY SERIES

Holder: *Wars* series (Nintendo, 1988 to present)

The first exposure gamers in the West had to Nintendo's *Wars* series was with the 2001 release of *Advance Wars* for the Game Boy Advance, yet in Japan the series dates back to 1988 with the release of *Famicom Wars* for the Nintendo Famicom console. There have been a total of 11 separate releases of *Wars* titles over the years, the most recent being 2008's *Advance Wars: Days of Ruin* for the DS.

TRIVIA TRAIL

The original *Worms* was based on *Total Wormage,* a game created by then-amateur game designer Andy Davidson as an entry for a computer magazine competition – he didn't win, but the game lead to Andy meeting (and eventually joining) the Team 17 crew.

»FASTEST WIN AGAINST THE COMPUTER IN ARCHON

Holder: John Sato (USA)

John Sato of Bellevue, Washington, USA, scored a win against his computer opponent on the C64 version of *Archon: The Light and the Dark* (EA, 1983) in a record time of just 55 seconds. John completed his super-fast victory on the early turn-based strategy title playing on 26 July 2008.

»FASTEST COMPLETION OF RISE OF NATIONS

Holder: Alex Nichols (USA)

Playing as France on the lowest difficulty level, Alex "AquaTiger" Nichols set the record for the fastest speed run on *Rise of Nations* (Microsoft, 2003) when he reached the end of the game's campaign mode in an amazing 41 min 40 sec on 28 April 2008. Despite his terrific time, Nichols believes it possible to shave down still further, possibly to below 40 minutes.

»BEST-SELLING CONSOLE TURN-BASED STRATEGY SERIES

Holder: *Yu-Gi-Oh!* (Konami, 2000 to present)

Yu-Gi-Oh! is an incredibly prolific game series based on the trading card franchise of the same name, which has sold over 14 million units worldwide as of September 2010. The series comprises 36 titles, including five that are available exclusively in Japan, where the game's fanatical fanbase is at its most substantial.

» NEW RECORD
» UPDATED RECORD

TOP 10 *ADVANCE WARS: DAYS OF RUIN* HIGH SCORES

	Player	Country	Score
1	Julian "Upertoonlink" Korten	Germany	11,017
2	Michele "ALAKTORN" Magnaterra	Italy	10,889
3	"MelonGx"	China	10,308
4	Eduardo "wadoludo" Nakagawa	Brazil	9,403
5	"floan"	France	8,594
6	Brandon "Shadowtje" Bongers	Netherlands	8,414
7	Matthew "Ephraim225" Adams	USA	8,327
8	Kevin "Cald" Caldwell	Germany	8,308
9	Ben Bayntun	UK	8,265
10	"Wellian"	UK	8,258

Source: http://www.cyberscore.me.uk/totaliser-group-2699.php

» NEW RECORD » UPDATED RECORD

"I'M A MARINE, SON. I'LL WALK ON WATER IF I HAVE TO."

WWW.GUINNESSWORLDRECORDS.COM/GAMERS **165**

REAL-TIME STRATEGY

WHEN THE ENEMY IS PLOTTING AGAINST YOU IN REAL-TIME, YOU MUST THINK FAST AND ACT QUICKLY TO WIN.

»FASTEST-SELLING REAL-TIME STRATEGY GAME

Holder: *StarCraft II: Wings of Liberty*
(Blizzard, 2010)
Hotly anticipated real-time strategy (RTS) title *StarCraft II* sold over 1 million copies in the first 24 hours of its worldwide release on 27 July 2010, giving it the record for the fastest-selling real-time strategy game. Expectations remain high that it will eventually eclipse the 11.3 million lifetime sales of the original *StarCraft* (Blizzard, 1998).

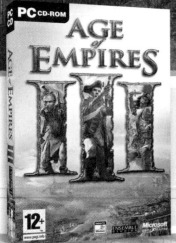

»FASTEST COMPLETION OF AGE OF EMPIRES III

Holder: Bart de Waal (Netherlands)
Strategy games are well known for their depth and complexity, yet the temptation is still there for players to try to finish them in record time. On 1 December 2008, Bart "The Void" de Waal managed to complete the story-based *Age of Empires III* (Microsoft, 2005) in Campaign mode on the "Easy" setting in 1 hr 31 min 52 sec. Amazingly, his speed-run saw him complete level 24, the last in the game, in just 1 min 12 sec.

»LONGEST-SERVING eSPORTS GAME

Holder: *StarCraft*
(Blizzard, 1998)
The first documented professional StarCraft tournament took place in South Korea in September 1999 (a full year before the commercial release of *Counter-Strike* (Sierra, 1999),

"WHOA! WHOA! SKULL KID, WAIT FOR ME! I'M STILL HERE!
TAEL, YOU CAN'T LEAVE WITHOUT ME!"

TOP 10 HIGHEST-RANKING PROFESSIONAL *STARCRAFT* PLAYERS

	Player	Gaming Name	Race	Points
1	Young-Ho Lee	Flash	Terran	3,740.5
2	Jae-Dong Lee	n.Die_Jaedong	Zerg	2,803.5
3	Jung-Woo Kim	EffOrt	Zerg	2,102.3
4	Myung-Hoon Jung	By.FanTaSy	Terran	1,989.0
5	Gu-Hyun Kim	GooJila (Kal)	Protoss	1,905.4
6	Yoon-Hwan Kim	Inter.Calm	Zerg	1,760.3
7	Jae-Ho Lee	Light[aLive]	Terran	1,744.5
8	Myung-Woon Kim	MenSol[Zero]	Zerg	1,581.8
9	Bo-Sung Yum	Sea[Shield]	Terran	1,499.6
10	Sung-Hoon Goo	HiyA[fOu]	Terran	1,439.3

Source: South Korean eSports Players Association KeSPA. All players from South Korea.

»FASTEST-SELLING CONSOLE STRATEGY GAME
Holder: *Halo Wars* **(Microsoft, 2009)**
This RTS game set in the Halo universe flew straight to the top of the Xbox 360 sales chart in the UK when released in February 2009. In doing so, *Halo Wars* sold three times as many copies on its debut as its nearest rival, *Command & Conquer 3: Tiberian Wars* (EA, 2007), making it the fastest-selling console strategy game. Three weeks after its release, Microsoft revealed that worldwide sales had passed the 1 million mark and more than 2.6 million multiplayer matches had been played – the equivalent of 118 years in total game time.

» NEW RECORD
» UPDATED RECORD

TRIVIA TRAIL

The map editor for *StarCraft II: Wings of Liberty* allows users to embed videos and, in June 2010, this feature resulted in a memorable jape as pranksters created a beta map entitled "DotA v.01". Eager gamers assumed that this was an updated version of the popular "Defence of the Ancients" mod. However, upon loading it up, players were greeted with the sight of 80s pop star Rick Astley performing "Never Gonna Give You Up", an internet phenomenon known as "Rickrolling".

»MOST INTERNATIONAL TOURNAMENT WINS ON AGE OF EMPIRES
Holder: **Byung-Geon Kang (South Korea)**
South Korean *Age of Empires* expert Byung-Geon "iamgrunt" Kang is one of the few players to be inducted into the World Cyber Games Hall of Fame for winning grand finals on two different games in a single series. Byung-Geon was first crowned champion on *Age of Empires II: The Age of Kings* (Microsoft, 1999) in 2001, aged just 18. He returned to win again in 2007, this time playing *Age of Empires III* (Microsoft, 2005). In his acceptance speech he thanked his parents for allowing him to focus on gaming rather than his schooling!

another eSports favourite). *StarCraft* remains a staple of the South Korean pro-gaming leagues over a decade later, with televised matches and star players. But *StarCraft*'s pre-eminent position as a professional electronic sports (eSports) title could soon be threatened by *Starcraft II*.

»MOST PROLIFIC STRATEGY SERIES
Holder: *Command & Conquer* **(EA, 1995 to present)**
With the release of *Command & Conquer 4: Tiberian Twilight* in March 2010, the *Command & Conquer* series now consists of 37 separate releases (including 2008's fan-favourite *Command & Conquer: Red Alert 3*, pictured), making it the most prolific strategy series. Its global sales of more than 30 million units also make it the **best-selling RTS series**. With a new game rumoured to be in the works, the series looks set to command (or conquer) a place in our record book for some time to come.

SIMULATION

WHAT WOULD YOU DO WITH OMNIPOTENT POWERS? SIMULATION GAMES GIVE YOU THE CHANCE TO FIND OUT.

»MOST BUILDING TYPES IN A CITY SIMULATION

Holder: *SimCity Societies* **(EA, 2007)**
In *SimCity Societies*, the fifth game in the main *SimCity* series, there are 400 different building types to choose from. The *Destinations* expansion pack released in June 2008 adds even more buildings, taking the total number to more than 500.

DID YOU KNOW?

SimCity 4 (EA, 2003) was the first game in the *SimCity* series to allow users to import their custom characters from *The Sims* and have them become part of the city's populace.

»LONGEST DEVELOPMENT PERIOD FOR A SIMULATION GAME

Holder: *Elite IV* **(Frontier Developments, 1997 to present)**
Fans have been waiting for more than 12 years to play the fourth game in the influential *Elite* series. David Braben (UK, pictured), co-creator of the original space trading sim, revealed in June 1997 that Frontier Developments was working on *Elite IV*, yet no firm information or assets have ever been released. Rumours circulated in May 2010 that the game had been put on hold, to which Braben told Eurogamer.net that although there had been staff changes, his commitment to *Elite* was as strong as ever.

FIRST "TYCOON" GAME
Holder: *Sid Meier's Railroad Tycoon* **(MicroProse, 1990)**
Sid Meier's Railroad Tycoon, which was developed and published by MicroProse in 1990, was such a commercial and critical success it soon inspired a boom in business simulators sporting the word "tycoon" in the title, few of

"WELL, I'VE REVIEWED YOUR CHART, LITTLE GIRL. THE BAD NEWS IS, WE'RE GOING TO HAVE TO REMOVE YOUR BRAIN... STRAP IT INTO AN ARMOURED BATTLE TANK, AND HAVE IT SHOOT DOWN INNOCENT CIVILIANS WITH ITS CONCENTRATED PSYCHIC DEATH BEAMS!"

»FIRST PEOPLE SIMULATOR

Holder: *Little Computer People* **(Activision, 1985)**
The Sims may be the most popular people simulator but it certainly wasn't the first. That particular honour belongs to *Little Computer People*, a game first released for the Commodore 64 computer by Activision in 1985. At the time of *The Sims'* release, designer Will Wright (USA) revealed that he had previously played *Little Computer People* and received valuable feedback from its creators.

»BEST-SELLING NINTENDO DS GAME

Holder: *Nintendogs* **(Nintendo, 2005)**
With worldwide sales in excess of 23.26 million since its launch in Japan in April 2005, the immensely popular pooch-petting simulator *Nintendogs* has become the best-selling Nintendo DS game of all time. However, hot on the wagging tail of the classic canine caper is *New Super Mario Bros.* (Nintendo, 2006), which has sold 22.49 million units. Even if *Mario* eventually outsells it, *Nintendogs* can still lay claim to the title of **best-selling simulation game on any platform**.

»BEST-SELLING CITY-BUILDING SERIES

Holder: *SimCity* **(Maxis Software, 1989)**
Since the original *SimCity* debuted in 1989, the series has sold more than 18 million units, making it the best-selling city simulation series. In the wider simulation field, *SimCity* is second only to its Maxis stablemate *The Sims* (2000), for which total series sales currently stand at a staggering 125 million.

HIGHEST POINTS HAUL IN M.U.L.E.

Holder: Jason Kelly (USA)
With a score of 68,273 points achieved on 2 February 2009, Jason Kelly of Memphis, Tennessee, USA, is recognized by Twin Galaxies as the champion of the Nintendo NES version of the seminal simulation game *M.U.L.E.* (EA, 1983). Kelly took the high score title from fellow American David Corbeill, who had registered a total of 63,336 points on 6 October 2008.

> "MY FAMILY AND I BOUGHT A DOG AND STARTED TAKING CARE OF IT AND THAT BECAME THE IMPETUS FOR THIS PROJECT." /LEGENDARY NINTENDO DESIGNER SHIGERU MIYAMOTO DISCUSSES THE INSPIRATION FOR THE BEST-SELLING *NINTENDOGS*.

TOP 10 BEST-SELLING GAMES IN THE *SIMS* SERIES

	Game	Sales
1	*The Sims* (PC)	16.08 million
2	*The Sims 2* (PC)	5.21 million
3	*The Sims: Unleashed* (PC)	3.76 million
4	*MySims* (DS)	3.55 million
5	*The Sims: Hot Date* (PC)	3.36 million
6	*The Sims: Vacation* (PC)	3.07 million
7=	*The Sims: Livin' Large* (PC)	2.99 million
7=	*The Sims: Superstar* (PC)	2.99 million
9	*The Sims 2: University* (PC)	2.86 million
10	*The Sims* (PS2)	2.68 million

Source: VGChartz

which had any connection to MicroProse, the original game or the Canadian game designer Sid Meier. In 2006, Meier commented that there had been so many *Tycoon* games that it had become a cliché, and so he decided to call the fourth game in the *Railroad Tycoon* series simply *Railroads!* (2K Games, 2006).

TRIVIA TRAIL

Spore (EA, 2008) was named as one of *Time* magazine's top 50 innovations of 2008. The renowned news weekly wrote of the EA-published god game: "It's blasphemy, brilliance or both to take the entire evolution of a species and turn it into a videogame. But that's exactly what [US game designer and Maxis co-founder] Will Wright has done."

» **NEW RECORD** » **UPDATED RECORD**

INDIE GAMING

INDEPENDENT GAMES ARE THOSE THAT HAVE BEEN DEVELOPED BY A SMALL TEAM OR AN INDIVIDUAL WITHOUT THE BACKING OF A PUBLISHER. WITH LESS COMMERCIAL PRESSURE, INDIE DEVELOPERS ARE FREE TO EXPERIMENT AND CRAFT THE KIND OF EXPERIENCES YOU WOULDN'T FIND IN MAINSTREAM GAMING.

DID YOU KNOW?

A key guide to what's going on in the thriving independent game movement is IndieGames.com, a website owned by UBM TechWeb, the people behind the Game Developers Conference and the Independent Games Summit. Edited by indie game experts Tim W and Michael Rose, the website serves up the latest indie gaming news, reviews of the cream of indie videogames and previews of projects indie developers have in the pipeline. It even has a blog section for the inside track on the cutting edge of gaming innovation.

THREE INDIE SUCCESS STORIES...

BRAID

Developer: Jonathan Blow (USA)
Initially released in 2008 via the Xbox Live Arcade service, *Braid* (right) tells the story of Tim, a man searching for his lost princess. Controlling Tim, the player has some limited power over time, which functions differently from level to level. Solving the game's numerous puzzles revolves around working out how to manipulate time to your advantage. Four years in the making, the entire game was the work of just two men, developer Jonathan Blow and artist David Hellman (USA). *Braid* has now been released for a variety of gaming platforms, from PC to PS3, and is still one of the top-rated games on Xbox Live Arcade.

WORLD OF GOO

Developers: Ron Carmel and Kyle Gabler (both USA)
Based around building small structures out of goo (what else?), *World of Goo* is the work of indie developers Ron Carmel and Kyle Gabler, collectively known as 2D Boy. On each gooey level, players must use their construction skills to build bridges, pyramids and towers out of little balls of goo, enabling any unused balls to traverse the structure to reach a goal point. A critical indie hit, *World of Goo* is available to play on WiiWare, Mac and PC, but it was in its PC incarnation that the game first adopted the "pay-what-you-want" price point that has now become common among indie developers seeking the widest possible audience for their wares.

CANABALT

Developer: Adam Saltsman (USA)
A simple PC game that has since been ported to the iPhone, *Canabalt* (below) tasks the player with prompting a free-runner to jump as he runs across the rooftops. The game, which needs just one button to play, generates its levels randomly so each playthrough is different, and there is no way to win as our hero never reaches any destination – it's simply a question of how far you can run before falling. Developed by Adam "Atomic" Saltsman, *Canabalt* has gone on to inspire a whole genre of one-button indie games.

"THERE'S ONLY ROOM FOR ONE BOSS. AND ONE SNAKE."

FIVE INDIE GAMES YOU SHOULD CHECK OUT...

MINECRAFT
Developer: Markus Persson (Sweden)
Featuring a 3D world full of pixel-like cubes, *Minecraft* (top right) is an online sandbox game that allows players to build anything they want. Friends can construct entire universes together and then battle monsters on their creations. The game is a work in progress with ongoing input from one-man development team Markus Persson.

VVVVVV
Developer: Terry Cavanagh (Ireland)
Created by Irish developer Terry Cavanagh, *VVVVVV* is a retro platformer with a twist – players cannot jump, but instead must flip gravity and walk on the ceiling to navigate their way around the various deadly spikes and malevolent space aliens. The aim of the game is to save your friends and put the universe to rights.

DARWINIA
Developer: Introversion Software
Set in a digital playground, *Darwinia* (bottom right) is a strategy game by UK developer Introversion Software in which the player has to guide little polygonal creatures known as Darwinians in a mission to destroy a deadly virus that is consuming their world. A multiplayer version of the game, called *Multiwinia*, is also available.

AUDIOSURF
Developer: Dylan Fitterer (USA)
An abstract racing game, *Audiosurf* uses your music collection to create its track. Developed by Dylan Fitterer, *Audiosurf* reads the music on your computer; it then analyses each of your sound files and converts them into roller-coaster-style environments, allowing you to surf along while listening to your favourite tunes.

SPELUNKY
Developer: Derek Yu (USA)
Spelunky is the work of famed indie developer Derek Yu. It's an action-adventure game in which players explore a series of randomly generated caves looking for treasure. There are plenty of traps waiting to catch the player but fortunately these can be negotiated with the help of a trusty whip when the going gets tough.

» NEW RECORD » UPDATED RECORD

> "WE... TAKE IDEAS AND INFLUENCES FROM OUTSIDE THE BOX AND INCORPORATE THEM INTO THE GAME." /CHRIS DELAY, LEAD DEVELOPER ON *DARWINIA*, ON WHAT MAKES INDEPENDENT GAMES DIFFERENT.

»MOST CRITICALLY ACCLAIMED INDIE GAME
Holder: *World of Goo* **(2D Boy, 2008)**
With a Metacritic rating of 94%, 2D Boy's *World of Goo* is currently the most highly regarded indie game. A total of 21 industry critics, including Eurogamer, *NGamer* magazine and Nintendo Life, all gave the game a perfect score.

»MOST PROLIFIC INDIE DEVELOPER
Holder: *Stephen Lavelle*
An unstoppable game-making machine, Stephen "increpare" Lavelle has released 118 games in total between 2008 and 2010. In the last year alone, Stephen has released over 40 freeware games. All his titles can be downloaded from Increpare.com.

Stephen got started in indie gaming when he began playing around with a piece of integrated development environment software called Delphi that came free with a computer game magazine. But despite all the effort he has put in, Stephen doesn't want to charge money for his games; instead he prefers to accept donations from fans of his work.

»BEST-SELLING XBOX LIVE INDIE GAME
Holder: *I MAED A GAM3 W1TH Z0MB1ES 1N IT!!!1* **(James Silva, 2009)**
You'll never guess what zombie-lover James "Jamezila" Silva (USA) has done. OK, you probably will, but more importantly he's made a game (with zombies in it) that has sold over 319,800 copies on Xbox

Live Arcade as of September 2010! Published under his developer name of Ska Studio, *I MAED A GAM3 W1TH Z0MB1ES 1N IT!!!1* is a lo-fi bird's-eye view shooter that supports up to four players. It even has its own rock theme song of the same name featuring the lines: "I made this game using XNA, it costs a dollar and I hope you'll pay."

INSTANT GAMING

NO NEED FOR MANUALS OR WALKTHROUGHS, JUST PICK UP AND PLAY – THIS IS GAMING AT ITS PUREST.

»LARGEST DOWNLOADABLE VIDEOGAME STORE

Holder: Apple App Store

As of September 2010, there are 37,362 games available for download via the Apple App Store, making it the world's largest downloadable videogame store. By comparison, PC games download service Steam offers around 1,100 titles, the Xbox Live Indie Arcade has slightly more at 1,300 and the Japanese Virtual Console store for Wii offers 576 titles covering a good chunk of the back catalogues of both Sega and Nintendo.

"MAN, THIS IS LIKE TRYING TO FIND A BRIDE IN A BROTHEL."

WHAT ARE THEY?

As games have developed over the years, there's been a tendency to make them richer, deeper and more involving. Gameplay is often multi-layered and the controls can be complex, meaning that players must invest time in learning how to actually play the game. This is a far cry from the early days of the arcade industry, when games were designed to be simple to play in order to appeal to as many people as possible. The influence of arcades may have dwindled over the decades, but these days, instant, pick-up-and-play gaming has made a fightback thanks to the prevalence of mobile devices and social network gaming.

WHO SAYS SO?

Martyn Carroll's (UK) first article on gaming was published in 1997, and since then he's contributed myriad features and reviews to many publications including *Retro Gamer*, *GamesTM*, *Micro Mart* and Eurogamer.net. Martyn has compiled records for the *Gamer's Edition* since it launched in 2008 and hopes to one-day emulate his high-score heroes with a videogame record of his own.

CONTENTS

FARMVILLE

CRITICAL HIT!

A SOCIAL GAMING PHENOMENON, FARMVILLE LETS YOU ESCAPE THE DAILY GRIND AS YOU SLOWLY BUILD A FARM.

» NEW RECORD
» UPDATED RECORD

» MOST POPULAR FACEBOOK GAME

Holder: *FarmVille* **(Zynga, 2009)**

Launched on 19 June 2009, farming simulator *FarmVille* quickly became the most popular application in the history of the social networking site Facebook, with an all-time high of 32,479,576 daily active users. As of September 2010, *FarmVille* has more than 60 million monthly active users, which is nearly twice that of its nearest competitor *FrontierVille* (Zynga, 2010). It has been estimated that if you lined up all the *FarmVille* players in the world shoulder-to-shoulder the line would stretch farther than 10,000 miles (16,100 km), equivalent to four times the distance from San Francisco to New York (both USA).

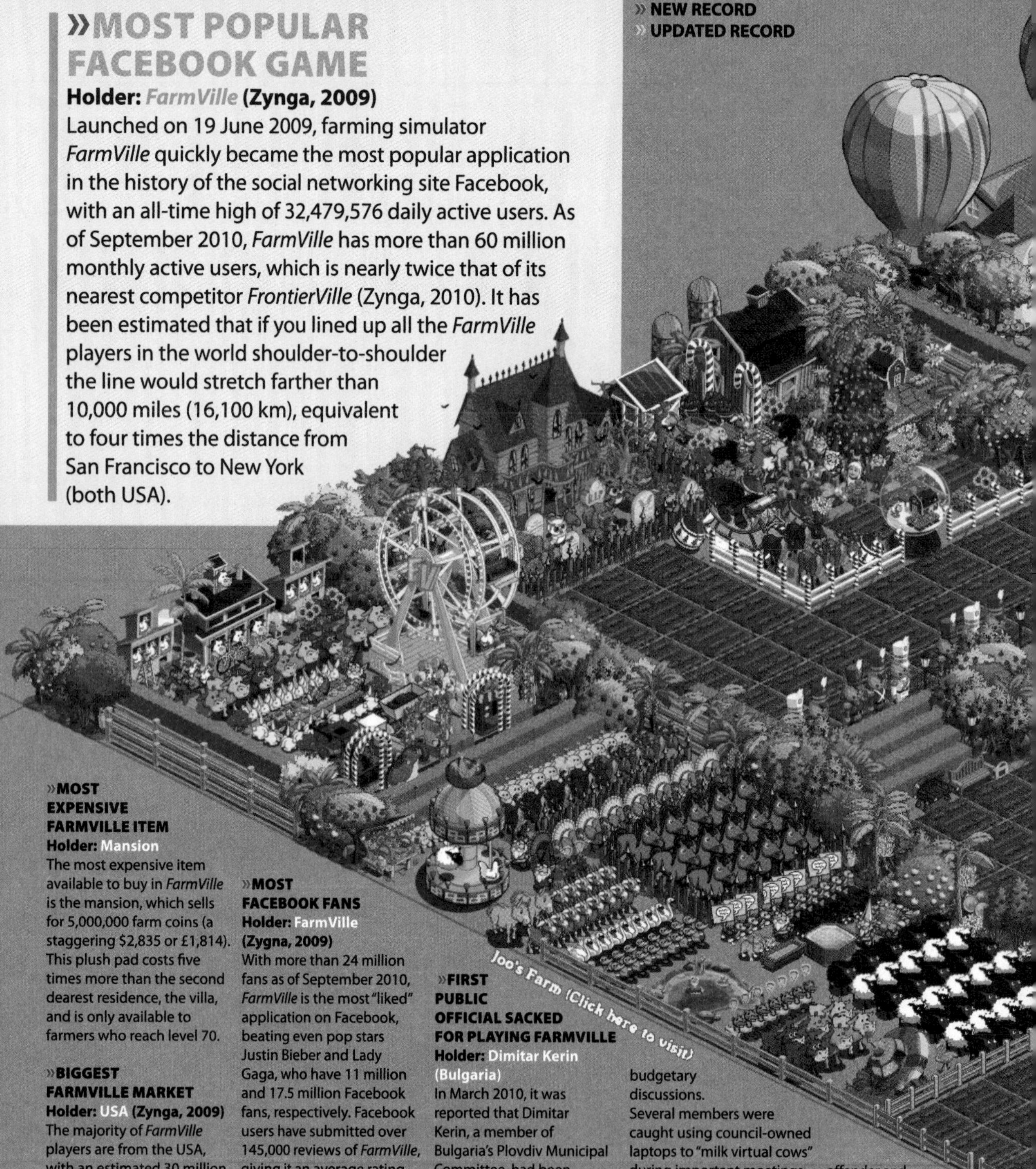

» MOST EXPENSIVE FARMVILLE ITEM

Holder: Mansion

The most expensive item available to buy in *FarmVille* is the mansion, which sells for 5,000,000 farm coins (a staggering $2,835 or £1,814). This plush pad costs five times more than the second dearest residence, the villa, and is only available to farmers who reach level 70.

» BIGGEST FARMVILLE MARKET

Holder: USA **(Zynga, 2009)**

The majority of *FarmVille* players are from the USA, with an estimated 30 million people playing the game – that's 10% of the population!

» MOST FACEBOOK FANS

Holder: FarmVille **(Zygna, 2009)**

With more than 24 million fans as of September 2010, *FarmVille* is the most "liked" application on Facebook, beating even pop stars Justin Bieber and Lady Gaga, who have 11 million and 17.5 million Facebook fans, respectively. Facebook users have submitted over 145,000 reviews of *FarmVille*, giving it an average rating of 3.9 out of 5 as of September 2010.

» FIRST PUBLIC OFFICIAL SACKED FOR PLAYING FARMVILLE

Holder: Dimitar Kerin **(Bulgaria)**

In March 2010, it was reported that Dimitar Kerin, a member of Bulgaria's Plovdiv Municipal Committee, had been removed from his post for playing *FarmVille* during budgetary discussions. Several members were caught using council-owned laptops to "milk virtual cows" during important meetings, but Kerin was identified as the most persistent offender and promptly voted off the committee.

Joo's Farm (Click here to visit)

"SHINE GET!"

83,755,953: THE ALL-TIME PEAK NUMBER OF MONTHLY ACTIVE USERS OF *FARMVILLE* ON FACEBOOK – AROUND 20% OF FACEBOOK'S TOTAL USERBASE.

TRIVIA TRAIL

In April 2010, a 12-year-old British boy made headlines after spending more than £900 ($1,370) on virtual items in *FarmVille*. After spending £288 ($440) of his own money, the anonymous youngster ran up a £625 ($950) debt on his mother's credit card without her knowledge.

TOP 10 MOST EXPENSIVE FARMING ITEMS IN *FARMVILLE*

	Item	Farm Coins	USD	GBP
1	Pheasant	2,000,000	$1,134.00	£725.76
2	Belted Cow	1,000,000	$567.00	£362.88
3	Arapawa Goat	500,000	$283.50	£181.44
4	Saddleback Pig	300,000	$170.10	£108.86
5	Biplane	30,000	$17.01	£10.89
6	Seeder	30,000	$17.01	£10.89
7	Harvester	30,000	$17.01	£10.89
8	Tractor	5,000	$2.84	£1.81
9	Pig	1,000	$0.57	£0.36
10	Forget-me-not	750	$0.43	£0.27

Source: FarmVille

Levi's Farm (Click here to visit)

"THE BIGGEST CHALLENGE HAS BEEN TO KEEP UP WITH THE GROWTH OF THE GAME... WE HAVE TO UNDERSTAND DEEPLY THE NATURE OF THE PROBLEM WE ARE FACING IN ORDER TO BUILD A SOLUTION THAT FIXES IT." /LUKE RAJLICH, ARCHITECT ENGINEER TALKING ABOUT *FARMVILLE'S* CONTINUAL GROWING PAINS.

"OH, THE LITTLE MAN IS COCKY NOW. PERHAPS YOU'D LIKE TO MEET HELGA ON THE WRESTLING MAT. LET'S SEE HOW COCKY YOU ARE, TWISTED UP LIKE A WET NOODLE."

CLASSIC ARCADE

ARCADE HISTORY BEGINS RIGHT HERE, WITH THE TIMELESS GAMES OF THE 1970s AND 1980s.

TAITO
TAITRONICS

»LONGEST-RUNNING GAME SERIES

Holder: *Space Invaders* **(Taito, 1978 to present)**
Since the original game blasted into Japanese arcades in 1978, *Space Invaders* has become one of the most successful and influential arcade games of all time. Such is its legacy that over the past three decades the game has been revamped, repackaged, re-released or ripped-off on almost every games platform ever created. The most recent release was *Space Invaders Extreme 2* (Taito, 2009) for the Nintendo DS. With a history stretching back more than 32 years, *Space Invaders* is the longest-running series of videogames in history.

"JUST ONCE, I'D LIKE FOR SOMEONE TO SAY 'YES, CERTAINLY, I'LL HELP YOU SAVE THE GALAXY! JUST LET ME GO GRAB MY STUFF!'"

TOP 10 HIGHEST SCORES ON *PAC-MAN*

	Player	Score	Verified
1	Billy Mitchell (USA)	3,333,360	3 July 1999
2	Rick Fothergill (Canada)	3,333,360	31 July 1999
3	Chris Ayra (USA)	3,333,360	16 February 2000
4	Tim Balderramos (USA)	3,333,360	28 August 2005
5	Donald Hayes (USA)	3,333,360	21 July 2005
6	David Race (USA)	3,333,360	15 August 2009
7	Jon Stoodley (UK)	3,227,000	29 May 2009
8	Ricky Mori (USA)	3,171,120	1 August 1982
9	Patrice Corbeil (Canada)	3,155,320	30 June 1985
10	Bryan Wagner (USA)	3,154,640	4 June 2004

Source: Twin Galaxies (3,333,360 is the highest possible score. Players ranked by date of achievement).

» NEW RECORD   » UPDATED RECORD

»HIGHEST SCORE ON DONKEY KONG

Holder: Steve Wiebe (USA)

Algebra teacher and renowned *Donkey Kong* (Nintendo, 1981) enthusiast Steve Wiebe (above) reclaimed the record for the highest score on the ape-based arcade classic from his long-time rival Billy Mitchell (USA) with a 1,064,500-point run on 30 August 2010. Wiebe's score marks the third time the record has changed hands this year following Hank Chein's (USA) score of 1,061,700 points in March and Billy Mitchell's 1,062,800 points in July. Bizarrely, Billy quit his game as soon as he set a new record, when he could have gone on and scored more.

»HIGHEST ASTEROIDS SCORE

Holder: John McAllister (USA)

On 5 April 2010, after a mammoth 58-hour session playing *Asteroids* (Atari, 1979), John McAllister amassed a new record score of 41,838,740 points. In doing so, he smashed the previous high score of 41,336,440 points set by Scott Safran (USA) on 13 November 1982. McAllister managed to beat the 27-year-old record by building up enough extra lives to enable him to leave the game unattended briefly while he ate food and visited the bathroom.

»HIGHEST SCORE ON GALAXIAN

Holder: Aart van Vliet (Netherlands)

With a score of 1,653,270 points, Aart van Vliet of The Hague, Netherlands, became the new *Galaxian* (Namco, 1979) high score record-holder on 27 May 2009. Aart achieved this impressive feat at the Funspot arcade in New Hampshire, USA, under the watchful eye of Twin Galaxies referee Kelly R Flewin. He took the title from noted *Galaxian* champion Gary Whelen (UK), who had previously held the top spot with a score of 1,114,550 points.

"SOME SAY I'M BEING COCKY. SOME SAY I'M BEING LAZY. I SAY, I'M BEING BILLY MITCHELL." /BILLY MITCHELL ON QUITTING HIS GAME RIGHT AFTER SETTING A DONKEY KONG RECORD.

»HIGHEST NEMESIS SCORE

Holder: Joe Martin (USA)

The top scorer on Konami's 1985 classic *Nemesis* is Joe Martin, who clocked up a 1,196,400-point haul on the side-scrolling shoot-'em-up on 28 January 2010. Playing a version of the game running on a Multiple Arcade Machine Emulator (MAME), Joe toppled the previous record of 1,195,500 points registered by Paul Ashworth (UK) in 1985. Martin also holds high score records in various other shoot-'em-up titles.

TRIVIA TRAIL

To celebrate 30 years of Namco's *PAC-Man* on 21 May 2010, Google changed its search engine logo to a playable version of the game. RescueTime, a time management software publisher, reported that visitors spent 4,819,352 hours playing *PAC-Man* during the day, equating to $120,483,800 (£78,278,400) in lost productivity.

MOST SUCCESSFUL COIN-OPERATED ARCADE GAME

Holder: *PAC-Man* (Namco, 1981)

From its launch in 1981 until 1987, a total of 293,822 *PAC-Man* arcade machines were built and installed in arcades around the world. Designed by Tōru Iwatani (Japan, pictured right) of Namco, the original game took eight people 15 months to complete. Namco estimate that *PAC-Man* has been played more than 10 billion times in its 30-year history.

MOBILE GAMING

POWERFUL SMARTPHONES HAVE MADE GAMING ON THE GO EASIER AND MORE ENJOYABLE THAN EVER.

»FASTEST-SELLING iPHONE/iPOD STRATEGY GAME

Holder: *Plants vs. Zombies* **(PopCap, 2010)**

With more than 300,000 paid downloads in its first nine days on sale in February 2010, PopCap's *Plants vs. Zombies* for the iPhone and iPod Touch is the highest-grossing strategy game launch in the history of Apple's App Store. Despite retailing at a pocket-money price of just $2.99 in the US (£1.79 in the UK), the tower defence title generated a cool $1 million (£650,000) for PopCap in a little over a week.

$455,660

Column Like You See 'Em

»MOST POPULAR APPLICATION MARKETPLACE

Holder: Apple App Store

With over 6.5 billion downloads since its launch in July 2008, the Apple App Store is the most popular downloadable app service in the world. As of September 2010 it hosts 259,470 apps for purchase or free download (a further 50,000 apps that were once available through the service have been discontinued). Of the apps currently available, 61 are flatulence simulators, a genre that includes such masterpieces as *Fart Machine*, *Fart Ocarina* and *iFart – Epic Rip Edition*…

TRIVIA TRAIL

The first mobile phone game was *Snake*, which appeared on the Nokia 6110 handset in 1997 and would slither its way on to an incredible 350 million phones. The first iPod game was *Brick*, an update of *Breakout* (Atari, 1976), which was included as a hidden feature, or Easter egg, on the original iPod model in 2001.

»FIRST 3D iPAD GAME

Holder: *Flight Control HD* **(Firemint, 2010)**

Flight Control HD from Firemint is the first iPad game with an option to display 3D visuals. The game, which casts players in the role of an air traffic controller in charge of an increasingly busy airport,

"YOU PATHETIC WRETCH… WHAT A WORTHLESS COWARD. I WILL MAKE YOUR POWER MINE… TIME TO DIE, BOY!"

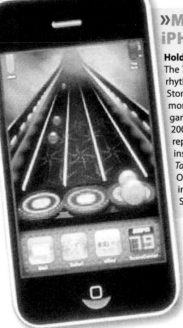

» MOST POPULAR iPHONE GAME SERIES

Holder: *Tap Tap Revenge* (Tapulous, 2008)
The *Tap Tap Revenge* series of music rhythm games is the most popular in App Store history, having been downloaded more than 15 million times since the first game in the series was released in July 2008. Market research firm comScore reports that the games have been installed by 32% of all iPhone/iPad users. *Tap Tap Revenge 3*, which was released in October 2009, hit No.1 in the App Store in the US, UK, Canada, Australia, Mexico, Singapore and Netherlands.

» MOST VIEWED VIDEOGAME WALKTHROUGH ON YOUTUBE.CO.UK

Holder: *Red Remover* (Gaz Thomas, 2009)
A guide to the Flash and iPhone/iPad physics puzzler *Red Remover* is the most viewed game walkthrough video on YouTube.co.uk, with 7,067,488 views as of 6 September 2010. The game can be played at www.thegamehomepage.com/play/red-remover/.

» NEW RECORD
» UPDATED RECORD

» MOST EXPENSIVE APP STORE GAME

Holder: *Alchemize* (Schiau Studios, 2009)
Most games in the App Store retail for less than $10 (£6.50), yet in October 2009 the puzzle game *Alchemize* was on sale for $39.99 (£25), making it the most expensive game available through the store. However, developers Schiau Studios listed the game at that high price for just two days in protest at customers who complained that the game's usual price of $2.99 (£1.88) was too expensive. Any extra revenue made from the inflated price was donated to charity.

"CLEARLY iPHONE PLUS iPOD TOUCH HAVE CREATED A NEW CLASS OF GAMING. IT'S A SUBSET OF CASUAL GAMING."
/STEVE JOBS, CEO OF APPLE, MASTERS OF THE APP STORE.

utilizes the traditional anaglyph 3D process, meaning that to experience the effect the player is required to wear red/cyan glasses. *Flight Control HD* launched alongside the iPad in April 2010. A version of the game was released on the PlayStation Network in September 2010.

TOP 10 SCORES ON THE iPAD/iPHONE VERSION OF *FLIGHT CONTROL*

	Player	Score
1	aguilas	82,383
2	volando-alto	80,891
3	Wolverine	68,674
4	danpho	30,039
5	smooth_criminal	28,543
6	cunbun	26,390
7	Nikom	24,161
8	johnmark58	24,042
9	TRUCMAN99	24,022
10	jonniejumbo	23,823

Source: http://flightcontrol.cloudcell.com

"FWAHAHAHA! THIS IS MY HIDEOUT! I PLANNED TO RESURRECT TEAM ROCKET HERE! BUT, YOU HAVE CAUGHT ME AGAIN! SO BE IT! THIS TIME, I'M NOT HOLDING BACK! ONCE MORE, YOU SHALL FACE GIOVANNI, THE GREATEST TRAINER!"

WWW.GUINNESSWORLDRECORDS.COM/GAMERS **179**

SOCIAL NETWORK GAMING

SOCIAL NETWORKS SUCH AS FACEBOOK AND MYSPACE INVITE US TO COMMENT, SHARE, CHAT... AND PLAY.

» NEW RECORD
UPDATED RECORD

TOP 10 HIGHEST-RANKING GUILDS IN *POXNORA*

	Guild	# Members	Rating
1	*dudes irritating*	32	1,322
2	*Mercs*	16	1,291
3	*High-Council*	36	1,211
4	*NotAGuild*	33	1,209
5	*Super-Extraordinary*	26	1,172
6	*Team Purple*	44	1,138
7	*Lords of The Tundra*	49	1,135
8	*Draksar Clan*	299	1,125
9	*Defenders of the Stronghold*	269	1,109
10	*Noob World Order*	37	1,106

Source: http://poxnora.station.sony.com

»HIGHEST-RANKING POXNORA GUILD

Holder: dudes irritating
PoxNora (Sony, 2006) is a collectible, turn-based, tactical online fantasy game that has registered a high of 604,000 people playing through Facebook every month (many hundreds of thousands of others play online). Currently, *PoxNora* has over 50 dedicated guilds vying to be top dogs within the game, of which the highest ranking is "dudes irritating" (see table, left).

"SUFFER, LIKE G DID."

»FASTEST-GROWING FACEBOOK GAME

Holder: *Treasure Isle* **(Zynga, 2010)**
After launch on 2 April 2010, Zynga's *Treasure Isle* attracted 980,000 players in just two days. By the end of its second week, this figure had risen to 5.8 million, and by June 2010 the game had more than 25 million people playing it daily. Thanks to this rapid rise in player numbers, *Treasure Isle* has become the fastest-growing Facebook application ever. The game sees players exploring islands in a bid to uncover valuable items, which can then be turned into virtual money.

"WITH OVER 35 MILLION [NOW 47 MILLION] UNIQUE USERS PLAYING OUR GAMES EVERY SINGLE DAY, SOCIAL GAMES ARE FAST BECOMING A LEADING SOURCE OF ENTERTAINMENT WORLDWIDE, SURPASSING MOST TELEVISION SHOWS."
/MARK PINCUS, FOUNDER AND CEO OF ZYNGA.

»MOST POPULAR SOCIAL GAMING NETWORK
Holder: Facebook
With 90% of all social games played on Facebook, the social networking website is far and away the biggest gaming platform of its kind. As of September 2010, Facebook has more than 500 million users spending over 700 billion minutes per month on the site, and the massive impact of games such as *FarmVille* (Zynga, 2009) and *Pet Society* (Playfish, 2009) is seen as one of the biggest contributors to the network's continued popularity. Facebook was launched by American Mark Zuckerberg in 2004.

»MOST PROLIFIC SOCIAL GAMING COMPANY
Holder: Zynga
Zynga is the biggest provider of social games, with 47 million people playing its 52 titles daily in September 2010. Zynga's closest rivals, Playdom and Electronic Arts, can only boast 38 and 35 titles, respectively. The list of most-played social games is dominated by popular Zynga titles such as *FarmVille*, *Texas HoldEm Poker* and *Treasure Isle*. An April 2010 report estimated that the company, based in California, USA, could be worth as much as $5 billion (£3.3 billion), despite only being founded in 2007.

»FIRST SOCIAL GAME TO BE OPTIONED AS A MOVIE
Holder: *Mafia Wars* **(Zynga, 2009)**
In June 2010, US film production company Radar Pictures announced that it had secured the rights to turn Zynga's *Mafia Wars* into a movie. Few details were revealed at the time, except that Radar Pictures planned to develop a "crime thriller" based on the hugely successful social game. When – and if – the film makes it to the big screen, Radar will certainly be hoping that some of the game's 21 million active users pop along to the cinema to see it.

»MOST POPULAR SOCIAL NETWORK GAME
Holder: *Happy Farm* **(Five Minutes, 2008)**
Surprisingly, the most popular social network game is not a Facebook chart-topper. *Happy Farm*, a farming sim, is played by 228 million users in China and Korea every month. The game is so popular with white-collar workers in China that an estimated 75 million man-hours per day are lost to picking pixellated potatoes.

TOP 50 CHARACTERS

TOP 50

On our website this year, we posed the question "Who is your all-time favourite videogame character?" and thousands of you took the time to post your answers – thanks to you all! So, over the next few pages we're counting them down, from number 50 through to number one. There are a few surprises in the list, and quite a few familiar faces, too. But all in all it makes for a pretty accurate rogues (and heroes) gallery of classic gaming characters over the years.

Top 50 Characters: 50 to 31	184
Top 50 Characters: 30 to 11	186
Top 50 Characters: 10 to 4	188
Top 50 Characters: Top 3	190

"FOR WHAT IT WAS WORTH, YOU DID A GREAT JOB ISAAC. SEE YOU AROUND... OR MAYBE NOT."

OUR SURVEY

GAMER'S EDITION

Over 13,000 votes were cast by gaming fans who visited our website: www.guinnessworldrecords.com/gamers

The most popular publisher in this year's survey is Nintendo, with 11 characters in the top 50. In second place is Sony with six characters, and third comes Capcom with five.

The best year for great characters was 1996, with five familiar faces in our top 50 making their first gaming appearance in that year. Other great years for gaming were 1987, 2001 and 2007 with four entries each.

But who are these great names in videogame history? Turn the page to find out how your favourite fared.

"THIS IS NOT A SERMON. I WILL OFFER NO INSIGHT. EVERY WORD I SPEAK, YOU ALREADY KNOW."

WWW.GUINNESSWORLDRECORDS.COM/GAMERS **183**

KICKING OFF OUR CHART, WE HAVE PRINCES, PRINCESSES, ALL MANNER OF WARRIORS AND EVEN A DRAGON!

SACKBOY
GAMER'S EDITION

Pliable Plaything

Completely Customizable:
Just like *LittleBigPlanet* itself, Sackboy can be modified as the player chooses, and has demonstrated a love of dressing up as other videogames characters.

First appearance: LittleBigPlanet (Sony, 2008)

50

RYU
GAMER'S EDITION

Street Fighter

Gadouken!:
It isn't just fast fists that are the key to Ryu's fighting – one of his main special moves is a surge blast of Chi energy that saps the life bars of his foes.

First appearance: Street Fighter (Capcom, 1987)

49

48

EDDIE RIGGS
GAMER'S EDITION

Rockin' Roadie

You Can't Kill the Metal:
A heavy metal roadie who comes back from the grave and saves the world, Eddie Riggs is voiced by Tenacious D's Jack Black.

First appearance: Brütal Legend (EA, 2009)

BOWSER
GAMER'S EDITION

King of the Koopas

Life's a Peach:
Mario's frequent foe, the top Koopa turtle just won't quit kidnapping Princess Peach or invading the Mushroom Kingdom.

First appearance: Super Mario Bros. (Nintendo, 1985)

47

AUGUSTUS COLE
GAMER'S EDITION

Alpha Male

Awesome Ally:
He might not be playable but Alpha Company's "Cole Train" provides both memorable quips aplenty and some much-needed extra firepower.

First appearance: Gears of War (Microsoft, 2006)

46

LARRY LAFFER
GAMER'S EDITION

Wannabe Lady's Man

Player:
He might be an older man, but Larry loves the ladies and there's little he won't stoop to in pursuit of a willing woman.

First appearance: Leisure Suit Larry in the Land of the Lounge Lizards (Sierra, 1987)

45

PRINCESS PEACH
GAMER'S EDITION

Mushroom Princess

Float Like a Butterfly:
Peach pulls no punches in 2D fighter *Super Smash Bros.*, using her parasol to float into a good attacking position.

First appearance: Super Mario Bros. (Nintendo, 1985)

44

JILL VALENTINE
GAMER'S EDITION

Zombie Killer

Finish Him:
Betrayed by the series' archvillain Albert Wesker in the first *Resident Evil*, Jill was on hand at his demise in *Resident Evil 5*.

First appearance: Biohazard/Resident Evil (Capcom, 1996)

43

MAX PAYNE
GAMER'S EDITION

Violent Vigilante

Revenge:
His wife and child were killed by drug dealers, now nothing's gonna stop Max Payne in his quest for vengeance.

First appearance: Max Payne (Rockstar, 2001)

42

GOKU
GAMER'S EDITION

Mixed-up Martial Artist

Plenty of Powers:
Goku has attained a variety of skills through his years of training, including super speed and energy blasts.

First appearance: Dragon Daihikyōe (Epoch, 1987)

41

}   "THE BIG ENEMY IS APPROACHING AT FULL THROTTLE. ACCORDING TO THE DATA, IT IS IDENTIFIED AS BUTSUTEKKAI. NO REFUGE."   }

31 MILLION: THE WORLDWIDE SALES OF THREE-FOLD GAME *POKÉMON RED/GREEN/BLUE* (NINTENDO, 1996), THE BEST-SELLING JAPANESE ROLE-PLAYING GAME.

GUINNESS WORLD RECORDS

"GHOST" RILEY — GAMER'S EDITION

Ghost-faced Killer

One-hit Wonder:
British special-ops soldier "Ghost" was betrayed and killed in his debut game. Not much chance of an encore, then.

First appearance: *Call of Duty: Modern Warfare 2* (Activision, 2009)

40

SPYRO — GAMER'S EDITION

Dynamic Dragon

Purple on Purpose:
What do you call a green dragon sitting on the grass? Invisible! Which is why Spyro became a purple dragon.

First appearance: *Spyro the Dragon* (Universal, 1998)

39

GUYBRUSH THREEPWOOD — GAMER'S EDITION

Wannabe Pirate

A Way with Words:
Over the *Monkey Island* games, Guybrush has developed a line of pithy retorts to help him outwit his pirate foes.

First appearance: *The Secret of Monkey Island* (LucasArts, 1990)

38

ASH KETCHUM — GAMER'S EDITION

Pokémon Trainer

Playing Catch-up:
As a punishment for being late for class, Ash was given the cheeky Pikachu as his first Pokémon.

First appearance: *Pokémon Red/Green* (Nintendo, 1996)

37

LEON S — GAMER'S EDITION

Zombie Slayer

Hard to Kill:
A battle-hardened Secret Service Agent, Leon S can only be killed by decapitation or in a Quick Time Event.

First appearance: *Biohazard/Resident Evil* (Capcom, 1996)

36

EZIO — GAMER'S EDITION

Accomplished Assassin

Renaissance Man:
An Italian nobleman, Ezio Auditore da Firenze makes use of the inventions of his friend Leonardo da Vinci on his missions.

First appearance: *Assassin's Creed II* (Ubisoft, 2009)

35

THE PRINCE — GAMER'S EDITION

Acrobatic Royal

The Nameless One:
Despite his royal blood, the title character in the original *Prince of Persia* was never given a name.

First appearance: *Prince of Persia* (Brøderbund, 1989)

34

DONKEY KONG — GAMER'S EDITION

Pixelated Primate

Dressed for Success:
No-one knows how DK ended up wearing a tie, but everyone assumes he did it himself because no-one would ever be brave enough to try to dress him.

First appearance: *Donkey Kong* (Nintendo, 1981)

33

SEPHIROTH — GAMER'S EDITION

Evil Angel

Heartless:
A vile villain who cruelly killed *Final Fantasy VII*'s lead character Aeris, Sephiroth brought tears to the eyes of gamers the world over.

First appearance: *Final Fantasy VII* (Square, 1997)

32

ZELDA — GAMER'S EDITION

Hylian Princess

Getting Tough:
No shrinking violet, Zelda gets tougher with each new game – possessing a suit of armour in her latest appearance.

First appearance: *The Legend of Zelda* (Nintendo, 1986)

31

SOME FAMILIAR FACES, AS WELL AS THE ODD SURPRISE, AS WE CONTINUE OUR CHARACTER COUNTDOWN.

ALTAÏR GAMER'S EDITION

Crusading Assassin

Sneak:
Altaïr Ibn-La'Ahad is a master assassin who can use his skills of concealment to become invisible; only you know when he's going to strike next.

First appearance: *Assassin's Creed* (Ubisoft, 2007)

30

NARUTO GAMER'S EDITION

Teen Ninja

Super Chakra:
Naruto hosts a demon fox spirit, giving him great reserves of chakra energy to fuel his surprising ninja abilities.

First appearance: *Naruto: Konoha Ninpōch* (Bandai, 2003)

29

28

DANTE GAMER'S EDITION

Paranormal Detective/Devil Slayer

Half Devil:
A professional devil slayer, not only does Dante carry guns and swords, he also has the "Devil Trigger", a range of powers due to his demon heritage.

First appearance: *Devil May Cry* (Bandai, 2003)

DUKE NUKEM GAMER'S EDITION

Just call him "The King"

Guns, Guns, Guns:
Duke Nukem isn't a complicated man, he's just here to shoot all manner of aliens and chew bubblegum – and he's all out of gum.

First appearance: *Duke Nukem* (Apogee, 1991)

27

JAK GAMER'S EDITION

Eco Warrior

Eco friendly:
Most of Jak's powers and abilities derive from Eco, the natural resource and main tool of the Precursor deities.

First appearance: *Jak and Daxter: The Precursor Legacy* (Sony, 2001)

26

SHADOW GAMER'S EDITION

Hypersonic Hedgehog

Evil Equivalent:
An artificial lifeform, super speedster Shadow is Sonic the Hedgehog's equal and rival in most things, but not his place in this top 50 list of characters…

First appearance: *Sonic Adventure 2* (Sega, 2001)

25

SAM FISHER GAMER'S EDITION

Super Spy

Silent, But Deadly:
Sam is a stealth expert and trained in unarmed combat, making him the ideal operative for work behind enemy lines.

First appearance: *Tom Clancy's Splinter Cell* (Ubisoft, 2002)

24

MEGA MAN GAMER'S EDITION

23

Robot Master

Proto-copier:
Mega Man automatically gains the abilities of defeated enemies. As a result, he has never needed to revise for an exam in his life!

First appearance: *Mega Man* (Capcom, 1987)

"CJ" JOHNSON GAMER'S EDITION

22

Smooth Criminal

Grove Street Shuffle:
A gangster on the rise, "CJ" knows the fastest way to make money in San Andreas is to take out crack dealers.

First appearance: *Grand Theft Auto: San Andreas* (Rockstar, 2004)

YOSHI GAMER'S EDITION

Sidekickasaurus

Baby Sitter:
Mario's best buddy and frequent sidekick, Yoshi has plenty of experience saving kids on tropical islands.

First appearance: *Super Mario World* (Nintendo, 1990)

21

"SUCH A PITY! SUCH A PITY!.. YOU CAN'T SEE HOW USELESS YOUR FEEBLE ENCHANTMENTS ARE AGAINST THE MIGHT OF THIS SCEPTRE!"

11.9 MILLION: THE NUMBER OF UNITS SOLD IN MICROSOFT'S XBOX 360 EXCLUSIVE *GEARS OF WAR* SERIES SINCE THE FIRST GAME WAS RELEASED IN 2006.

GUINNESS WORLD RECORDS

PIKACHU
GAMER'S EDITION

Lightning Mouse

20

Gotta Get 'em All:
Pikachu always manages to be the centre of attention, even when he's not the star of the game in question.

First appearance: Pokémon Red/Green (Nintendo, 1996)

MARCUS FENIX
GAMER'S EDITION

COG Master

19

Strong Stomach:
Marcus is immune to nausea, even when faced with the goriest scenes. Gears of War 2 saw him cheerfully eviscerating a Stone Worm – from the inside!

First appearance: Gears of War (Microsoft, 2006)

KIRBY
GAMER'S EDITION

Denizen of Dream Land

18

Heavy Breathing:
Kirby's powerful lungs allow him to inhale enemies and steal their powers. He can also hold his breath for ages.

First appearance: Kirby's Dream Land (Nintendo, 1992)

CAPTAIN PRICE
GAMER'S EDITION

Solid Soldier

17

Unbreakable:
Not even five years in a gulag can put Price out of action. Just don't get in the way of his nuclear powered payback.

First appearance: Call of Duty 4: Modern Warfare (Activision, 2007)

NATHAN DRAKE
GAMER'S EDITION

Audacious Adventurer

16

Illustrious Ancestors:
Nathan Drake can allegedly trace his ancestry to the English sea captain, pirate and adventurer Sir Francis Drake.

First appearance: Uncharted: Drake's Fortune (Sony, 2007)

RATCHET
GAMER'S EDITION

Last of the Lombax

15

Old Skool:
The last of his kind, Ratchet doesn't follow trends. He's still doing 3D platformers like it's 2002.

First appearance: Ratchet & Clank (Sony, 2002)

SAMUS ARAN
GAMER'S EDITION

Bounty Hunter

14

Surprise:
Few of her foes suspect that under her armour, Samus is actually all woman.

First appearance: Metroid (Nintendo, 1986)

NICO BELLIC
GAMER'S EDITION

Economic Migrant

13

Living the Dream:
Nico is a man who is determined to make his American Dream a reality – Second Ammendment style.

First appearance: Grand Theft Auto IV (Rockstar, 2008)

"SOAP" MacTAVISH
GAMER'S EDITION

Serious SAS Specialist

12

Don't Mess:
He's taken down terrorists and corrupt US Army Generals – are you going to tell him he has a silly haircut?

First appearance: Call of Duty 4: Modern Warfare (Activision, 2007)

CRASH
GAMER'S EDITION

Genetically Modified Marsupial

11

His Own Bandicoot:
Originally intended to be Sony's mascot character to rival Nintendo and Sega's Mario and Sonic, Crash never quite became a company man.

First appearance: Crash Bandicoot (Sony, 1996)

"WHAT IS A MAN? A MISERABLE LITTLE PILE OF SECRETS! BUT ENOUGH TALK, HAVE AT YOU!"

WWW.GUINNESSWORLDRECORDS.COM/GAMERS   **187**

INTO THE TOP 10, WE HAVE SCIENTISTS, GHOSTS AND ONE HUNGRY BALL OF PIXELS.

10

SONIC
GAMER'S EDITION

The Blue Dude with 'Tude

Put a Ring on it:
The fastest hedgehog in town, swifter than the speed of sound. Everyone knows that Sonic is super, but when you collect those rings he's Super Sonic!

First appearance: *Sonic the Hedgehog* (Sega, 1990)

9

KRATOS
GAMER'S EDITION

Ghost of Sparta

This is Madness:
Kratos isn't going to back down from a fight – he's taken down Ares and replaces him as the God of War. The bigger they are the harder they fall…

First appearance: *God of War* (Sony, 2005)

8

GORDON
GAMER'S EDITION

Theoretical Physicist

Nothing to Say:
He might be a brilliant scientist, but in the face of headcrabs and various other nasties infesting the Black Mesa facility Gordon Freeman remains tight-lipped.

First appearance: *Half-Life* (Valve, 1998)

7

LARA CROFT
GAMER'S EDITION

Tomb Raider

Star Power:
A multi-media phenomenon, Lara makes it into the top 10 off the back of movies, advertising deals, merchandising, oh, and great games.

First appearance: *Tomb Raider* (Eidos, 1996)

"NOBLE TWO TO NOBLE SIX.
YOU'VE GOT INCOMING TANGOS!"

26 MILLION: THE NUMBER OF VIDEOGAMES STARRING LARA CROFT THAT HAVE BEEN SOLD WORLDWIDE AS OF SEPTEMBER 2010.

GUINNESS WORLD RECORDS

PAC-MAN
GAMER'S EDITION

6

Powerful Eating Machine

Greedy:
He may be 30 years old, but his appetite shows no sign of diminishing – even on the original arcade version, PAC-Man hit a kill screen before he felt full.

First appearance: *PAC-Man* (Namco, 1980)

CLOUD STRIFE
GAMER'S EDITION

5

GUINNESS WORLD RECORDS 2011

Moody Mercenary

Not Interested:
Cloud says little and is consumed by inner guilt and many secrets. He might want to tear his adversary Sephiroth apart, but he doesn't want to talk about it.

First appearance: *Final Fantasy VII* (Square, 1997)

"BY CREATING… KAWAII (CUTE) CHARACTERS WE THOUGHT WE COULD APPEAL TO WOMEN…"
/TŌRU IWATANI EXPLAINS HOW HE DEVELOPED THE IDEA FOR PAC-MAN.

SOLID SNAKE
GAMER'S EDITION

4

Clone Baby

A Follower of Fashion:
It takes a certain type of man to carry off the moustache/eyepatch combo – Snake makes them work, taking after his nemesis and clone father Big Boss.

First appearance: *Metal Gear* (Konami, 1987)

"WARS ARE LIKE BOMBS. THE FUSE GETS LIT BEFORE YOU ACTUALLY HEAR THE BANG AND SOMETIMES THE FUSE CAN BE PRETTY LONG."

WWW.GUINNESSWORLDRECORDS.COM/GAMERS **189**

SO, HERE WE ARE AT THE TOP OF THE LIST WITH A SPARTAN, A HYLIAN AND A CERTAIN PLUMBER CALLED MARIO...

MASTER CHIEF

GAMER'S EDITION

Genetically Engineered Supersoldier

Gun Show:
The Master Chief's fists cause more damage than his rifle.

The mysterious supersoldier and thrice saviour of humanity, John-117 is the archetypal action hero. Too bad he wasn't around to help his Spartan brothers on the planet Reach.

First appearance: *Halo: Combat Evolved*
(Microsoft, 2001)

3

GUINNESS WORLD RECORDS 2011

2

LINK

GAMER'S EDITION

Hero of Time

Good Communicator:
Link can always make himself understood with his little grunts and shouts.

Star of countless critically acclaimed games, Link the Hylian has taken the form of many creatures over the years, including a wolf, a rabbit, a plant, a rock, an evil god, a midget and even a fishperson!
First appearance: *The Legend of Zelda* (Nintendo, 1986)

"OH NO!"

GUINNESS WORLD RECORDS

MARIO

GAMER'S
EDITION

TRADING CARD GAME

Polymath Plumber

Versatile:

Over the years, Mario has showed off his skills at so many different things: jumping, kart racing, rescuing princesses, athletics, tennis, soccer, baseball, painting and even being a doctor. But we've never actually seen him do any plumbing… is he even qualified?

One of gaming's longest-serving superstars, the artist known as Jumpman in his gaming debut has proven time and again that charisma is what counts. That and a stack of endlessly replayable games are probably the reasons that hundreds of you voted for him.

First appearance: *Donkey Kong* (Nintendo, 1981)

GUINNESS WORLD RECORDS 2011

"I'M SORRY. I DIDN'T REALIZE YOU WANTED HIM TO SHOOT YOU. I CAN CALL IN SOME MORE GUARDS IF YOU LIKE."

TWIN GALAXIES SCOREBOARDS

ON CONSOLE OR IN THE ARCADE, OLD SCHOOL OR 7TH GENERATION – TWIN GALAXIES HAVE THE HIGH SCORES.

"I WAS JUST READING A COLLECTION OF ESSAYS ON THE SCIENCE-FICTION GENRE. THERE WAS ONE QUOTE ATTRIBUTED TO A NOVELIST I FOUND REMARKABLE. 'THOUGH LOVE MAY LOSE, KINDNESS WINS.' I FIND THAT PHILOSOPHICAL AND, AT THE SAME TIME, COMPASSIONATE."

WHO ARE TG?

Founded in 1981, Twin Galaxies International are a world-leading authority on player rankings, gaming statistics and championship events. They hold pinball statistics dating back to the 1930s and videogame records from the 1970s.

Guinness World Records Gamer's Edition is extremely pleased to partner with Twin Galaxies every year and values the passion, integrity and commitment with which they scrutinize every entry in their database.

HOW THEY WORK

This year we've made a small change to our Twin Galaxies high scores tables. Instead of one long A to Z of scores, we have split the entries up into different console manufacturers, making it easier for you to find the high score you're looking for. We have also included some "Old School" records for the videogame historians among you.

It's been a busy year for high scores and record attempts, and over the past 12 months Twin Galaxies have charted some of the most exciting records they've ever seen. In some of the most heavily contested categories they've indicated how scores on the same game under the same conditions stack up against each other, which is why you'll see scores marked out as 1 , 2 , 3 in some cases.

CONTENTS

THE LATEST TWIN GALAXIES HIGH SCORES ACROSS NINTENDO'S FINEST PLATFORMS.

GOLDENEYE 007

(Nintendo, 1997)
With a 95.35% score on review aggregator site GameRankings.com, GoldenEye 007 is the **most critically acclaimed shooter for the N64**, it's also the second most critically acclaimed N64 game overall behind Super Mario 64 (Nintendo, 1996), which has a score of 95.95%.

IKARUGA

(Treasure, 2001)
The GameCube version of the danmaku shooter Ikaruga featured support for 480p resolution, giving gamers the choice of playing it as either a widescreen side-scroller or, by twisting their monitor to the side, they could play "TATE mode" in a top-scrolling format similar to that employed by the original arcade machine.

NINTENDO RECORDS A TO I

Game	Platform	Setting/Variation	Record	Player (Country)	Date
10-Yard Fight	NES	Biggest Blowout [Super Bowl]	56	Kyle Goewert (USA)	20 Jul 2009
Actraiser 2	SNES	Fastest Completion	48 min 30 sec	Patrick DiCesare (USA)	12 Aug 2010
Arkanoid DS	DS	Points [Clear Mode]	164,630	Daniel Phillips (USA)	11 Sep 2009
Bart Simpson's Escape From Camp Deadly	Game Boy	Points	245,600	Brian Picchi (USA)	6 Mar 2010
Bases Loaded II: The Second Season	NES	Biggest Blowout	25	Andrew Furrer (USA)	16 Sep 2009
Battletoads in Battlemaniacs	SNES	Fastest Completion	20 min 43 sec	Patrick DiCesare (USA)	16 Jan 2010
Bejeweled 2	WiiWare	Action	465,100	William Willemstyn III (USA)	20 Aug 2010
Big Brain Academy	DS	Biggest Brain [Test Mode]	1,826 grams	Tim Kujac (USA)	1 Aug 2009
Bomberman	NES	Points [Marathon]	1,135,928,900	Ryan Johnson (Canada)	14 Feb 2010
Bonk's Adventure	NES	Fastest Completion	28 min 5 sec	Eric Cummings (USA)	16 Sep 2009
Chiller	NES	Points	1,472,900	Terence O'Neill (USA)	29 Aug 2010
Chunkout 2	NES	Points [Easiest Mode]	3,181,400	Nicole Ashdown (USA)	22 Mar 2010
City Connection	NES	Points	1,518,000	Ryan Johnson (Canada)	5 Feb 2010
Contra	NES	Fastest Completion	10 min 51 sec	Matt Turk (USA)	29 Dec 2009
Donkey Kong 3	NES	Points	5,391,500	Andrew Furrer (USA)	15 Jun 2010
Double Dragon	Game Boy	Points	138,020	Graham Ogilvie (USA)	13 Apr 2010
Double Dragon Advance	Game Boy Advance	Most Wins [Survival Mode]	206	Douglas Kirk (USA)	18 Jan 2010
Dr. Mario	NES	Points [Low Speed]	4,000,000	Nik Meeks (USA)	11 Apr 2009
Dr. Mario	NES	Points [Medium Speed]	2,010,400	Will Nichols (USA)	1 Mar 2010
Dr. Mario	NES	Points [High Speed]	1,602,600	Patrick Stanley (USA)	10 Jun 2010
Earthbound	SNES	Fastest Completion	6 hr 38 min 16 sec	Chris Corsi (USA)	30 Jul 2010
Elevator Action	NES	Points	101,300	Brian Picchi (USA)	3 Jun 2010
Fast Draw Showdown	WiiWare	Fastest Draw	0.030 seconds	JC Padilla (USA)	3 Jun 2010
Flying Dragon: The Secret Scroll	NES	Points	19,345,000	Tom Votava (USA)	26 Feb 2010
Ghostbusters: The Video Game	Wii	1 Player; Fastest Completion	3 hr 3 min 58 sec	Andrew Furrer (USA)	7 Feb 2010
GoldenEye 007	Nintendo 64	Fastest Completion [Agent/Facility]	1 min 33 sec	Matthew Runnels (USA)	4 Feb 2010
Hatris	Game Boy	Points	89,568	Ryan Johnson (Canada)	18 Jan 2010
Hook	SNES	Points	1,460,100	Graham Ogilvie (USA)	5 Apr 2010
HyperZone	SNES	Points	10,003,490	Patrick DiCesare (USA)	15 Dec 2009
Ikaruga	GameCube	Points	1 5,134,730	Kasper van Rijckevorsel (Netherlands)	6 Jun 2009
			2 2,247,860	Joey Anderson (USA)	7 Jul 2010
			3 1,454,260	Mark Stacy (USA)	15 Apr 2010

NINTENDO RECORDS J TO L

Game	Platform	Setting/Variation		Record	Player (Country)	Date
Jackal	NES	Points	1	6,553,500	Tom Votava (USA)	29 Mar 2010
			2	6,478,800	Andrew Furrer (USA)	16 Mar 2010
Jordan vs Bird: One on One	NES	Biggest Blowout	1	1,002	Andrew Furrer (USA)	21 Jan 2010
			2	992	Rudy Ferretti (USA)	28 Dec 2009
Just Dance	Wii	"A Little Less Conversation"		14,405	Brooke Mitchell (USA)	8 Aug 2010
Just Dance	Wii	"Acceptable in the 80s"		855	Jared Bowling (USA)	8 Aug 2010
Just Dance	Wii	"Can't Get You Out of My Head"		10,027	Brooke Mitchell (USA)	8 Aug 2010
Just Dance	Wii	"Cotton Eye Joe"		9,861	Brooke Mitchell (USA)	8 Aug 2010
Just Dance	Wii	"Dare"		11,661	Elizabeth Bolinger (USA)	8 Aug 2010
Just Dance	Wii	"Eye of the Tiger"		12,123	Aaron Jackson (USA)	8 Aug 2010
Just Dance	Wii	"Fame"		7,443	Jodi McFarlane (USA)	8 Aug 2010
Just Dance	Wii	"Funplex"		8,125	Matt Ringering (USA)	8 Aug 2010
Just Dance	Wii	"Girls & Boys"		7,093	Matt Ringering (USA)	8 Aug 2010
Just Dance	Wii	"Girls Just Want to Have Fun"		9,162	Brooke Mitchell (USA)	8 Aug 2010
Just Dance	Wii	"Groove Is In the Heart"		13,011	Brooke Mitchell (USA)	8 Aug 2010
Just Dance	Wii	"Heart of Glass"		14,330	Brooke Mitchell (USA)	8 Aug 2010
Just Dance	Wii	"Hot N Cold"		10,633	Nate Golomski (USA)	8 Aug 2010
Just Dance	Wii	"I Like to Move It"		9,293	Amanda Walker (USA)	8 Aug 2010
Just Dance	Wii	"Jerk It Out"		11,443	Brooke Mitchell (USA)	8 Aug 2010
Just Dance	Wii	"Kids in America"		11,457	Amanda Walker (USA)	8 Aug 2010
Just Dance	Wii	"Lump"		8,416	Amanda Walker (USA)	8 Aug 2010
Just Dance	Wii	"Mashed Potato Time"		12,016	Jacob Chaney (USA)	8 Aug 2010
Just Dance	Wii	"Pump Up the Jam"		13,030	Brandon Pace (USA)	8 Aug 2010
Just Dance	Wii	"Ring My Bell"		14,647	Brooke Mitchell (USA)	8 Aug 2010
Just Dance	Wii	"Surfin' Bird"		15,842	Brooke Mitchell (USA)	8 Aug 2010
Just Dance	Wii	"That's the Way (I Like It)"		12,707	Brooke Mitchell (USA)	8 Aug 2010
Just Dance	Wii	"U Can't Touch This"		17,380	Aaron Jackson (USA)	8 Aug 2010
Just Dance	Wii	"Wannabe"		11,541	Heather Kellar (USA)	8 Aug 2010
Just Dance	Wii	"Who Let the Dogs Out?"		14,672	Brooke Mitchell (USA)	8 Aug 2010
Just Dance	Wii	"Womanizer"		14,687	Brooke Mitchell (USA)	8 Aug 2010
Kid Icarus	NES	Points		1,611,700	Andrew Furrer (USA)	13 Apr 2010
Kirby's Adventure	Wii Virtual Console (NES)	Points		862,630	William Powell (USA)	14 Aug 2010
Kirby's Avalanche	SNES	Points		112,434	Geoffrey Lin (USA)	5 Apr 2010
Lifeforce	NES	Points [Tournament Settings]		6,553,800	Tom Votava (USA)	29 Mar 2010

JUST DANCE
(Nintendo, 2009)
Surprisingly, Nintendo's *Just Dance* doesn't feature the Lady Gaga track of the same name, which would seem to be a missed opportunity. However, it does feature 32 tracks on the disc.

KIRBY'S ADVENTURE
(Nintendo, 1993)
He might look cute, but don't be fooled – Kirby's key characteristic is his ability to steal the powers of his enemies by inhaling them! Nintendo have been exhaling *Kirby* hits since 1993, although there have been a couple of sharp intakes along the way – two Kirby titles developed for the N64, *Kirby 64* and *Kirby's Air Ride*, failed to see the light of day, although the latter was released as *Kirby Air Ride* (Nintendo, 2003) for the GameCube.

"I HEAR IT'S AMAZING WHEN THE FAMOUS PURPLE STUFFED WORM IN FLAP-JAW SPACE WITH THE TUNING FORK DOES A RAW BLINK ON HARA-KIRI ROCK. I NEED SCISSORS! 61!"

WWW.GUINNESSWORLDRECORDS.COM/GAMERS **195**

OUR SECOND CHUNK OF NINTENDO RECORDS TAKES US FROM LOOPZ TO THE ANIMATED TATSUNOKO UNIVERSE.

MEGA MAN 6

(Nintendo, 1993)
The last of the *Mega Man* series developed and launched for the NES, *Mega Man 6* featured two power-up adaptors that combined Mega Man and his dog Rush into two alternative forms. Jet Mega Man gives the player the power to fly or hover briefly and Power Mega Man gives the player a powerful, short-range punch attack.

RAYMAN RAVING RABBIDS 2

(Nintendo, 2007)
In this sequel to the 2006 original, the Rabbids plan to take over the earth and set up their base in a shopping mall. Players can choose to play as Rayman or the Rabbids.

NINTENDO RECORDS L TO R

Game	Platform	Setting/Variation	Record	Player (Country)	Date
Loopz	NES	Points [Game B]	94,840	Patrick Stanley (USA)	9 Feb 2010
Mach Rider	NES	Points [Endurance Course]	401,360	Ryan Johnson (Canada)	8 Jul 2010
Mad Dog McCree Gunslinger Pack	Wii	Mad Dog McCree	10,200	Kelly R Flewin (Canada)	25 Mar 2010
Madden NFL 10	Wii	Biggest Blowout	121	Andrew Furrer (USA)	15 Nov 2009
Mario Bros.	Wii Virtual Console (NES)	Points [1 Player]	10,147,660	Timothy Hykes (USA)	17 Sep 2009
Mario Strikers Charged	Wii	Domination Mode [Biggest Blowout]	133	Fred Bugmann (Brazil)	19 Mar 2010
Mega Man 9	WiiWare	Endless Mode - Most Screens Cleared	3,621	Steven Ellis (USA)	27 Jul 2010
Mega Man 6	NES	Fastest Completion	48 min 26 sec	Simeon King (USA)	20 Nov 2009
Mega Man X2	SNES	Fastest Total Completion	54 min 14 sec	Brendan Blakemore (USA)	21 Oct 2009
Midway Arcade Treasures [Roadblasters]	GameCube	Points	314,970	John Brissie (USA)	8 Mar 2010
Monster In My Pocket	NES	Points	8,185	Rudy Ferretti (USA)	16 Jan 2010
Monster Party	NES	Points	629,700	Daniel Brown (USA)	2 Nov 2009
Ms. PAC-Man	SNES	Points [Strange Mode]	85,770	Ryan Johnson (Canada)	10 May 2010
Namco Museum [Galaga]	Game Boy Advance	Points [Marathon]	277,230	John Brissie (USA)	10 Mar 2010
Need for Speed Underground	GameCube	Fastest Race [Circuit Mode; Inner City]	1 min 40.37 sec	Fred Bugmann (Brazil)	4 Jan 2010
NES Play Action Football	NES	Biggest Blowout	514	Andrew Furrer (USA)	22 Jul 2009
New Super Mario Bros.	DS	Minimalist Speedrun	32 min 53 sec	Adam Colton (USA)	17 Apr 2010
New Super Mario Bros. Wii	Wii	Fastest Completion	32 min 10 sec	Ronald Hastings (USA)	15 Jun 2010
New Super Mario Bros. Wii	Wii	Points [Twin Galaxies Extreme Settings]	1 9,428,480	Chris Helmin (USA)	7 Aug 2010
			2 5,033,720	Brandon LeCroy (USA)	6 Aug 2010
Ninja Gaiden 3: The Ancient Ship of Doom	SNES	Fastest Completion	20 min 51 sec	James Sorge (USA)	22 Feb 2010
Pocky & Rocky	SNES	Points	790,460	Patrick DiCesare (USA)	15 Dec 2009
Pokémon Snap	N64	Points [Beach]	3,309,360	Craig Rout Gallant (Canada)	31 Dec 2009
Q*Bert	NES	Points [TGTS]*	96,760	Mason Cramer (USA)	22 Apr 2010
Q*Bert 3	SNES	Points	115,725	Brandon LeCroy (USA)	22 Apr 2010
R.B.I. Baseball	NES	Biggest Blowout	34	Adam Vlcek (USA)	6 Jul 2010
Rayman Raving Rabbids 2	Wii	Points [Spider Rabbid]	24,236	Gregrey Hall (USA)	15 Dec 2009

"IT STINKS LIKE ROTTEN MEAT, BUT LOOKS LIKE THE LOST DEIMOS BASE. LOOKS LIKE YOU'RE STUCK ON THE SHORES OF HELL. THE ONLY WAY OUT IS THROUGH."

118.69 MILLION: THE LIFETIME
SALES OF THE GAMEBOY – LAID END TO END, THEY WOULD
CIRCLE THE GLOBE MORE THAN ONE-AND-A-QUARTER TIMES.

GUINNESS WORLD RECORDS

NINTENDO RECORDS S TO T

Game	Platform	Setting/Variation		Record	Player (Country)	Date
Street Fighter II: The World Warrior	SNES	Points [TGTS]*		1,239,700	Eric Schafer (USA)	26 May 2010
Super Adventure Island	SNES	Points		390,400	Jared Oswald (USA)	5 Feb 2010
Super Ghouls 'n Ghosts	SNES	Points		736,700	Daniel Brown (USA)	2 May 2010
Super Mario All Stars [Super Mario Bros. 3]	SNES	Minimalist Speed Run		12 min 53 sec	Jordan Horstman (USA)	20 Mar 2010
Super Mario Bros.	NES	Points [5 life limit]		1,201,350	Patrick Scott Patterson (USA)	27 Apr 2010
Super Mario Bros. 3	NES	Points [TGTS]*		2,568,080	Kyle Goewert (USA)	5 Dec 2009
Super Mario Bros.: The Lost Levels	Wii Virtual Console (NES)	Points [TGTS]*		4,031,350	Scott Fowler (USA)	14 Aug 2010
Super Mario Kart	SNES	Fastest Race [Mario Circuit 2]		1 min 19.54 sec	Brandon Skar (USA)	24 Aug 2009
Super Mario World	SNES	Points [TGTS]*		4,415,900	Mason Cramer (USA)	25 Jul 2010
Super R-Type	SNES	Points		1,220,700	Steven Ellis (USA)	11 Dec 2009
Super Smash Bros.	N64	Board the Platforms [Yoshi]		18.110 seconds	Craig Rout Gallant (Canada)	31 Dec 2009
Super Smash Bros. Brawl	Wii	Fastest completion of 10-Man Brawl in a two player team		22.95 seconds	Michael & Shailey Petik (USA)	3 Dec 2009
Super Smash Bros. Brawl	Wii	NTSC – Stadium – Multi-Man Brawl – Endless Brawl – Kills	1	259	Joel Pugh (USA)	8 Aug 2010
			2	252	Thomas Trovato (Canada)	12 Jan 2010
Super Smash Bros. Brawl	Wii	Endless Brawl - Kills		233	Andrew Furrer (USA)	15 Nov 2009
Super Street Fighter II Turbo Revival	Game Boy Advance	Break the Car		9.320 seconds	Kelly R Flewin (Canada)	25 Mar 2010
T & C Surf Designs	NES	Points	1	999,999 (1st perfect game)	Logan Chard (USA)	7 Apr 2008
			2	999,999 (2nd perfect game)	Brian Picchi (USA)	17 Feb 2010
			3	999,999 (3rd perfect game)	Kevin Hanley (USA)	20 Aug 2010
Tatsunoko vs Capcom: Ultimate All-Stars	Wii	Points	1	1,350,370,000	Leonardo Bugmann (Brazil)	19 Aug 2010
			2	1,226,068,000	Victor Delgado (USA)	22 Jul 2010
			3	241,820,000	Ted Dallaire (USA)	19 Mar 2010
Tatsunoko vs Capcom: Ultimate All-Stars	Wii	Survival Mode [Most Victories, 8-star difficulty]		44	Christoper C Tirpak (USA)	22 Aug 2010

TRIVIA TRAIL

Renowned for their cross-franchise fighters, Capcom took on the Japanese animation studio Tatsunoko, home of armoured soldier Tekkaman Blade (above), in the Wii title *Tatsunoko vs Capcom: Ultimate All-Stars* (Capcom, 2008).

*TGTS = Twin Galaxies Tournament Settings

SUPER SMASH BROS. BRAWL

(Nintendo, 2008)
Nintendo's 2D fighter for the Wii finally gave you the chance to see who would win in a fight between the villainous Wario (below) and *Metal Gear*'s Solid Snake!

"LOOK AT THIS PLACE. FIFTY-THOUSAND PEOPLE USED TO LIVE IN THIS CITY, NOW IT'S A GHOST TOWN. I'VE NEVER SEEN ANYTHING LIKE IT."

WWW.GUINNESSWORLDRECORDS.COM/GAMERS

NINTENDO III

OUR THIRD SLICE OF NINTENDO RECORDS TAKES US ON A WHISTLE-STOP TOUR OF THE WORLD OF Wii GAMES.

TRIVIA TRAIL

Tetris Party Deluxe (Hudson Soft, 2008) for the Wii cleverly combines modern gaming peripherals and classic puzzle gaming. The inclusion of a Wii Balance Board *Tetris* game mode enables players to control the tumbling tetrominoes by shifting their bodyweight.

TOMENA SANNER

(Konami, 2010) Businessman Hitoshi Susumu is having a bad day, but that's not going to stop him getting his dance on in this lo-fi, rhythm-based, one-button 2D side-scroller. Cheap and silly, the appeal of its nine standard levels might be limited, but the endless mode is the stuff high-score hounds crave to pile up the points.

NINTENDO RECORDS T TO W

Game	Platform	Setting/Variation		Record	Player (Country)	Date
Tatsunoko vs Capcom: Ultimate All-Stars	Wii	Time Attack Mode		7 min 22.55 sec	Victor Delgado (USA)	22 Jul 2010
Tecmo Super Bowl	SNES	Biggest Blowout		174	Ryan Johnson (Canada)	10 May 2010
Tetris	NES	Most Lines		296	Ben Mullen (USA)	20 Mar 2010
Tetris	NES (Tengen version)	Most Lines		1,502	Thor Aackerlund (USA)	12 Aug 2010
Tetris	NES	Points	1	999,999 (1st perfect score)	Harry Hong (USA)	19 Apr 2009
			2	999,999 (2nd perfect score)	Jonas Neubauer (USA)	16 Jul 2009
Tetris	NES (Tengen version)	Points		3,591,504	Thor Aackerlund (USA)	12 Aug 2010
Tetris Party Deluxe	Wii	Marathon – 150 Lines	1	690,750	Isaiah "Triforce" Johnson (USA)	6 Aug 2010
			2	283,821	Shane Muir (USA)	8 Aug 2010
			3	212,260	Kevin Kirwin (USA)	8 Aug 2010
The Castlevania Adventure: Rebirth	WiiWare	Points		335,030	Mark Stacy (USA)	11 Jun 2010
The Karate Kid	NES	Fastest Completion		4 min 1 sec	Brian Picchi (USA)	15 Apr 2010
The New Tetris	N64	Ultra		11 min 57 sec	John Pompa (USA)	13 Jul 2010
Tomena Sanner	WiiWare	Normal Mode – Endless	1	5,673,100	William Willemstyn III (USA)	29 Jul 2010
			2	5,095,060	Shane Muir (USA)	7 Aug 2010
Urban Champion	NES	Points		8,694	Brian Vaughn (USA)	24 Jan 2010
Wayne Gretzky and the NHLPA All-Stars	SNES	Biggest Blowout		113	Jonathon Plombon (USA)	12 Sep 2009
Wii Fit / Wii Fit Plus	Wii	Rhythm Boxing – 6 minutes		713	Melissa Patterson (USA)	24 May 2010
Wii Fit / Wii Fit Plus	Wii	Rhythm Kung Fu – Advanced		840	Noora Hele Suoniemi (Finland)	1 Apr 2010
Wii Fit / Wii Fit Plus	Wii	Super Hula Hoop – 3 minutes		901	Brooke Mitchell (USA)	6 Aug 2010
Wii Fit Plus	Wii	Snowball Fight – Advanced		49	David Caudwell (USA)	6 Aug 2010
Wii Fit Plus	Wii	Super Hula Hoop – 3 minutes	1	901	Brooke Mitchell (USA)	6 Aug 2010
			2	898	Matt Den Hartog (USA)	6 Aug 2010
Wii Play	Wii	Find Mii		68	John Eden (Australia)	29 Oct 2009
Wii Play	Wii	Tanks!		190	Dave Survinski (USA)	13 Feb 2010
Wii Sports	Wii	Baseball [Hitting Home Runs]	1	6,041	Craig Rout Gallant (Canada)	28 Jun 2010
			2	5,762	Kevin Conner (USA)	6 Apr 2010

"WELL...I GUESS THIS IS FAREWELL, HUH? LIGHT AND SHADOW CAN'T MIX, AS WE ALL KNOW. BUT...NEVER FORGET THAT THERE'S ANOTHER WORLD BOUND TO THIS ONE."

11: THE NUMBER OF GAMES MARIO'S FRIEND YOSHI HAS STARRED IN OVER THE YEARS, ENABLING THE LITTLE DINOSAUR TO CLAIM SALES OF 22 MILLION GAMES IN HIS OWN NAME.

NINTENDO RECORDS W TO Z

Game	Platform	Setting/Variation		Record	Player (Country)	Date
Wii Sports	Wii	Baseball [Biggest Blowout]		24	Lance Eustache (USA)	27 May 2010
Wii Sports	Wii	Golf [Hitting the Green]		32	John Eden (Australia)	21 Mar 2010
Wii Sports Resort	Wii	Archery [Expert]	1	106	Ronnie Dalbianco (USA)	26 Dec 2009
			2	105	Brandon Skar (USA)	24 Aug 2009
Wii Sports Resort	Wii	Basketball [3-Point Shootout]	1	39	Kimberley Sanders (USA)	6 Aug 2010
			2	29	Andrew Pete Mee (UK)	2 Jan 2010
Wii Sports Resort	Wii	Bowling [100 Pin Bowling]	1	3,000 (perfect score)	Ryan Sullivan (USA)	13 Feb 2010
			2	2,999	Kimberley Sanders (USA)	21 Jan 2010
Wii Sports Resort	Wii	Frisbee Dog	1	1,500 (perfect score)	Ronnie Dalbianco (USA)	28 May 2010
			2	1,350	Craig Rout Gallant (Canada)	6 May 2010
			3	1,310	Vinnie Hirt (USA)	22 Aug 2010
Wii Sports Resort	Wii	Frisbee Golf		49	David Nelson (USA)	26 Aug 2010
Wii Sports Resort	Wii	Power Cruising [Beach]		212	Craig Rout Gallant (Canada)	2 Aug 2010
Wii Sports Resort	Wii	Power Cruising [Marina]		179	Andrew Pete Mee (UK)	10 Dec 2009
Wii Sports Resort	Wii	Skydiving		241	Pekka Luodeslampi (Finland)	13 Apr 2010
Wii Sports Resort	Wii	Table Tennis [Match]		1,484	Kristian Farnan (UK)	21 Jan 2010
Wii Sports Resort	Wii	Table Tennis [Return Challenge]	1	999 (1st perfect score)	Brandon Skar (USA)	24 Aug 2009
			2	999 (2nd perfect score)	Andrew Pete Mee (UK)	2 Jan 2010
Wizards & Warriors	NES	Points	1	999,999 (1st perfect score)	Tom Votava (USA)	17 Sep 2002
			2	999,999 (2nd perfect score)	Rudy Ferretti (USA)	29 May 2010
WWE Day of Reckoning 2	GameCube	Fastest Victory [1 Player; Exhibition Mode; Normal Difficulty]		11 seconds	James Bouchier (UK)	13 Jul 2010
Yoshi	NES	Points [Game A]	1	31,145	Daryl Kiddey (USA)	30 Aug 2010
			2	30,960	Ryan Johnson (Canada)	1 Aug 2010
			3	28,805	Patrick Stanley (USA)	14 Aug 2010
Zombie Nation	NES	Points		517,900	Rudy Ferretti (USA)	29 May 2010
Zombie Panic in Wonderland	Wii	Arcade Mode		48,770	Ginger Stowe (USA)	18 Jun 2010
Zombies Ate My Neighbors	SNES	Points		3,115,064	Eric Schafer (USA)	19 Aug 2010

DID YOU KNOW?

Boasting sales of over 27 million units worldwide, the mini-game compendium *Wii Play* (Nintendo, 2006) is the sixth best-selling videogame of all time. The game owes its sales success to the fact it comes with a "bonus" second controller, which allows gamers to take full advantage of the various multiplayer challenges in this and other Wii titles.

ZOMBIES ATE MY NEIGHBORS

(Konami, 1993)

A game that became a cult classic on the NES and Mega Drive/Genesis, *Zombies Ate My Neighbors* has recently been brought back from the grave itself thanks to a re-release on the Wii's virtual console.

GET OUT YOUR PLAYSTATION OR YOUR PSP AND SEE IF YOU CAN GET CLOSE TO THESE HIGH SCORES.

TRIVIA TRAIL

Released in 1996 for PlayStation, demolition derby sequel *Twisted Metal 2* earned a rating of 86.44% on review aggregator website GameRankings.com. The game was applauded by the Gamespot reviewers, who described it as "among the best PlayStation games of the season".

WIPEOUT PURE

(Sony, 2005)
This futuristic racer was a launch title for the PSP in North America. The game is a streamlined version of previous games in the *Wipeout* series, hence the *Pure* in the title. It utilized the PSP's Wi-Fi capability to allow multiplayer racing and was also the first PSP game to support downloadable content.

SONY RECORDS A TO M

Game	Platform	Setting/Variation		Record	Player (Country)	Date
2010 FIFA World Cup South Africa	PlayStation 3	Biggest Blowout vs. computer	1	5	Dakota Bunnell (USA)	8 Aug 2010
			2	2	Stephen Cani (USA)	8 Aug 2010
After Burner Climax	PS3 Network	Arcade Mode – Points	1	307,000	Zach Sloan (USA)	7 Aug 2010
			2	305,150	Joey Testa (USA)	7 Aug 2010
			3	185,820	Aaron Sloan (USA)	7 Aug 2010
After Burner Climax	PS3 Network	Score Attack – Points	1	792,850	Zach Sloan (USA)	7 Aug 2010
			2	606,460	Dakota Bunnell (USA)	7 Aug 2010
			3	578,860	Joey Testa (USA)	7 Aug 2010
Blur	PlayStation 3	Fans		9,380	Aaron Sloan (USA)	8 Aug 2010
Blur	PlayStation 3	Most Career Fans	1	1,685	Sean Hendrickson (USA)	5 Aug 2010
			2	680	Zach Sloan (USA)	5 Aug 2010
Capcom Classics Collection (Vol 1)	PlayStation 2	SFII: Champion Edition; hardcore diff.		881,900	Paulo Valmir (Brazil)	11 Dec 2009
Joe Danger	PS3 Network	Back in the Saddle – High Score		18,283,200	Dustin Campbell (USA)	8 Aug 2010
Joe Danger	PS3 Network	Has He Still Got It? – High Score	1	106,262,300	Sean Hendrickson (USA)	6 Aug 2010
			2	27,940,325	Draven Jones (USA)	6 Aug 2010
			3	5,327,500	Tyler Rose (USA)	6 Aug 2010
Joe Danger	PS3 Network	Joe Danger Returns – High Score	1	63,995,000	Dustin Campbell (USA)	8 Aug 2010
			2	40,638,400	Sean Hendrickson (USA)	6 Aug 2010
			3	12,032,900	Tyson Faoro (USA)	8 Aug 2010
Joe Danger	PS3 Network	Joe Danger Rides Again – High Score	1	808,725	John Wen (USA)	6 Aug 2010
			2	546,700	Allen Salden (USA)	6 Aug 2010
			3	321,000	Shelby Majors (USA)	6 Aug 2010
Joe Danger	PS3 Network	Mostly Dangerous – High Score		43,028,750	Sean Hendrickson (USA)	6 Aug 2010
Lumines Supernova	PS3 Network	Challenge Mode; Advanced		150,065	Sophie Wormer (Netherlands)	23 Jun 2010
Madden NFL 09	PlayStation 2	Play Now Mode [Biggest Blowout]		103	Matthew Runnels (USA)	14 Jun 2010
Midway Arcade Treasures [Toobin']	PlayStation 2	4 bars		1,223,968	Shaun Michaud (USA)	9 May 2010
ModNation Racers	PlayStation 3	Alpine Drop – Fastest Lap		42.813 sec	Brian Kellar (USA)	7 Aug 2010
ModNation Racers	PlayStation 3	Boardwalk – Fastest Lap	1	39.005 sec	Shelby Majors (USA)	7 Aug 2010
			2	40.333 sec	John Wen (USA)	7 Aug 2010

"THESE ARE THE FACES OF EVIL. YOU MUST CONQUER EACH."

SONY RECORDS M TO W

Game	Platform	Setting/Variation		Record	Player (Country)	Date
ModNation Racers	PlayStation 3	Farm Frenzy – Fastest Lap		24.371 seconds	Troy Scoggin (USA)	7 Aug 2010
ModNation Racers	PlayStation 3	Island Dash – Fastest Lap	1	37.567 seconds	Draven Jones (USA)	7 Aug 2010
			2	39.162 seconds	John Wen (USA)	7 Aug 2010
			3	42.491 seconds	Brian Kellar (USA)	7 Aug 2010
ModNation Racers	PlayStation 3	Mod Circuit – Fastest Lap	1	20.416 seconds	Zach Sloan (USA)	7 Aug 2010
			2	21.020 seconds	Troy Scoggin (USA)	7 Aug 2010
			3	22.691 seconds	Shelby Majors (USA)	7 Aug 2010
ModNation Racers	PlayStation 3	Village Run – Fastest Lap	1	35.892 seconds	Brian Kellar (USA)	7 Aug 2010
			2	37.198 seconds	Edward Bell (USA)	7 Aug 2010
PaRappa The Rapper	PlayStation Portable	Stage 1; normal mode		87	Kevin Brisley (Canada)	8 Feb 2010
Pinball Hall of Fame: The Williams Collection	PlayStation 2	Funhouse		132,675,750	Justin Evancy (USA)	9 Oct 2009
Pro Pinball: Big Race U.S.A.	PlayStation	Normal		142,154,350	Steve Germershausen (Canada)	6 Jan 2010
Ridge Racer V	PlayStation 2	99 Lap; Sunny Beach; Regular Track		1 hr 40 min 31.224 sec	Dick Moreland (USA)	16 Nov 2009
Super Stardust HD	PS3 Network	Arcade Mode		7,322,000	Wouter Lugtenaar (Netherlands)	23 Jun 2010
Super Street Fighter IV	PlayStation 3	Arcade Mode – Points		1,119,600	John Lapsey (USA)	28 Aug 2010
Taito Legends	PlayStation 2	Battle Shark		6,751,130	Shaun Michaud (USA)	28 Aug 2009
Tiger Woods PGA 11	PlayStation 3	Pebble Beach – Fewest Strokes	1	102	Aaron Sloan (USA)	8 Aug 2010
			2	100	Phil Geraci (USA)	8 Aug 2010
Twisted Metal 2	PlayStation	Holland [Fastest Completion]		4 min 22.000 sec	Brian Serfass (USA)	9 Mar 2010
Wipeout Pure	PlayStation Portable	Blue Ridge		2 min 7.870 sec	Kevin Brisley (Canada)	21 Mar 2010

DID YOU KNOW?

Gameplay in *PaRappa the Rapper* (Sony, 1996) follows a "call and response" format in which players have to repeat a sequence of sounds and button presses in the correct order and with accurate timing. Results are then judged on the "U Rappin'" meter.

"U RAPPIN' GOOD. U RAPPIN' COOL. U RAPPIN' BAD."

/PARAPPA KNOWS ABOUT RAPPING.

MODNATION RACERS

(Sony, 2009)

ModNation Racers was revealed to the world at Sony's 2009 E3 press conference, where it was billed as "a thoroughly modern take on kart racing". The game is part of Sony's "Play. Create. Share." genre of games, which also includes *LittleBigPlanet* (Sony, 2008), and, as with that game, the focus is on user-developed content – pretty much everything can be modded: racer, kart, track – you name it!

ON XBOX 360 AND THROUGH XBOX LIVE ARCADE, TWIN GALAXIES BRING YOU THE LATEST HIGH SCORES.

TRIVIA TRAIL

Capcom's 2010 fighter *Super Street Fighter IV* was originally intended to be an update for *Street Fighter IV* (Capcom, 2008) but became too large during development so was released separately.

TRIALS HD

(Microsoft, 2009)
Trials HD is a physics-based motorcycle racing game with over 50 tracks in which explosions, crashes and injuries cannot be avoided.

XBOX RECORDS A TO I

Game	Platform	Setting/Variation		Record	Player (Country)	Date
2010 FIFA World Cup South Africa	Xbox 360	Biggest Blowout		4	Burt Jameson (USA)	24 Jun 2010
After Burner Climax	XBLA	Arcade Mode		704,600	JC Padilla (USA)	3 Jun 2010
After Burner Climax	XBLA	Score Attack Mode		1,210,850	JC Padilla (USA)	4 Jun 2010
Boom Boom Rocket	XBLA	Standard: 1812 Overdrive		17,513,285	Joel Pugh (USA)	6 Aug 2010
Boom Boom Rocket	XBLA	Standard: Carmen Electric		10,673,543	Shelby Majors (USA)	6 Aug 2010
Boom Boom Rocket	XBLA	Standard: Game Over Beethoven		13,844,260	Andrew Kaake (USA)	6 Aug 2010
Boom Boom Rocket	XBLA	Standard: Hall of the Mountain Dude		18,473,420	Brian Ho (USA)	6 Aug 2010
Boom Boom Rocket	XBLA	Standard: Rave New World		15,670,332	Joel Pugh (USA)	6 Aug 2010
Boom Boom Rocket	XBLA	Standard: Smooth Operetta		12,585,625	Zach Sloan (USA)	6 Aug 2010
Boom Boom Rocket	XBLA	Standard: Tail Light Sonata		13,859,511	Andrew Kaake (USA)	6 Aug 2010
Boom Boom Rocket	XBLA	Standard: Toccata and Funk		15,900,452	Kevin Kirwin (USA)	6 Aug 2010
Boom Boom Rocket	XBLA	Standard: Valkyries Rising		8,230,987	Andrew Kaake (USA)	6 Aug 2010
Boom Boom Rocket	XBLA	Standard: William Tell Overload		16,970,290	Brian Ho (USA)	6 Aug 2010
Call of Duty 4: Modern Warfare	Xbox 360	Mile High Club [Arcade Mode]		92,730	Brett Smith (USA)	24 Jan 2010
Crackdown 2	Xbox360	Rooftop Race: Bound Over the Bay	1	1 min 54.975 sec	Zach Sloan (USA)	7 Aug 2010
			2	2 min 41.959 sec	Ryan Yeoman (USA)	7 Aug 2010
Geometry Wars: Retro Evolved 2	XBLA	Pacifism		206,976,750	Jeffrey D Lowe Jr (USA)	13 Nov 2009
Geometry Wars: Retro Evolved 2	XBLA	Sequence		31,648,350	Jordan Baranowski (USA)	13 Aug 2010
Hydro Thunder Hurricane	XBLA	Ring Master: Lake Powell – Novice	1	1 min 57.550 sec	Zach Sloan (USA)	7 Aug 2010
			2	1 min 58.790 sec	Elton Renaud (USA)	6 Aug 2010
			3	2 min 0.650 sec	Aaron Sloan (USA)	6 Aug 2010
I MAED A GAM3 W1TH Z0MB1ES 1N IT!!!1	XBLA Indie	Points	1	881,760	Dave Vogt (USA)	8 Aug 2010
			2	848,760	Chris Yeoman (USA)	8 Aug 2010
			3	842,440	Tim Bishop (USA)	8 Aug 2010

"RELAX? RELAX? HAVE YOU EVER BEEN IN A TURKISH PRISON, MATE? IF WE GET CAUGHT, THEY WILL LOCK US UP AND THROW AWAY THE SODDING KEY, YOU DO REALIZE THAT, DON'T YOU?"

XBOX RECORDS M TO U

Game	Platform	Setting/Variation		Record	Player (Country)	Date
Madden NFL 10	Xbox 360	Biggest Blowout	1	56	Patrick Scott Patterson (USA)	20 Jan 2010
			2	54	Jennifer Jones (USA)	30 Apr 2010
Metal Slug XX	XBLA	Main mission		1,020,680	Lance Eustache (USA)	30 May 2010
Mirror's Edge	Xbox 360	Playground 1 [Time Trial]		1 min 1.510 sec	Daniel Collotte (USA)	23 Oct 2009
Need for Speed Underground	Xbox	Inner City [Fastest Race]		1 min 39.600 sec	Fred Bugmann (Brazil)	4 Dec 2009
Need for Speed Underground 2	Xbox	Freemount – Forward Track [Fastest Race]		1 min 32.060 sec	Fred Bugmann (Brazil)	17 Mar 2010
NHL 08	Xbox 360	Biggest Blowout		14	Nathan Weygandt (USA)	24 Jul 2010
PAC-Man Championship Edition	XBLA	Championship Mode	1	338,810	Michael Sroka (USA)	14 Mar 2010
			2	336,740	Tim Balderramos (USA)	7 Aug 2010
			3	286,880	Daniel Rogers (USA)	5 Oct 2009
Resident Evil 5	Xbox 360	The Mines [Mercenary Mode]		31,740	Gullermo Cepeda (USA)	25 Oct 2009
Soul Calibur IV	Xbox 360	Arcade Mode [Points]		511,890	Lance Eustache (USA)	30 May 2010
Soul Calibur IV	Xbox 360	Fastest Completion [Arcade Mode]		4 min 16.280 sec	Anthony Palmer (USA)	19 Mar 2010
Street Fighter IV	Xbox 360	Arcade Mode [Tournament settings]	1	3,038,600	Jeffrey D Lowe Jr (USA)	17 Jan 2010
			2	1,671,800	Emerson Duarte (Brazil)	10 Nov 2009
Street Fighter IV	Xbox 360	Win Steak [Live event]		300	Justin Wong (USA)	3 Jun 2009
Super Street Fighter IV	Xbox 360	Arcade Mode [Tournament settings]	1	2,014,700	Jeffrey D Lowe Jr (USA)	24 Jul 2010
			2	1,079,400	John Lapsey (USA)	5 Aug 2010
Taito Legends	Xbox	Super Qix [Points]		167,480	Perley Walsh (Canada)	13 Feb 2010
Trials HD	XBLA	Delivery mode	1	970.27 feet	Zach Sloan (USA)	6 Aug 2010
			2	959.83 feet	Chris Mincks (USA)	6 Aug 2010
			3	905.37 feet	Alex Baird (USA)	6 Aug 2010
UFC Undisputed 2010	Xbox 360	Exhibition - Fastest Victory	1	14 seconds	Kelly R Flewin (Canada)	8 Aug 2010
			2	14 seconds	Patrick Scott Patterson (USA)	8 Aug 2010
			3	15 seconds	Chris Yeoman (USA)	8 Aug 2010
UFC Undisputed 2010	Xbox 360	Fastest Knockout [Expert]		6 seconds	TJ Wilt (USA)	6 Aug 2010

NHL 08
(EA, 2007)
This 2007 version of EA's mega ice hockey franchise saw the introduction of a "goalie mode", which allowed players to control their goalie with a third-person camera, as well as a feature allowing the creation of custom plays.

UFC UNDISPUTED 2010
(THQ, 2010)
Capitalizing on the continued success of mixed martial arts, THQ teamed up with the Ultimate Fighting Championship once again for some full-on fighting action.

OLD SCHOOL CONSOLE

TIME FOR A SIT DOWN? THOSE ARCADE CLASSICS HAVE MADE THEIR WAY INTO YOUR LIVING ROOM.

GALAXIAN

(Namco, 1983)
This port of the 1979 arcade hit was faithful to the cabinet-based original. In the style of the earlier smash *Space Invaders* (Midway, 1978), a lone cannon attempts to fend off hordes of swarming aliens, except with *Galaxian* the aliens would come swooping down to attack you and there were no shields to hide behind.

SEWER SHARK

(Sony Imagesoft, 1992)
In this first-person rail shooter, players make their way through the underground world to a resort location known as "Solar City"; all the time their performance is being assessed by the city's commander and a co-pilot. It was the first console game to use full-motion video.

OLD SCHOOL CONSOLE RECORDS A TO G

Game	Platform	Setting/Variation	Record	Player (Country)	Date
After Burner II	Sega Genesis	Points	30,213,110	Dan Lee (USA)	11 Jun 2004
Air Raiders	Atari 2600	Points [Game 1, Difficulty B]	122	Steve Germershausen (Canada)	18 Dec 2010
Alien	Atari 2600	Points [Game 1, Difficulty B]	211,753	Greg Troutman (USA)	11 Jun 2004
Alien 3	Sega Genesis	Points	157,360	Magnus Andersson (Sweden)	25 May 2009
Alien Crush	TurboGrafx-16	Points	999,999,900	Todd Rogers (USA)	29 Nov 2003
Alien vs. Predator	Atari Jaguar	Points [Marine]	1,310,200	Ron Corcoran (USA)	15 May 2001
Arcus Odyssey	Sega Genesis	Fastest Completion	38 min 49 sec	Ryan Sullivan (USA)	28 May 2010
Armor Attack	Vectrex	Points [Game 1]	566,400	John Brissie (USA)	2 Jan 2010
Ayrton Senna's Super Monaco GP II	Sega Genesis	NTSC Australia [Fastest Lap]	36.150 seconds	John Brissie (USA)	1 Jul 2010
Ayrton Senna's Super Monaco GP II	Sega Genesis	NTSC - San Marino [Fastest Lap]	40.940 seconds	John Brissie (USA)	25 Mar 2010
Ayrton Senna's Super Monaco GP II	Sega Genesis	PAL - USA [Fastest Lap]	40.790 seconds	Magnus Andersson (Sweden)	20 Jul 2010
Baku Baku Animal	Sega Saturn	Points [NTSC Expert]	30,397	Nik Meeks (USA)	16 Apr 2004
Batman Returns	Sega Genesis	Points	53,400	Jared E Oswald (USA)	17 Aug 2010
Berzerk	Atari 2600	Points [Game 1]	1,000,950	Paul Zimmerman (USA)	10 May 2010
Communist Mutants From Space	Atari 2600	Points [Game 1, Difficulty B]	15,130	E Williams (USA)	25 Sep 2010
Cosmic Crisis	Colecovision	Points [Skill 1]	92,500	Tom Duncan (USA)	15 Oct 2004
Crossbow	Atari 7800	Points	1,698,000	Paul Zimmerman (USA)	18 May 2010
Donkey Kong	Atari 2600	Points [Game 1, Difficulty B]	1,234,800	Steve Germershausen (Canada)	31 Mar 2010
Double Dragon	Atari 7800	Points	110,420	Shane Shaffer (USA)	11 Nov 2004
Fantasy Zone	TurboGrafx-16	Points	98,265,100	Brandon Fish (USA)	11 Jun 2004
Frantic Freddy	Colecovision	Points [NTSC/PAL, Skill 1]	83,280	Tom Duncan (USA)	8 Dec 2004
Frogger	Sega Genesis	Points	17,770	Jared E Oswald (USA)	17 Aug 2010
Frogger	Vectrex	Points	12,890	Nik Meeks (USA)	17 Mar 2009
Galaxian	Atari 2600	Points [Game 1, Difficulty B]	2,696,100	George Riley (USA)	13 Jan 2010
Guardian Heroes	Sega Saturn	Fastest Completion [Hard Difficulty]	54 min 45 sec	Adam R Wood (USA)	4 Jun 2005

TRIVIA TRAIL

Launched in 1988, the Sega Mega Drive (aka the Genesis in the USA) originally came with controllers that featured a directional pad, a start button and three function buttons (far left). In 1993, Sega released a controller with six function buttons (left) that matched the button layout of arcade fighting machines, to complement their version of *Street Fighter II: Special Champion Edition* (Capcom, 1993).

"IRONIC ISN'T IT? THAT YOUR GREATEST ENEMY KEPT YOU SAFE FROM HARM. BUT NOW YOU'VE TAKEN MY LIFE, AND IN THE PROCESS, ENDED YOUR OWN."

OLD SCHOOL CONSOLE RECORDS H TO V

Game	Platform	Setting/Variation	Record	Player (Country)	Date
Hard Drivin'	Sega Genesis	Points	154,527	Jared Stanley (USA)	1 Jul 2010
M*A*S*H	Colecovision	Points [Copter Pilot, Game 3 Skill 1]	1,966	Tom Duncan (USA)	14 Apr 2005
Mario Bros.	Colecovision	Points	1,873,570	Terence O'Neill (USA)	14 Aug 2010
Masters of the Universe	Intellivision	Points [Novice]	363,050	Terence O'Neill (USA)	26 Jul 2010
Mr. Do's Castle	Colecovision	Points, Skill1 [Default]	117,160	Kim M Mooney (USA)	10 Aug 2009
NHL '94	Sega Genesis	Biggest Blowout	39	John Balawejder (USA)	8 Mar 2010
Night Stalker	Intellivision	Points	1,167,200	Matthew Miller (USA)	15 May 2010
Operation Wolf	Sega Master System	Points	88,550	E. Williams (USA)	29 Aug 2010
PAC-Land	TurboGrafx-16	Points	2,641,810	Daniel Delavera (USA)	11 Jun 2004
Paperboy	Atari Lynx	Points [Default]	59,690	Jason C Dove (USA)	25 Feb 2009
Pole Position	Vectrex	Points	77,100	Terence O'Neill (USA)	15 Jan 2009
Pro Pinball / Pro Pinball: The Web	Sega Saturn	Points	982,500,550	John Brissie (USA)	8 May 2010
Robotron 2084	Atari 7800	Points	32,078,500	Ben Strobel (USA)	11 Nov 2004
Sewer Shark	Sega CD	Points	4,088,394	Jon Piornack (USA)	26 Nov 2007
Sonic R	Sega Saturn	Radiant Emerald - Fastest Race	1 min 41.64 sec	Elijah Parker (USA)	19 Jun 1998
Sonic the Hedgehog	Sega Genesis	Points [TGTS]*	404,980	Michael Sroka (USA)	28 May 2010
Street Fighter Alpha 2	Sega Saturn	Points [PAL, TGTS]*	62,100	Andrew Pete Mee (USA)	15 Sep 2009
The Need for Speed	Sega Saturn	Autumn Valley - Fastest Lap	1 min 21.6 sec	John Brissie (USA)	18 Apr 2010
The Steel Empire	Sega Genesis	Points	3,154,300	Jared Stanley (USA)	1 Jul 2010
Time Gal	Sega CD	Points	1,493,000	Adam Dubicki (USA)	11 Jun 2004
Todd's Adventure in Slime World	Atari Lynx	Points [Default settings]	4,321,400	James Carter (USA)	11 Jun 2002
Tron Deadly Discs	Intellivision	15 minute limit	1,050,700	Matthew Miller (USA)	20 Jun 2010
Vectorman	Sega Genesis	Points	44,080	Ryan Sullivan (USA)	28 May 2010
Vigilante	Sega Master System	Points	122,700	Brandon LeCroy (USA)	17 Jul 2010

VECTORMAN

(Sega, 1995)
Vectorman is an ordinary green orbot who has been left on Earth to clear up toxic waste after the human population has gone off to find a cleaner environment in which to live. His job should be simple, but for an evil, insane orbot known as Warhead, who has taken control of other orbots and wants to rule the world!

*TGTS = Twin Galaxies Tournament Settings

GUARDIAN HEROES

(Sega, 1996)
Released for the Sega Saturn in 1996, side-scrolling beat-'em-up *Guardian Heroes* achieved an aggregate score of 89.20% on GameRankings.com, making it the third highest-ranking Saturn game on the website. GameRankings.com itself describes *Guardian Heroes* as "much more than just a beat-'em-up, [it] is the perfect blend of action and adventure".

DID YOU KNOW?

A side-scrolling shmup, *Fantasy Zone* (Sega, 1985) was something of a surreal take on arcade classic *Defender* (Williams, 1982). The hero of the game is Opa Opa, a portly egg-shaped ship that flies around the Fantasy Zone, taking on the enemy and coming up against huge boss characters such as evil snowmen and giant blocks of wood.

"IT'S BEEN A WHILE, BOY. YOU HAVE DONE WELL TO SNEAK INTO MY FORTRESS AND WRIGGLE YOUR WAY ALL THE WAY UP HERE. I SUPPOSE THE LEAST I CAN DO IS COMMEND YOU FOR YOUR RECKLESS COURAGE. MY NAME IS GANONDORF..."

WWW.GUINNESSWORLDRECORDS.COM/GAMERS **205**

OLD SCHOOL ARCADE

THE ORIGINAL WAY TO PLAY VIDEOGAMES WAS STANDING UP IN A STORE ON THE HIGH STREET. FANCY THAT!

ASTEROIDS

(Atari, 1979)
This vector-based arcade classic from Atari is a 24-carat nugget from the golden age of videogames. As with all good things, it left everyone wanting more, and they got it too, as the multi-directional shooter has been ported to many different devices including the Xbox via Xbox Live Arcade and, almost inevitably, mobile phones.

ALIEN SYNDROME

(Sega, 1987)
Two-player gameplay sees the characters Ricky and Mary fight their way through eight scrolling levels as they try to rescue their comrades from the clutches of evil aliens. A sequel to the game bearing the same name was released for Wii and PSP in 2007.

OLD SCHOOL ARCADE RECORDS A TO E

Game	Settings/Variation		Record	Player (Country)	Date
1943: The Battle of Midway	Points [Single player only]		2,947,360	Brian Chapel (USA)	23 Jun 1988
720 Degrees	Medal Count		363	Matthew J Angiulo (USA)	24 Jun 2010
Alien Syndrome	Points [Single player only]		2,269,200	Donn Nauert (USA)	2 Feb 1998
Alpine Racer	Gate Racing [Expert]		2 min 9 sec	Ken Patrick (USA)	20 Apr 1997
Area 51	Points [Single player only]	1	324,700	Frank Bryan (USA)	20 Apr 1997
		2	321,475	Michael Walker (USA)	20 Apr 1997
		3	314,075	Herb Branan (USA)	20 Apr 1997
Arkanoid	Points		1,658,110	Zachary B Hample (USA)	13 Mar 2000
Asteroids	Points		41,838,740	John McAllister (USA)	22 Apr 2010
Centipede	Points		16,389,547	Jim Schneider (USA)	1 Aug 1984
Chase H.Q.	Points		3,596,680	Brian Kuh (USA)	1 Jun 2006
Cloak & Dagger	Points [TGTS]*		1,497,744	John McAllister (USA)	7 Apr 2009
Contra	Points [Single player only]		2,029,900	Charlie D Wehner (USA)	2 Jul 2010
Crazy Kong	Points		568,400	JJ Cahill (USA)	20 Mar 2010
Crazy Taxi	Most money earned		$106,833.09	JC Padilla (USA)	17 Nov 2009
Crisis Zone	Fastest completion		16 min 15 sec	Adam Uppahad (USA)	1 Apr 2001
Cruis'n USA	Appalachia [Fastest race]		1 min 49.43 sec	Geoffrey Miller (USA)	20 Apr 1997
Crystal Castles	Points		910,722	Frank Seay (USA)	17 Mar 1988
Dig Dug	Marathon		5,136,150	Ken House (USA)	6 Dec 2009
Donkey Kong	Points	1	1,064,500	Steve Wiebe (USA)	30 Aug 2010
		2	1,062,800	Billy Mitchell (USA)	31 Jul 2010
		3	1,061,700	Hank Chien (USA)	8 Mar 2010
Donkey Kong Junior	Points	1	1,307,500	Mark Keihl (USA)	19 Jul 2010
		2	1,270,900	Billy Mitchell (USA)	31 Jul 2010
		3	1,190,400	Steve Wiebe (USA)	14 Feb 2010
Double Dragon	Points: 2-player team		129,660	Mike Vacca (USA) & JoJo Simoncelli (USA)	16 May 2010
Eagle	Points		259,070	Tongki Linderman (USA)	6 Jun 2010

TRIVIA TRAIL

Taito's 1987 arcade beat-'em-up *Double Dragon* has spawned a series of sequels and been ported to a number of home consoles, including the Nintendo Entertainment System in 1988, which was then made available on the Wii Virtual Console in 2008. The franchise has also been adapted for a range of other media, including an animated television series, a comic published by Marvel and a live-action feature film; there was even a CD released featuring the music from the original arcade version of the game.

{ "IN THE SULTAN'S ABSENCE, THE GRAND VIZIER JAFFAR RULES WITH THE IRON FIST OF TYRANNY. ONLY ONE OBSTACLE REMAINS BETWEEN JAFFAR AND THE THRONE: THE SULTAN'S BEAUTIFUL YOUNG DAUGHTER." }

OLD SCHOOL ARCADE RECORDS E TO V

Game	Settings/Variation		Record	Player (Country)	Date
Elevator Action	Difficulty 1		149,350	Steve Wagner (USA)	24 Aug 2010
Frogger	Points		896,980	Pat Laffaye (USA)	1 Jan 2010
Galaga	TGTS*		3,275,720	Phillip Day (USA)	1 Nov 2009
Ikari Warriors	Points		1,445,600	Noah Banwarth (USA)	10 Jul 2010
Lock 'N Chase	Points		89,580	Patrick Scott Patterson (USA)	4 Jun 2010
Mario Bros.	Points		4,678,440	Tom Votava (USA)	27 Nov 2009
Missile Command	Tournament Mode	1	4,472,570	Tony Temple (UK)	10 Aug 2010
		2	1,874,925	Jeffrey Blair (USA)	15 Jun 2010
Moon Patrol	Points	1	1,414,660	Tom Votava (USA)	1 Jan 2010
		2	1,014,820	Ben Falls (USA)	14 Sep 2009
PAC-Man	Fastest Perfect Game		3 hr 34 min 8 sec	David Race (USA)	26 Feb 2010
PAC-Man Plus	Points		3,376,780	David Race (USA)	12 Apr 2010
Popeye	Points		1,238,110	Perry Rodgers (USA)	17 Jun 2010
Raiden Fighters Jet	Normal difficulty		15,308,468	Cliff Reese (USA)	28 Nov 2009
Robotron: 2084	Tournament		1,236,950	John McAllister (USA)	27 Dec 2009
Space Duel	Doubles		53,480	Rusty Nunnelee & Kevin Moore (both USA)	10 Jul 2010
Space Harrier	Points	1	42,384,290	Phillip Campbell (UK)	13 Aug 2010
		2	39,495,060	Nick Hutt (UK)	30 Apr 2010
Splatterhouse	Normal difficulty		234,000	Jérôme Pastorel (France)	14 Jul 2010
Star Castle	Easy chip		10,001,110	John McAllister (USA)	25 Sep 2009
Stocker	Points		54,202	Andrew D O'Neil (USA)	3 Oct 2009
Swimmer	Points		132,830	Steve Wagner (USA)	22 Apr 2010
Timber	Points		5,005,555	Vincent Vassallo (USA)	31 May 2009
Track & Field	Points [one round of events only]		95,350	Hector Rodriguez (USA)	23 Jan 2009
Vs. Super Mario Bros.	5 life limit	1	2,600,200	Isaiah "Triforce" Johnson (USA)	6 Jun 2010
		2	2,595,850	Andrew Gardikis (USA)	5 Jun 2010

SPACE HARRIER
(Sega, 1985)
Gameplay in this rail shooter was set in a bright, checkerboard world called the "Fantasy Zone" with your character running, jumping or flying towards the distant horizon trying to avoid the giant millipede-like dragons that came rushing at you head on.

*TGTS = Twin Galaxies Tournament Settings

MISSILE COMMAND
(Atari, 1980)
Missile Command tapped in to some of the Cold War paranoia that was strong in 1980 with its simple premise of cities under attack from ballistic missiles. Only your counter-missiles can save them.

ON YOUR MARK, GET SET...
W I N
Konami/cenwn
TRACK & FIELD
cenwn

DID YOU KNOW?
Konami's 1983 offering *Track & Field* brought athletics into the arcade in a frenzy of button-bashing fun. A digitized take on the Olympics, *Track & Field* featured six events that encompassed running, jumping and throwing – 100 metres, long jump, javelin, 110 metres hurdles, hammer and high jump. Players would build up speed by hitting the two "run" buttons alternately as fast as possible and then jump or throw using a third "action" button. The key to success was a combination of speed and timing.

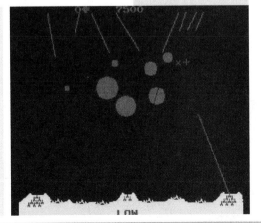

PRO-GAMING TABLES

YOU THINK YOU'VE GOT GAME? WAIT 'TIL YOU'VE SEEN WHAT HAPPENS WHEN THE PROS COME OUT TO PLAY.

IT'S BEEN ANOTHER BUMPER YEAR FOR ELECTRONIC SPORTS, WITH HUNDREDS OF GAMING PROS AROUND THE WORLD WITH THEIR EYES ON THE BIGGEST PRIZES. HERE ARE OUR HIGHLIGHTS OF THE PAST YEAR'S PRO-GAMING EVENTS.

MAJOR LEAGUE GAMING

Major League Gaming has been running tournaments since 2002. The 2009 season finals were held in Orlando, Florida, USA, in January 2010, with competitions in *Halo 3* (Microsoft, 2007) and *Gears of War 2* (Microsoft, 2008). After the 2009 tournament, it was announced that the 2010 event would feature fighting games, such as *Super Smash Bros. Brawl* (Nintendo, 2008).

HALO 3 4v4 MLG RANKINGS: 2009 SEASON

Rank	Team
1st	Believe The Hype
2nd	Classic
3rd	Carbon
4th	Instinct
5th	Triggers Down
6th	Str8 Rippin
7th	Dynasty
8th	Final Boss
9th	Status Quo
10th	Active Rush

GEARS OF WAR 2 4v4 MLG RANKINGS: 2009 SEASON

Rank	Team
1st	THE NSAN3Z (above)
2nd	Type-Z VisioN
3rd	Get Bronco
4th	Infinity
5th	MbN: The Business
6th	LeGaCy
7th	Raw Talent
8th	AmazYn
9th	Simply UnderRated
10th	Less Than Zero

TRIVIA TRAIL

The eSports World Championships 2008 featured an attempt on the record for the **longest LAN party**. Participants successfully set the record at 36 hours, but their feat has since been bettered by the 40-hour stint by attendees at Cyber Fusion 2009 in Malaysia.

FIFA INTERACTIVE WORLD CUP (FIWC) 2010 WINNERS

As the biggest pro-gaming tournament in the world, the FIWC 2010 saw over 775,000 entrants competing for $20,000 (£13,000) in prize money, a trip for two to the FIFA World Player Gala 2010 and a host of other prizes.

Rank	Player
1st	Nenad Stojkovic (USA, right)
2nd	Ayhan Altundağ (Germany)
3rd	Bruce Grannec (France)
4th	Danny Taylor (UK)

"UM... HAS ANYONE SEEN A FLOATING SARCASTIC SKULL AROUND HERE?"

WORLD CYBER GAMES

The World Cyber Games began in South Korea in 2000. The 2010 competition took place in Los Angeles, California, USA, although it was organized from South Korea, and featured events across 13 different titles.

FIFA 10 (PC) 1v1

Rank	Player
1st	daimonde (Germany)
2nd	Zola (China)
3rd	bl4ck_p01nt (Slovakia)
4th	Gimli (Austria)

TEKKEN 6 (XBOX 360) 1v1

Rank	Player
1st	Knee (South Korea, below)
2nd	AO(ALI) (Japan)
3rd	honnda (Japan)
4th	Leck (Spain)

FORZA MOTORSPORT 3 (XBOX 360) 1v1

Rank	Player
1st	d.DaveySkills (UK)
2nd	Johnson (Germany)
3rd	Handewasser (Netherlands)
4th	Yggdrasil (France)

GUITAR HERO 5 (XBOX 360) 1v1

Rank	Player
1st	Acai28 (USA)
2nd	ti.Monkey (UK)
3rd	Kaos.Boyke (Netherlands)
4th	rudeism (Australia)

eSPORTS WORLD CUP 2010 COUNTRY RANKINGS

Rank	Team	G	S	B	Total
1st	France	10	7	10	27
2nd	USA	7	5	3	15
3rd	South Korea	5	2	2	9
4th	Sweden	4	9	4	17
5th	Germany	4	4	7	15
6th	Netherlands	4	1	4	9
7th	Poland	3	1	0	4
8th	Russia	2	3	4	9
9th	Denmark	2	2	4	8
10th	Brazil	1	4	0	5

eSPORTS WORLD CUP

Established in 2003, the eSports World Cup deftly quashed rumours of its demise in 2009 by putting on its 2010 grand final at Disneyland Paris, France. The PC-heavy games line-up included *Trackmania*, (Nadeo, 2002), *Need for Speed: Shift* (EA, 2009) and two *WarCraft III* (Blizzard, 2002) tournaments: one for the expansion "The Frozen Throne" and one on the fan modification "Defense of the Ancients". The total prize purse was $213,500 (£134,848) split between 10 games. In the women's *Counter-Strike* (Valve, 2004) event, the girls of US-team SK Gaming (below, left to right: Benita Novshadian, Alice Lew, Jennifer So, Christine Chi and Stephanie Harvey) took home $14,000 (£8,800) between them.

SUPER STREET FIGHTER IV

Rank	Player
1st	Jwong (USA)
2nd	Marn (USA)
3rd	Luffy (France)
4th	Infiltration (South Korea)

NEED FOR SPEED: SHIFT

Rank	Player
1st	Steffan (Netherlands)
2nd	Husky (Germany)
3rd	Silver (Germany)
4th	Lecho (Poland)

COUNTER-STRIKE WOMEN

Rank	Team
1st	SK Gaming
2nd	fnatic
3rd	Millenium
4th	Mousesports

WANT TO KNOW WHERE TO FIND ALL YOUR FAVOURITE GAMES? LOOK NO FURTHER THAN OUR EXTENSIVE INDEX.

Bold entries in the index indicate a main entry on a topic, and entries in **BOLD CAPITALS** indicate an entire chapter.

QUOTES QUIZ ANSWERS

SO, IF YOU'VE AVOIDED SNEAKING A PEEK ALREADY, HERE ARE THE QUIZ ANSWERS YOU'VE BEEN WAITING FOR...

HAVE YOU BEEN BAFFLED BY THE QUOTES RUNNING ALONG THE BOTTOM OF EACH PAGE? OR DO YOU THINK YOU KNOW WHO SAID EVERY ONE? HERE'S WHERE YOU FIND OUT – WE'VE LISTED THE PAGE ON WHICH THE QUOTE APPEARS FOLLOWED BY THE CHARACTER WHO FIRST SAID IT AND THE GAME IT'S FROM.

Page 6
Pigsy
*Enslaved:
Odyssey to the West*

Page 7
Introduction
Ultima Underworld

Page 8
Psymon
SSX Tricky

Page 9
Falsetto
Eternal Sonata

Page 10
Issun
Okami

Page 11
Theresa
Fable II

Page 12
Jonathan Morris
*Castlevania:
Portrait of Ruin*

Page 13
Lara Croft
*Tomb Raider:
Underworld*

Page 14
Henpecked Hou
Jade Empire

Page 15
Cryptosporidium
Destroy All Humans

Page 16
Loading screen
*Guitar Hero III:
Legends of Rock*

Page 17
Snake
*Metal Gear Solid 4:
Guns of the Patriots*

Page 18
Meryl Silverburgh
Metal Gear Solid

Page 19
Faith
Mirror's Edge

Page 20
The Joker
Batman: Arkham Asylum

Page 21
Mondu
Tongue of the Fatman

Page 22
Sora
Kingdom Hearts II

Page 23
Jacqueline Natla
*Tomb Raider:
Anniversary*

Page 24
Peppy Hare
*Starfox/Starwing/
Lylat Wars*

Page 25
Old Man
The Legend of Zelda

Page 26
Wadsworth
the robot butler
Fallout 3

Page 27
Random dialogue
The Elder Scrolls: Daggerfall

Page 28
Imperial Guard
*The Elder Scrolls:
Morrowind*

Page 29
Barry Burton
Resident Evil

Page 30
Kratos
God of War

Page 31
Tony Montana
*Scarface:
The World is Yours*

Page 32
Cats
Zero Wing

Page 33
Lynch
Kane and Lynch

Page 34
Koga
*Pokémon HeartGold/
SoulSilver*

Page 35
Daxter
*Jak and Daxter:
The Precursor Legacy*

Page 36
Arkvoodle
Destroy All Humans 2

Page 37
Gambit
Marvel vs. Capcom

Page 38
Carl Johnson
*Grand Theft Auto:
San Andreas*

Page 39
Crazy Ivan
*Command & Conquer:
Red Alert 2*

Page 40
Commentator
World Class Leader Board

Page 41
Safety Advice
Wii Sports

Page 42
Morty
Pokémon Gold/Silver

Page 43
Wallace
Pokémon Ruby/Sapphire

Page 44
Rahm Kota
Star Wars: The Force Unleashed

Page 45
Announcer
Mortal Kombat

Page 46
Dr. Fred Eddison
Day of the Tentacle

Page 47
Ben Throttle
Full Throttle

Page 48
Phoenix Wright
*Phoenix Wright: And
Justice for All*

Page 49
Cranky Kong
Donkey Kong 64

Page 50
Introduction
Captain Comic

Page 51
Eddie Riggs
Brütal Legend

Page 52
Sinistar
Sinistar

Page 53
Announcer
Gauntlet

Page 54
Ace
Space Ace

Page 55
Tommy Vercetti
Grand Theft Auto: Vice City

Page 56
Captain Thygh
*Leisure Suit Larry 7:
Love for Sail*

Page 57
Sarah Kerrigan
StarCraft

Page 58
Ryu Hayabusa
Ninja Gaiden

Page 59
HK47
*Star Wars: Knights of the
Old Republic*

Page 60
Silver
*Sonic the Hedgehog
(2006 version)*

Page 61
Mark Lawrenson
commentating
Pro Evolution Soccer

Page 62
Kyle Hyde
Hotel Dusk: Room 215

Page 63
Travis Touchdown
No More Heroes

Page 64
John Marston
Red Dead Redemption

Page 65
Brucie Kibbutz
Grand Theft Auto IV

Page 66
Lord Vyers/Midboss
*Disgaea: Afternoon of
Darkness*

Page 67
The Prince
*Prince of Persia:
The Sands of Time*

Page 68
Gary Smith
Bully/Canis Canem Edit

Page 69
Nico Collard
*Broken Sword:
The Shadows of the
Templars*

Page 70
Cloud Strife
Final Fantasy VII

Page 71
The G-Man
Half Life 2

Page 72
Leon S. Kennedy
Resident Evil 2

Page 73
Duke
Duke Nukem 3D

Page 74
Redda
Skate 2

Page 75
The Heavy
Team Fortress 2

Page 76
Introduction
*Bad Dudes vs.
Dragon Ninja*

Page 77
Fuuka
Persona 3

Page 78
Dormin
Shadow of the Colossus

Page 79
Ico
Ico

Page 80
Ethan
Heavy Rain

Page 81
Urdnot Wrex
Mass Effect

Page 82
Kheldar Ironfist
Neverwinter Nights 2

Page 83
Banshee
StarCraft II

Page 84
Kratos
God of War II

Page 85
Steven Heck
Alpha Protocol

Page 86
Gunnery Sergeant
Edward Buck
Halo 3: ODST

Page 87
Dominic Santiago
Gears of War

Page 88
Ed DeLuca
Dead Rising

Page 89
Sam Fisher
Splinter Cell Essentials

Page 90
Quizmaster
Buzz

Page 91
Prince Laharl
*Disgaea:
Hour of Darkness*

Page 92
Announcer
Soul Calibur

Page 93
King of all Cosmos
Katamari Damacy

Page 94
Gene
God Hand

Page 95
Instructions
WarioWare: Smooth Moves

Page 96
Prison Guard
Mafia II

Page 97
Toad
Super Mario Bros.

Page 98
Flea Market Rap
PaRappa the Rapper

Page 99
Conker
Conker's Bad Fur Day

Page 100
Blaze
Streets of Rage 3

Page 101
Minsc
Baldur's Gate

Page 102
Stonehead
Alex Kidd in Miracle World

Page 103
Leon
Dead or Alive 4

Page 104
Master Roshi
*Dragonball Z Budokai
Tenkaichi 3*

Page 105
Captain Falcon
Super Smash Bros. Brawl

SO YOU CALL YOURSELF A GAMER?

How many quotes did you guess correctly? Give yourself half a point for each character you got right and half a point for each game, then add them up and see how you fare on our game-themed ranking system:

0: n00b; 1-10: Goomba; 11-20: Brain Trainer; 21-30: Rookie; 31-40: Padawan; 41-50: Recruit; 51-60: Shy-guy; 61-70: Mid-boss; 71-80: Game quote tycoon; 81-90: Psychonaut; 91-100: Rampant A.I.; 101-110: Big Boss; 111-120: Professor Layton; 121-130: Shadow Broker; 131-140: Psycho Mantis; 141-150: Jedi Consular; 151-160: Avatar; 161-170: Game Genie; 171-180: Robot Master; 181-190: Spider Mastermind; 191-200: Mother Brain; 201+: Prophet of Truth.

PICTURE CREDITS

Page	Picture Credit
4	Paul Michael Hughes/GWR
8	Josh Meyer/GWR
10	Dave Benett/Getty Images
11	www.Penny-Arcade.com
11	Matt Carr/Getty Images
17	Timothy A Clary/Getty Images
36	Paul Michael Hughes/GWR
47	Dana Edelson/NBC
68	Tomohiro Ohsumi/Getty Images
82	Ryan Schude/GWR
94	Shinsuke Kamioka/GWR
96	Mathieu Reynes
112	© Disney
142	Shinsuke Kamioka/GWR
152	Ranald Mackechnie/GWR
176	Arcade Flyer
177	Kevin Parry/Getty Images
192	Jason Scott
206	Arcade Flyer
206	Arcade Flyer
206	Arcade Flyer
207	Arcade Flyer
207	Arcade Flyer
208	Action Images
216	Suzi Deaves/GWR

ACKNOWLEDGEMENTS

Guinness World Records would like to thank the following individuals, groups and websites for their help in the creation of *Guinness World Records Gamer's Edition 2011*:

James Anderson, Colin Barker, Luci Black, Richard Booth, Olivia & Alex Boulton, Pete Bouvier, Matt Bradford, Zuraida Buter, Dominic Carey, Charles Cecil, Letty Cherry, Sophie Choudry, Brian David-Marshall, Walter Day, Jesse Divinch, Natalie Edwards, Phil Elliott, Eurogamer.net, Geraint Evans, Gamesindustry.biz, Gamespress.com, Gametrailers.com, Abid Gangat, Rachel Gosling, Jim Hawker, Daan Hendrikse, Chris Higgins, Mel Johnson, Seth Killian, Kiyoshi Kodama, Simon Livesey, Mike Lorimer, Pete Low, Daisy McBurney, Eddie May, Media Molecule, Tjerk Mellink, Izzy Miller, Robbert Minderhoud, Ruby Mulraine, Darren Murph, Michael O'Dell, Karen O'Donovan, Andrew Oliver, Jack Patillo, Stefano Petrullo, Geoff Ramsey, Peter Rosengard, Roosterteeth.com, Dean Shaw, Greg Short, Iain Simons, Thea Smith, Simon Smith Wright, Sony Computer Entertainment, Jennie Sue, Leo Tan, Ciji Thornton, Norie Tomoka, Twin Galaxies International, Alex Verrey, VGChartz.com, Mark Ward, Kate White, Kevin Williams, Mark Wooldridge, Tom Woolley and Geoff Zatkin.

STOP PRESS

»MOST "F" WORDS IN A VIDEOGAME

Holder: *Scarface: The World is Yours* **(Sierra, 2006)**
Following the internet interest created by Roosterteeth.com's video of swearing in *Mafia II* (2K, 2010), we received a new claim just as we were wrapping up book production for *Guinness World Records Gamer's Edition 2011*. The letter was from games designer Pete Low claiming he had a contender for the title of the most foul-mouthed game. Pete was the lead designer on the 2006 open world game *Scarface: The World is Yours* and he provided us with a copy of its script. Out of its 31,716 lines of dialogue, the script contains an unbelievable 5,688 uses of the "f" word. By contrast, the word "the" appears just 5,187 times. The game doesn't just contain bad language in English either, Spanish and Jamaican vulgarities are also used.

»LONGEST WINNING STREAK ON BLAZBLUE: CONTINUUM SHIFT

Holder: Kyle Dixon (UK)
On 30 October 2010, Kyle "Kyzertron" Dixon (pictured centre) amassed an impressive haul of 30 victories in one hour on 2D fighter *BlazBlue: Continuum Shift* at the MCM Expo, London, UK. Kyle played as Λ-11 throughout the attempt and managed to pull off a savage 63-hit juggle combo against one opponent playing as Iron Tager.

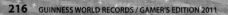